Am I a Hindu?

Ed Viswanathan

© Halo Books 1992

San Francisco

Library of Congress Cataloging-in-Publication Data

Viswanathan, Ed. (Edakkandiyil), 1944-
    Am I a Hindu? : the Hindu primer / by Ed Viswanathan.
       p.   cm.

    ISBN 1-879904-06-3 (soft) : $13.95
    1. Hinduism. I. Title.
BL1202.V57   1992
294.5--dc20

92-8587
CIP

© Halo Books, San Francisco, 1992

HALO BOOKS
73691 Sawmill Canyon Way • Palm Desert, CA 92260

Cover art by Sue Larson
Typography by Karen Mandel

Table of Contents 🙏

Publisher's Foreword ॐ

One of the last major publishing vacuums--a definitive primer on Hinduism--is being filled by this book. Until now, American-born children of Hindu families have had no reliable literary guide to their own roots. Students of religion have been required to wade through voluminous texts, often on highly specific aspects of Hinduism.

You now hold a book that, in slightly over 300 pages, covers it all. *Am I a Hindu?* approaches the vast scope of Hinduism with thoroughness, clarity and understanding. The author, who has studied, practiced and experienced the many facets of Hinduism both in his native India and in the United States, approaches the subject head-on: what it means to be a Hindu.

As Lord Krishna spoke to Arjuna on the battlefield of Kurukshetra, as the great *rishis* imparted wisdom to their disciples, so too this book is traditionally framed as an instructional discussion. The lively dialogue is between an American-born teenager and his father.

This highly readable, thought-provoking volume will ensure that Hinduism's lofty ideals and profound wisdom remain in the minds and hearts of people everywhere.

Preface ॐ

Dear Readers:

For the last so many years I have been looking for a special book dealing with all aspects of Hinduism, one that would try to answer every conceivable question one could have on Hinduism and on life in general, but I found none. So after years of rigorous research and by the blessings of the Almighty I managed to write this book. I humbly wish to present this before you for your kind perusal.

My book is written in a "question and answer" format between a fourteen-year old American-born Indian teenager and his well-settled middle-aged father. Every part of Hinduism right from the Vedas all the way to the Tantras is dealt with in this book. Throughout the book, the inquisitive son is grilling his father with all kinds of questions. All questions and answers are brief and direct.

All answers in this book are authentic. There is absolutely no dogma or demagoguery in the answers. Throughout this book I have repeatedly stated that Hinduism is a way of life and not an organized religion. In fact, Hinduism is the culture of Indians in India.

For my part I have read quite a number of books on Hinduism as well as on other religions. I feel all true religions of the world tell one and the same truth, but in Hinduism the truth is explored scientifically by a large number of ancient scientists called Rishis, who conducted all research without the use of a single test tube or a microscope.

I have absolutely no fanatical love affair with Hinduism and I am willing even to say that we should be ready to give up Hinduism if we can find a different source which will address all the problems in life and provide instant remedies. I do not mean to say that Hindu scriptures have answered every question to the satisfaction of all. My argument is that those scriptures have at least tried to answer every conceivable question one may have with the language of the Vedic age. Again we all know that we cannot understand in words that truth which is above the mind.

Even the very abstract scientific truths of today we are only understanding through equations and mathematics. Of course understanding is strictly personal and we understand things by way of comparison. When we talk about one object we compare it with another known object in order to understand it. For example, when I talk about the "fifth generation of computers," you may think about robots and all those space adventure movies. If I talk about God, there is nothing to compare it with, so we try to compare it with natural powers like lightning and thunder or try to visualize the image of Jesus, Krishna, Moses, Buddha or Mahavira. So we all know how limited languages are in conveying truths, and as such, scriptures are not at fault if we cannot grasp the truths from them.

If all religions were made today, they would have been treated like physics or chemistry with universality in nature. Religions have airtight divisions not because of their prophets, but because of the fanatic work of the zealot followers. Neither Rishis nor Moses nor Buddha nor Christ nor Mohammed nor Guru Nanak intended their revelations to go to a chosen few, but to the whole of humanity. When they asked their followers to preach their word, they did not intend to destroy the existing schools of thought, but to strengthen the existing beliefs and practices. It is unimaginable to even think that Buddha or Christ could have said something different from Lord Krishna since there is only one truth and one God.

For example, I am of the opinion that the Hindu Maya and the Christian original sin are one and the same. Maya means illusion or false knowledge. According to Hinduism, we witness duality in the world such as "right and wrong," "good and bad," "yin and yang," all due to Maya. If you look very deeply, you will see that the whole story of Adam and Eve in Genesis deals with Maya. God said to Adam that he could eat the fruits of every tree in the garden, except for the "tree of knowledge of good and evil" (Genesis 2:15). Adam disobeyed, and by eating that forbidden fruit Adam and Eve came to know right and wrong, good and bad, etc. That caused the downfall of man. That capability to discern right and wrong is the perception of duality in Hinduism, which is indeed Maya. What Adam and Eve attained in the garden by eating the forbidden fruit is "false knowledge," and it is that false knowledge which is causing the downfall of every man. So Maya is indeed the original sin. That is the reason why man became aware of his nakedness in the Garden of Eden and lost the knowledge of his true nature. The serpent only depicts the inert weakness in the man which is to indulge in material things. There is no subject more liable to cause the Christian theologians to tear their hair out, and Christians to profess their outspoken disbelief, than the original sin. But if the Christian theologians would try to explain the original sin as false knowledge or Maya, many Christians would understand the magnanimity of the symbolism behind the story of Adam and Eve. Maya is indeed the original sin described in Genesis, and true knowledge is the only way to get rid of it.

My book may seem to you a mixture of many facts without a proper order. That is because Hinduism itself is a mixture of so many things. It is a summation of all types of thoughts and all types of religions. On one hand you will see the existence of the primitive worship of reptiles and other pests, yet on the other hand you will see thoughts and ideas excelling Bohr's theory of nuclear structure and reactions. This atmosphere is generated due to three reasons. 1. Hinduism allowed and still allows the free flow of thoughts. 2. It allowed and still allows the coexistence of all kinds of thoughts. 3. Hinduism has never ever had a "house-cleaning" like other religions, which have had that periodically.

The objective behind writing this book is to open up the free thinking spirit in the reader as well as to open up the vast spiritual heritage of Hinduism to anyone who is interested in further research. I have tried to answer many questions in this book, but I know that understanding the ultimate truth is beyond the mind and as such beyond any verbal explanations. As a writer I can only repeat exactly what is written in ancient scriptures and explain them as I see and understand them.

I am dedicating this book to the poor and sick of India and contributing part of all profits from this book to charity because I believe that without food and proper health a person can never have knowledge, and at the same time ignorance is the root of all evils in the world.

I thank again the Almighty for giving me the opportunity to write this book. In fact I am only a compiler of facts and figures and I do not want to develop any unnecessary ego about this book, for as a great saint once said, "Ego is ego in whatever form it comes." I thank you very much for taking time to read my humble book.

Sincerely,
Ed. Viswanathan

1 ॐ
Introduction to Hinduism

DADDY, MAY I TALK TO YOU?

Of course you may.

I WANT TO ASK YOU A LOT OF QUESTIONS REGARDING OUR RELIGION.

Please go ahead and ask me any question you want.

WHERE DO I START?

Start with the first question that comes to your mind.

OK. WHAT AM I, A HINDU?

Of course you are. We follow Hinduism, so we are called Hindus, just like the people who follow Christianity are called Christians.

Looking at it in one way, Hinduism is the relentless pursuit after truth. As such, it is the religion forever. There is only one God and one truth. The Hindu Vedas proclaim, "Ekam Sat, Viprah Bahudha Vadanti" (There is one truth, only men describe it in different ways). So a Christian, a Hindu, a Muslim and a Jew are all one and the same. Looking at it in another way, Hinduism is not a religion but a way of life. For argument's sake, one can state that if all Hindu scriptures are destroyed one day, this age-old religion will still come back to life again within a few years, since it pursues only absolute truth. Right now, Hinduism is more a culture than a religion.

DADDY, BEFORE I PROCEED FURTHER, I WANT TO WARN YOU THAT I AM A TEENAGER BORN IN THE U.S.A., SO SOME OF MY QUESTIONS MAY SOUND AGGRESSIVE. I HOPE YOU WON'T BE OFFENDED.

Son, you can ask me any question you want. Just think of yourself as a district attorney, interrogating me on the witness stand. Trust me, none of your questions will offend me. I will answer all your questions as directly as possible. I will also never give you any retaliatory answers. Furthermore, I shall bring other religious ideas and science into my answers. I hope you will be satisfied.

HONESTLY, CAN HINDUISM STAND GRILLING QUESTIONS?

Hinduism has no problem facing any type of question. It does not have to hide behind unpronounceable Sanskrit words or spiritual dogma. Instead, it absorbs new ideas like a sponge.

Believe it or not, Hinduism recharges itself with modern thoughts. Technology, psychology, parapsychology, modern astronomy, the new physics and genetics all enrich Hinduism.

Within Hinduism, you can think and argue on any subject. You can even make statements like "There is no Krishna or Rama" and still be a Hindu. It has no hierarchy, it has no establishment and it has no governing body.

In Hinduism, one will seldom come across a statement starting with "Thou shalt not." As you study Hinduism, from one end to the other you will find it to be filled with all kind of ideas. It has highly spiritualistic Advaita and Raja Yoga on one side and highly materialistic, atheistic, hedonistic Charvaka philosophy, which does not believe in God or the Vedas, on the other side. On one side, idolatry is a part of Hinduism, and on the other, as expressed by the German philosopher Max Muller, "The religion of the Vedas knows no idols." The Jahala Upanishad says, "Images are meant only as aids to meditation for the ignorant."

The ancient Hindu mythology is filled with all kind of stories. On one side, Advaita talks about Brahman (the Infinite) alone, and again on the other side, mythology talks about thousands of gods. It is indeed a religion with unity in diversity. Picking up subjects randomly from Hindu scriptures could confuse you. But if you sit down and study them all, you will be able to understand the actual truth behind all Hindu scriptures. Today there is quite a large number of books on Hinduism available in English and in so many other languages that even the knowledge of Sanskrit is not a must to understand Hindu scriptures.

DADDY, BEFORE YOU PROCEED FURTHER, I WANT TO ASK YOU ONE VERY CRUCIAL QUESTION. PLEASE DON'T FEEL HURT. MY QUESTION IS, WHAT AUTHORITY DO YOU HAVE TO TALK ABOUT HINDUISM?

I am happy that you asked me this question. Arjuna, the warrior-prince of the epic Mahabharata, asked the same question of Lord Krishna during the narration of the Bhagavad Gita, the Hindu holy bible. Lord Krishna, as an answer to Arjuna, showed him his Viswaroopa (the great Formless Form or Shapeless Shape) and a stunned Arjuna saw the whole world revolving on the body of God. Arjuna got more of an answer than he had bargained for. Well, I cannot show you any such thing to prove any of my points.

You may laugh, but since even Arjuna asked about Lord Krishna's authority, it is perfectly all right for you to ask me the same question. On my part, I can only say that I am a humble aspirant of truth like so many people. Of course I have read many books (about 500) regarding Hinduism and all other religions. My only intention is to lay out before you the history of Hinduism as well as the most salient points about it. After listening to my answers, you on your part should investigate the validity of my statements. At this juncture, let me repeat a scriptural stanza, in which a Guru told his inquisitive disciple:

> Nobody knows what is right or what is wrong;
> Nobody knows what is good or what is bad;
> There is a deity residing within you;
> Find it out and obey its commands.

That is my answer. Please understand that the deity mentioned in the stanza above is none other than the "inner voice" about which Aurobindo, the modern Hindu mystic, wrote volumes. It is indeed the Christ within, or to put it in better words, it is the immortal Holy Ghost. I just wanted to point out to you that all final answers are within. Like a Zen master, I wish to say that to seek answers outside of oneself is futile and idiotic. Zen Buddhists say that truth cannot be taught by word of mouth and that true knowledge only comes from personal experience.

Again, please do not take the above stanza as a green light for licentiousness and doing things as one's emotions dictate. Emotions within a person are very deceptive. They can come out with
intellectual authority and make every silly action look meaningful. They even dupe great saints and seers into believing in their own personal egoistic sentiments and acting very foolishly. So be very cautious of the verses I quoted above.

IS HINDUISM THE ONLY WAY TO GOD-REALIZATION?

Once a gentleman told the famous American philosopher Emerson that he had studied almost all philosophies and religions of the world, and was finally convinced that Christianity was the only one. Emerson replied, "That only shows, my friend, how narrowly you have read them." The same statement goes for Hinduism. Nobody has the right to say that Hinduism is the only way. In fact, Hindus consider it absurd to state that any other true religion of the world is false.

The Bhagavad Gita (4:11) says, "Whatever and whichever way men approach Me, even so do I accept them; whatever paths they may choose finally lead to Me, oh! Arjuna [his disciple]." From these lines, one can easily understand that Hinduism does not project itself as the only way to God-realization. It claims no monopoly on wisdom. It tolerates all forms of thoughts. A Hindu Yogi will never try to convert a person from another religion to Hinduism. Instead he will try to make a person's faith steadfast in his/her own religion. The Gita says, "In whatever form a devotee seeks to worship Me with faith, I make his faith steadfast in that form alone." So in Hinduism, you can worship the Almighty, which is formless and timeless, as Krishna, Jesus, Allah, Moses, or as anyone or anything. As long as you have faith in that form of the Almighty, you will be following a true religion and you will ultimately realize the truth, even if you are following a crude form of worship. No one can be lost according to Hinduism. In whichever way one may seek God, one is always in the path of God.

In India, saints often say that if you visualize "It" (God) and call "It" forth intensely as a buffalo, then "It" will appear in front of you as a buffalo. In fact, legends say that God appeared to American Indians as Buffalo.

When someone calls "It" Jesus Christ, "It" comes as Jesus Christ; when someone calls "It" Lord Krishna, "It" comes as Lord Krishna. Even the most popular devotee of India, the sage Narada, called God by the word Asmin, meaning "That," in the second Sutra of the Narada Bhakti Sutra. The great Muslim mystics, the Sufis, said, "Wheresoever you turn, there is the Face of Allah."

In all forms of worship, ultimately the worshipper will transcend the name and form of his/her personal god. Look at the writings of Saint Francis of Assisi or the Sufi mystics or Lord Chaitanya or Sri Ramakrishna Paramahamsa. Lord Chaitanya cried for Vital and Ramakrishna cried for Mother Kali. But if one studies all the above works, one can see that the Absolute they were after has no name and no form and is beyond human description. All of them started with their attachment to a personal god and finally ended up with an Almighty which is timeless and formless.

The word Islam means "submitter to the will of Allah," and Allah has no proper definition. A true Muslim worships that formless, nameless entity called Allah, which is indeed the Supreme Power. Moslems object to the term "Mohammedanism" because that word implies worship of Mohammed. Moslems never ever worshipped the prophet Mohammed. All Moslems believe in the following cardinal statement: "I bear witness that there is no God but Allah, and Mohammed is His prophet." Allah is like the Tao of Taoism, the Brahman of Hinduism, the Ayin of Jewish Kabbalah mysticism, or the Jehovah ("I Am") of the Old Testament. It is an unnameable, undefinable pure being or power out of which all else emerges.

No religion has any monopoly on God. To say that is exactly like saying "The sun only rises in New York and sets over the Honolulu beaches." The sun that shines on New York mansions and Beverly Hills swimming pools also shines in the dark ghettos of Calcutta, the dry deserts of Saudi Arabia and the killing fields of Cambodia. Similarly, the God in the Bhagavad Gita is the same God you see in the Bible and in the Koran.

DOES HINDUISM BELIEVE IN FORCIBLE CONVERSIONS?

Not at all. A true Hindu never proselytizes, but Hindus gladly greet anyone who wants to join Hinduism out of love for Hindu ideals. The Bhagavad Gita urges everyone to follow the religion in which he/she was born. Hindus never make false promises to convert someone to Hinduism.

Just like Hindus, Jews are also very tolerant of believers of other faiths. Jews do not persuade others to join their religion. Of course, there are many converts to Judaism, but Jews never actively propagate their faith. To some extent, just like Hinduism, Judaism is also a way of life.

Again, Hindus look at religion as a basic science. Have you ever heard of somebody being converted into Indian Chemistry, or British Physics? So it is absurd to even discuss conversions. There is only one truth. All of us have an equal right to that truth, just as all of us have an equal right to the Indian Raman's Effect, the German Jew Einstein's Quantum Theory, or the American Edison's experiments. The Bhagavad Gita, the Holy Bible, the Koran, the Torah, the Dharmapada and other scriptures are open to all.

All of us have an equal right to quote Christ and Krishna and Lao-Tse and Socrates and Mohammed in the same sentence. Just like all sciences are open to everyone, so are all religions.

IS HINDUISM TOLERANT OF OTHER RELIGIONS?

In Hinduism, tolerance is not simply a matter of policy but an article of faith. Historians like H.G. Wells say that Hindu kings actually welcomed with open arms Christian missionaries and Muslim fakirs and Buddhist monks for free exchange of ideas. In fact, the greatest Hindu king, Ashoka (269-232 B.C.), changed his religion to Buddhism and propagated Buddhism throughout India. The "Laws of Dharma" or righteousness and epigraphic inscriptions which Ashoka left on various rocks and pillars throughout India are as historic as the "Bill of Rights" of the United States of America. Son, if you intend to study about only one king in the whole of Indian history, then it should be King Ashoka. H.G. Wells, who did not praise any king in his world history, made an exception regarding Ashoka and wrote, "The name of Ashoka shines almost alone, a star in the world history."

Another great Hindu king of Kerala, Cheraman Perumal (742-826 A.D.), converted to Islam, left India, and died in Mecca. One of the great apostles of Jesus Christ, Saint Thomas, came all the way to Madras, India, propagated Christianity, and finally died at Mylapore in Madras. It is indeed a fact that in 70 A.D., when Romans were feeding Christians to lions in Europe, in Kerala Christians were praying in churches to Saint Thomas.

Even today, when Jews are persecuted all over the world, in Cochin, India, they have absolute liberty to worship in their synagogues. (Jews came to India in the year 5 A.D.) In fact, some of the Jews who went to Israel from Kerala have come back to India because it is a land of such tolerance. Today, when a Jew cannot be converted to Christianity in Israel, when one cannot even carry a copy of the Holy Bible to Saudi Arabia, and when one cannot convert a Muslim to Christianity in Malaysia, thousands of Hindus in India are being converted to

Christianity. India today has the greatest number of major Catholic seminaries in the world--exactly 3,856.

A true Hindu never condemns any true religion. He/she accepts the truth behind all religions. A Hindu saint will only be happy to read the Bible or the Koran to his devotees.

Swami Vivekananda said, "I am proud to belong to a religion which has taught the world both tolerance and universal acceptance. We believe not only in universal toleration, but we accept all religions as true. As different streams having different sources all mingle their waters in the sea, so different paths which men take through different tendencies, various though they appear, crooked or straight, all lead to God."

DADDY, ARE HINDUS ALLOWED TO STUDY OTHER RELIGIONS?

Of course, my son. Hinduism not only allows but actually encourages one to seek truths from all sources. Hinduism strictly forbids comparison of different methods of God- realization, since all methods are true and all take devotees to God-realization. After studying Hinduism well, a Hindu should read and study all other true religions. Then he/she will be able to see Hinduism as the encyclopedia of religions, and to fully grasp the greatness of Jesus Christ, the sacrificial nature of the Sufi saints, and the importance of the ten commandments. If one knows Hinduism well, then the Bible, Koran, and Adi Grantha (the holy book of the Sikhs) will be interesting to read.

One of the great Hindu Puranas, the Srimad Bhagavatam says, "Like a honey bee gathering trickles of honey from different flowers, the wise man accepts the essence of different scriptures and sees only the good in all religions." With that kind of ideology, a Hindu should be eager to read all the religious books in the world.

DADDY, DO HINDUS HAVE A POPE?

No. As I told you before, in Hinduism there is no hierarchy. One of the ancient Hindu saints, Adi Sankara, set up four monasteries in different corners of India, which are popularly known as Sankaramaths. They are at Sringeri (Mysore), Badrinath (Himalayas), Dwaraka (Gujaret) and Puri (Orissa). The chief priest of each monastery is called Sankaracharya, and the priests there teach Hindus all aspects of Hinduism. Of course, these monasteries have no power to rule over the individual will of any Hindu. There are many monasteries in India apart from the four I mentioned above. All of them are independent of each other, and all propagate Hindu ideals in their own individual ways without criticizing each other.

Nobody is excommunicated from Hinduism, and nobody is persecuted in Hinduism. Hinduism has had revolutionaries like Buddha (who refused to acknowledge the authority of the Vedas) and Adi Sankara (who propagated Advaita philosophy), but it has never had a Martin Luther and never will, for it is open to all types of criticism from all quarters.

DADDY, IS IT POSSIBLE TO EXPRESS "SUBTLE TRUTHS" IN SIMPLE LANGUAGE? CAN THE HUMAN MIND REALIZE ULTIMATE TRUTHS?

I have to answer "no" to your question. Hinduism started with Sruti, "that which is heard." The Christ-like masters of the Vedic age, called Rishis, heard eternal truths in their hearts and taught their disciples telepathically, by actual transfer of thoughts. Only later did languages like Sanskrit and Pali emerge. For long periods of time there were no written texts. The Vedas and Upanishads were taught in chanted lyrics.

We know that thought is the best medium of realizing true knowledge, but since we cannot transfer thoughts, we express them in languages. Verbal language is better than written language in expressing thoughts. Sanskrit, Pali, Latin, Greek and Hebrew were used to express thoughts in ancient days. It is said that Jesus Christ spoke in Armenian and that a few years after his crucifixion the New Testament was written in three languages: Hebrew, Aramaic and Greek. The New Testament still preserves some important Aramaic statements such as "Eli, Eli, Lama Sabachthani"--"My God, my God, why hast Thou forsaken me?" (Matthew 27:46). During the 15th century, the first English version of the Bible was written by William Tyndale (1525). Unfortunately, he was accused of blasphemy and later burned at the stake!

After Tyndale, seven subsequent English versions of the Bible were written, the last of which was the most popular King James version, compiled by a large number of theologians under the leadership of King James of England in 1611. Unluckily, even the first edition of the King James version had more than three hundred errors in it (*How We Got the Bible*, Neil R. Lightfoot). This only shows how difficult it is to write thoughts in words. Apart from that, the Holy Bible is full of numerical symbolism. For example, 666 stands for the Antichrist and 12 stands for spiritual faculties. All good things in the Bible are associated with the number twelve: twelve apostles, twelve sons of Jacob, twelve tribes of Israel, etc. With such underlying symbolism, translation of the Bible is even more difficult.

English right now is spoken by the vast majority of people--its vocabulary has developed abundantly, and it has become the prime means of conveying thoughts. So English may be the only language in the world which can express truths in a more understandable format. Luckily for us, we also have mathematics, physics and other sciences to aid us in understanding subtle truths today.

Again, understanding is something very personal. For example, "$E=mc^2$" may be just a few letters for common folks, but to students of science they speak volumes. So eternal truths can be understood only if we evolve high enough to understand them. This is true of Hinduism, Christianity, Islam and all other religions.

Taoism states that impressions of life cannot be conveyed by words. The Chinese mystic Lao-Tse said, "He who knows never tells. He who tells never knew." This shows that subtle truths are indeed difficult to express in words, since words try to limit their size. It will be correct to conclude that the human mind can never conceive the ultimate truths of the universe.

Indeed, Einstein tried to develop a unified field theory to explain all the riddles in the universe, but he failed miserably. Finally he accepted defeat and said, "The human mind is not capable of grasping the universe. We are like a little child entering a huge library." Gauthama Buddha very clearly stated that only by transcending human existence can one understand the supreme reality. That may be reason why Buddha, who left the country as a young prince to get instant remedies for old age and death, came back with his famous eightfold path to Nirvana. If there are ready-made answers to the riddles of the universe, great masters like Buddha and Christ would surely have given them to the world. Since their answers are ambiguous to almost all of us, we have to face the fact that ultimate truths are beyond mind and beyond duality perception.

Today, confined to his wheelchair, unable to speak, paralyzed by an incurable disease, the great British physicist Stephen Hawking seeks the Grand Unification Theory that will explain all the riddles of the universe. Will he succeed? Will he be able to unlock the mysteries of the universe? That is the one billion-dollar question. Isaac Newton's universe was perfect, linear and predictable. Einstein's universe became somewhat unpredictable and took on wave patterns. Today's scientists claim that the universe is somewhat chaotic and unpredictable.

DO YOU REALLY THINK WORDS CAN BE MISINTERPRETED AND MISUNDERSTOOD?

Yes indeed. Due to the lack of sufficient words in the Aramaic language, Christ was forced to use words like "My kingdom" and "I am the King" to explain subtle truths about spirituality to people. But the same words made the Romans angry, for "kingdom" and "king" had a different meaning to them altogether.

Look at the lives of the Sufis. Just like a realized Hindu master who says "I am Brahman" (the Spirit), each of them said "I am God." But the Islamic fundamentalists of that age could not fully grasp the true meanings of the utterances of those great Sufi masters, and all of them were put to death. Throughout history, you can find many such examples of misunderstanding due to the lack of vocabulary in language. Christ told parables, and we also have mythological stories to explain the subtle truths of the universe. I feel that if Christ or Krishna or Buddha came back today, they · would use electrons, DNA, electro-magneticism and other scientific concepts to explain subtle
truths.

DADDY, DO YOU THINK HISTORY AND TRADITION HAVE A VITAL ROLE IN EVERY RELIGIOUS SCRIPTURE?

Very surely so. The history of Hinduism is a very slowly-developed thought process. That is the reason why, in the Rig Veda, we see a nomad community just settling on the banks of the Indus, worshipping all natural gods and stating, "After all, who knows, and who can say, from where it all came and how creation takes place?"

Look at one of the oldest Hindu scriptures, Manusmriti. The "Code of Manu" is indeed the history of a nomad society taking roots on the banks of the River Indus. During the Rig Vedic period the Aryans were constantly engaged in battles, and drinking and gambling were part and parcel of their culture. Those who drank Sura were known as Suras or Devas, and those who refused to drink this beverage were known as Asuras. You will see that Manu restricted the freedom of women in so many ways. He also put down the foundation stone of the modern-day caste system.

Similarly, look at Exodus in the Old Testament. In telling us of the exodus of the Jews from Egypt, it describes a society which condoned slavery. The Old Testament is the true history of the Jews in those times. So I fully agree with you, almost all scriptures in the world are part and parcel of history and tradition.

IS METAPHOR A PART OF SCRIPTURAL LANGUAGE?

Many may disagree with me, but I must say that metaphor is a part and parcel of all religious scriptures. The poet within the saint has taken off and written things in almost all the religious scriptures in the world. One will come across lines similar to the "Lotus Eaters" of Tennyson in all religious scriptures.

So religious scriptures should be properly scanned to get proper meanings rather than considered as true in every written word. We will make grave errors if we try to analyze the literal meaning of the scriptures. In fact, on December 14, 1990, Pope John Paul cautioned Christians against literal interpretation of the Holy Bible. He said,

"The books of the Bible have God as their author, but the men who composed them were also true authors." He added that the essential message of the Bible is lost in interpretations that are strictly based on observable facts.

ARE YOU SAYING THAT THERE IS A POET IN EVERY SAINT, AND THAT ALL WRITINGS CAN CONSIST OF TRUTH AS WELL AS FIGMENTS OF THE SAINT'S IMAGINATION?

You said it right. I could not have said it in better words. So all scriptures should not be followed word for word, but they have to be scanned for truth. This is true of Hinduism and all other religions including Christianity.

DADDY, WHO IS AN ATHEIST? ARE AN ATHEIST AND AN AGNOSTIC ONE AND THE SAME?

The word "theism" means "belief in a god or gods." So the word "atheism" means absence of theistic belief, or the belief that there is no god or gods of any kind. So in a nutshell, a person who does not believe in the existence of a God is an atheist.

An agnostic, on the other hand, is a person who believes that there are things beyond the human mind. An agnostic may or may not believe in a God. So an agnostic can be a theist or an atheist. The terms "gnostic" and "agnostic" were actually coined by the philosopher-thinker Thomas Huxley in 1869. "Gnostic" came from the Greek root word "gnosis," meaning "to know."

The best explanation of both terms comes from the Catholic Encyclopedia and it is as follows: "An agnostic is not an atheist. An atheist denies the existence of God; an agnostic professes ignorance about His existence. For the latter, God may exist, but reason can neither prove nor disprove it."

WOULD YOU SAY MOST PEOPLE ARE AGNOSTIC?

I would say some intellectuals are agnostic, but at the same time, most of the uneducated masses are believers. Most religions use the fear of God and hell to make people believe in them. This you will never come across in Hinduism, where a believer, an atheist and an agnostic can happily coexist. Let us look at the case of Bertrand Russell. Many saw him as an atheist, but he was actually an agnostic. He questioned everything and he never came to any conclusions. The only mistake he made was to write a book named *Why I Am Not a Christian*. He should not have named the book in that way, because he had no right to hurt the feelings of millions of devoted Christians around the globe. He should have named the book *The Doubts I Have About World Religions*. That would have saved him from unnecessary criticism from many religious quarters as well as from being denied a job in New York City.

Anyway, I don't think he ever wrote that there is no God. For that would be against his style, denying or approving something of which he had no idea or definition. Russell did not deny God, since he could not define God. Standing in Hinduism, one can easily respect and admire people like Russell, Freud and Darwin.

Hinduism has its share of atheists and agnostics. The Charvaka philosophy and to some extent the Vaisesika philosophy question the existence of a personal God. Kanada, the founder of Vaisesika philosophy, only mentioned God as "That" in all of his writings.

DADDY, DO YOU MEAN TO SAY THAT AN AGNOSTIC WILL STAY AN AGNOSTIC FOREVER?

All Hindu scriptures point to the fact that agnosticism is the starting point of a relentless pursuit after truth. Just like a pinch of salt which goes to find out the depth of the ocean and then becomes part and parcel of the ocean, an agnostic will finally realize eternal truths if he persists in his search of truth. But just like Buddha, he won't be able to explain the truth he finds out to the world, since that truth is beyond description or comparison. I feel most agnostics will finally become personalities like J. Krishnamurti and Buddha, provided they do not try to seek intellectual answers to the riddles of the universe. As an orphan, Krishnamurti was hand-picked by the late Annie Besant to become a great leader of the Theosophical Society. But as time went on, Krishnamurti transcended all positions and power and questioned the integrity of every minute thing in every religion. Finally he became an institution in himself, without an iota of ego. Of course, Krishnamurti was not an agnostic at all. He was a logician with great capabilities. So as far as Hinduism is concerned, agnosticism is the starting point of the relentless pursuit after truth.

DADDY, DO YOU BELIEVE IN GOD?

Son, I come from a very religious family and as such I believe in God and sometimes even in a very personal God. Sometimes I see God as an entity without any feelings or consciousness. According to the time and place, my concept of God changes. When I was a teenager I did not have any problem visualizing "It" as Lord Krishna, but when I became older I began to see "It" as a power source, something beyond my wildest imaginations. Of course, I have no problem listening to a person who describes "It" as Lord Krishna or Jesus Christ or Allah or Jehovah or Buddha or anything else, nor do I have any problem listening to anyone who describes "It" as a formless, imperishable, timeless, unborn, indescribable entity. One thing I know for certain. We are all part and parcel of nature. We are just instruments of an unknown entity or energy or power or something beyond definition. On one side we are just an amalgamation of chemicals, we are just an array of DNA molecules. On the other side, we are conscious entities.

Honestly, I am at total loss whenever I think of God. To begin with, I do not know where to start, and the more I read about "It," the more I study modern science, the more curious I am about God and the universe. That does not mean religion has all the answers. All religions of the world have not fully explained many of their fundamental principles. Anyway, the lack of proper answers makes me a very humble person. Today, I know for sure that we know very little about ourselves or about the universe.

2 ❧
Christianity in India

DADDY, WHEN AND HOW WAS CHRISTIANITY SPREAD
IN INDIA?

Son, as I mentioned earlier, in 70 A.D. when the
Romans under Emperor Nero were feeding Christians to
angry lions, in Kerala, India, Christians were worshipping
in churches. Long before any part of Europe came to
know about Jesus Christ and his wonderful teachings, the
southeastern part of India, Malabar, had a flourishing
Christianity. In 65 A.D., Malabar had many Christian
churches.

In India, Saint Thomas the Apostle started Christianity. According to a very ancient Syriac work, *The Acts
of Judas Thomas*, the apostles who were together in
Jerusalem after the ascension of Jesus Christ cast lots to
decide where each should go and preach the Gospel.
India fell to the lot of Thomas, who did not want to go.
Legends say that later Thomas had a dream, in which
Christ asked him to go to India. It may be the irony of
fate that poor Thomas was purchased as a slave by a
merchant from the northwest of India and forcefully taken
there. After coming to India Thomas converted his master
to Christianity, and later took a boat to Malabar in the year
52 A.D. He reached a place very close to Cochin, and
later established churches all over Kerala. He travelled to
China and finally died at Mylapore, Madras in 72 A.D.

Most of the teachings of Saint Thomas in India had
a very close resemblance to Hindu teachings. The world
knows very little of the teachings of Thomas today. Some
parts of the lost original text of the Gospel of Thomas
were found in 1945. What the archaeologists found is
similar to Hindu ideals and principles. A very good book
on the Thomas gospels and other Gnostic gospels is
available on the market today. The book is *The Gnostic*

Gospels, written by Elaine Pagels and published by Vintage Books.

It is said that by 189 A.D., much of South India had a very large population of Christians. It is said that a bishop from India attended the great Council of Nicaea in 325 A.D.

Christianity really spread by leaps and bounds after the Portuguese under Vasco de Gama came to my own town, Calicut, in 1498. Another great preacher of Christianity in India was Saint Francis Xavier of Goa. By 1599, the Catholic Church was well-established in India.

I am one of those who always thank the Christian missionaries for bringing mass education to India. Christian missionaries worked along with liberal Hindu theologians to eradicate the evils in Hindu society. Hindu reformers like Raja Rammohan Roy, Keshab Chandra Sen, Ramakrishna Paramahamsa, Vivekananda and Gandhi were influenced by the compassionate aspects of Christianity.

3
Birth and Development of Hinduism

WHO IS THE FOUNDER OF HINDUISM?

Nobody in particular. It is the research output of many learned men known as Rishis, all of whom were Christ-like masters.

WHEN WAS HINDUISM BORN?

An exact date cannot be given. There are many theories regarding the birth of Hinduism. If you go by Hindu mythological stories, Hinduism is trillions of years old. Some state that it started immediately after the ending of the last ice age. Some date its origins to 6000-7000 years before Christ. Some theologians like Max Muller of Germany trace the beginnings of Hinduism to the third millennium B.C. According to this theory, nomad tribes of European descent came to India and settled on the banks of the Indus, Ganges, and Brahmaputra Rivers. These tribes were called Aryans ("Noble Ones"). After their settlement, they started a "thinking process" which was later known as Hinduism.

Who really started this great thinking process in India? Did the nomad Aryans who settled in India start it, or was it actually started by the dark-colored Indians, known as Dravidians, who always lived in India? That is a million-dollar question. According to many Hindu theologians, knowledge has always existed in India from antiquity. According to them, the early settlers of North India mixed their knowledge with the civilization of the dark-colored people of South India, the Dravidians, and started Hinduism.

The astonishing discovery of the Indus valley civilization at Mohenjodaro and Harappa dates back to 6000-7000 years before Christ. The Mohenjodaro and

Harappa excavations declare the Indus valley civilization as not only non-Aryan but pre-Aryan on the basis of: (a) the presence of beautiful cities, (b) the absence of iron in these cities, and (c) the absence of horses. From the artifacts excavated at Harappa, we know today that Indus valley people worshipped Lord Siva as Lord Rudra, worshipped a mother goddess, built ceremonial baths, practiced Yoga, and had fire pits. The cities had paved roads and underground sewers.

According to some theologians, the people of the Mayan civilization were mighty navigators and in fact had once conquered parts of India, which resulted in the intermingling of Mayan and Aryan civilizations. Valmiki in his beautiful epic Ramayana refers to the Danava invasion of India. Some believe that the Danavas were in fact Mayans. In another story, the Mahabharata warrior Arjuna fought against the Danavas at Hiranyapura. Some believe the Mayans wrote the Sourya-Siddhanta, an ancient treatise on astronomy in India.

Dravidians might have started the "thinking process" of Hinduism, but it was later influenced by Aryan, Mayan, Egyptian and Greek civilizations. Several points show that:

1. "There is only one God, but that God is expressed in different forms" may be an offspring of the Egyptian civilization.
2. The theory of life after death may be an Egyptian idea which the Greeks worked on and which finally became part and parcel of Aryan civilization.
3. The Rudra, the God of Annihilation who was worshipped by the Aryans, is actually a Dravidian god. Rudra was later known as Siva in the later scriptures of Hinduism.
4. Gods like Varuna (water) and Vayu (air) have corresponding gods in Greek mythology.

Today, all great religions of the world are a mixture of contradictory ideas and thoughts. Even Christianity is a complex blend of Judaism, Platonism (philosophy of Plato), Gnosticism, and Roman paganism. In fact, according to Encyclopedia Britannica, the early Christian theologian Augustine of Hippo (354-430 A.D.), "fused the religion of the New Testament with the Platonic tradition of Greek philosophy." Most pagan influence on Christianity happened after Emperor Constantine of Rome (306-327 A.D.) became a Christian in 312 A.D.

WHO ARE DRAVIDIANS?

As I said before, all people in South India can be called Dravidians. But taking into account the location of all the temples of Lord Siva and the development of Saivism, I should say Madras and its surroundings are the prime locations of the Dravidian civilization.

The best scripture in Dravidian civilization is Thirukural, written in the Tamil language by a saint named Thiruvalluar during the first century B.C. Thirukural is considered to be the holy bible of Saivites (people who worship Lord Siva--the God of Annihilation).

DID ARYANS AND DRAVIDIANS LIVE IN AMITY?

I wish to answer yes, but even today there is misunderstanding between South Indians and North Indians on some aspects of religion. Many Hindus consider Lord Siva to be a Dravidian god and Lord Vishnu to be an Aryan god. As such, some Dravidians, especially in Madras, feel that most of the Hindu mythology has gone into purposefully ridiculing Lord Siva, because in almost all mythological stories Lord Siva always winds up on the losing side of battles, especially with his close ties to demons like Ravana and Narakasura. Whereas in all those mythological stories, Lord Vishnu comes out a winner and lovable. Maybe all these stories are mere coincidences and people today are reading things into ancient scriptures and finding out fresh meanings to those episodes of mythology. Anyhow, most Saivites today do not give much importance to the Bhagavad Gita, maybe due to its dominance by Lord Vishnu.

DADDY, HOW WAS HINDUISM STARTED?

According to Hindu scriptures, it started with Sruti. Sruti literally means "that which is heard." The great scientists of those days called Rishis who had perfected themselves by meditation are said to have heard in their hearts eternal truths, and these truths were taught to their disciples telepathically. For long periods of time there was no literature on them. The Vedas and Upanishads were in Sruti format for long periods of time. In fact the word Upanishad means Upa (near), Ni(down), Shad (sit). It means the teachings of the Upanishads are conveyed from Guru to disciple when the disciple sits very close to the Guru.

According to Christian theologians, the Holy Bible is a Holy Spirit or Holy Ghost-inspired book. II Peter 1:21 reads, "For the prophecy came not in old time by the will of man; but holy men of God spake as they were moved by the Holy Ghost." II Timothy 3:16 states that "All scripture is given by inspiration of God."

Similarly, all Sruti literature is considered as the revealed truth of God. The Vedic literature, according to one school of thought (Nyaiyayikas), was composed by the Almighty God. According to the Mimamsa school of thought, all Sruti existed all through eternity in the form of sounds. Therefore the sounds of the words of the Vedas and Upanishads are very important.

WHAT WAS THE ORIGINAL NAME OF HINDUISM?

Sanathana Dharma, meaning "righteousness forever" of "that which has no beginning or end," was its original name. It was the Persians who invaded India in the sixth century B.C. who gave the name Hinduism. This word originated from the root word "Indus." Some say that this word originated from a Persian word meaning "river people."

By the name Sanathana Dharma, Hinduism is proclaiming to the world that eternal truths are forever, and Rishis happened to be the first to tap into them. Saint Augustine on his part said, "True religion always existed and became Christian after the appearance of Jesus Christ." So the same truths can be found out by anyone who is in relentless pursuit after truth, even if he/she has absolutely no idea of Hinduism. Just like scientists around the world sometimes stumble across similar discoveries, eternal truths are known to the Sufis, Buddha, Socrates, Christ, Nanak and others even though they may or may not have known one word of Hindu scriptures. Personally I feel Sanathana Dharma is the most appropriate name for Hinduism.

WHAT IS THE LANGUAGE IN WHICH HINDU SCRIPTURES ARE WRITTEN?

Sanskrit. It is an ancient language like Hebrew and Latin. Sanskrit has fifty-two alphabets, and believe it or not the first words of the English language, "father" and "mother," came from the Sanskrit words "pitha" and "mata" as per the book *The Story of English*. Almost all sixteen languages of India have come out of Sanskrit.

ARE ALL HINDU SCRIPTURES WRITTEN BY SPECIFIC
AUTHORS?

We have only speculative guesses on the authorship
of different Hindu scriptures. Almost all Hindu scriptures
are written by anonymous authors. Through all Hindu
scriptures one can see the authors deliberately trying to
avoid signing their names anywhere.

Again, including the Bhagavad Gita, all scriptures
are written with a third person narrating format. In the
Bhagavad Gita, Lord Krishna (first person) is advising
warrior-prince Arjuna (second person), and that advice is
heard and seen telepathically by a saint named Sanjaya
(third person) and narrated to King Dhartharashtra (fourth
person).

Another epic, the Ramayana, is written as a
narration of the story of Lord Rama by a small bird who
has just lost its lover to the arrow of a wicked hunter.
The scripture Yoga Vasishtha which came out of the
Ramayana is a discussion between Lord Rama and the
saint Vasishtha. The most dramatic narration one can find
in the Srimad Mahabhagavatam, where Saint Suka is
describing the whole story of the ten Avatars of Lord
Vishnu to the doomed King Pareeshit in seven days. On
the seventh day the king was killed by the serpent
Thashakan.

Indirectly, the Srimad Mahabhagavatam is
proclaiming to the world that all of us are like the
doomed King Pareeshit, with very limited time to live on
this earth, so God-realization is the most important duty
of all of us.

Nobody can clearly say why this deliberate attempt
to conceal the authorship of scriptures was made by
almost all saints of Hinduism. Perhaps it could be to
avoid the emergence of unnecessary ego, or perhaps it
was a statement to the world that all these stories are

eternal truths and as such no authorship question should arise.

IS HINDUISM CONFUSING AND CONTRADICTORY?

Absolutely not. To a person who reads the Hindu scriptures haphazardly, Hinduism may seem to be somewhat confusing and contradictory. However, to someone who has researched the scriptures, Hinduism stands as an embodiment of truth. Since Hinduism is a slowly-developed thought process, in it you can see the existence of primitive religion as well as very advanced religion. Of course Hinduism also allows literally hundreds of contradictory thoughts to coexist within it. Hinduism is like modern science. Just like hundreds of scientists around the world are doing research on different and sometimes conflicting ideas, in Hinduism the Rishis used to work on different conflicting aspects of the riddles of the universe.

Hinduism has never had a "house cleaning" in its five thousand-year history. That is also the reason why it looks like a great soup. On one side you see strict morality, and on the other Tantric eroticism. On one side there is the personal God, and on the other side Hinduism talks about a Brahman with no feelings. Christianity, on its part, had yearly house cleanings from the day it was born. Since the first Council at Nicaea in 325 A.D., it has thrown out anyone who does not literally follow the Church. That is the reason why Jehovah's Witnesses and Mormons are out of the mainstream of Christianity.

Again, contradictions are seen in every scripture in the world. The Old Testament is in direct contrast to the New Testament in many aspects. When the New Testament talks about showing "the other cheek" when attacked, the Old Testament talks about "an eye for an eye" ideology. When the Old Testament details all types of sexual activity including incest, the New Testament upholds very high morality. The Old Testament God demanded and allowed human sacrifices. But you will see a very compassionate and understanding God in the New Testament. Apart from that, the Gospel of Saint Thomas ("Doubting Thomas") is somewhat different from the Gospels of Matthew, Mark, Luke and John. Of course, the Saint Thomas Gospel is not included in the New Testament, maybe due to its differences with other gospels.

Once again, it is wrong to judge any scripture in the world by quoting lines from it here and there. We have to look at the summation of ideas of the whole scripture and not the word meaning of each specific line.

IS HINDUISM A RELIGION LIKE CHRISTIANITY?

No. It is more a way of life than a specific religion. As I told you before, in Hinduism you can find all religions of the world. Jainism, Buddhism and Sikhism emerged from Hinduism. Sikhism was originated by Guru Nanak by combining the good and prominent aspects of Hinduism and Islam.

Similarly, both Christianity and Islam came out of Judaism. It is from Judaism that both Christianity and Islam inherited many religious principles, morals and practices. Without studying Judaism, it is very difficult for one to have a very clear picture of both Christianity and Islam. In fact, I should conclude that both Hinduism and Judaism are the two mothers of all world religions.

DADDY, WHAT IS THE MOST IMPORTANT ASPECT OF HINDUISM?

Since there are very many aspects of Hinduism, it is very difficult to say that one aspect is better than others.

Still, I feel that being truthful to oneself is the most important aspect of Hinduism.

WHICH IS EASIER, TO BECOME A BELIEVER OR A NON-BELIEVER?

To become a non-believer is quite easy. Just say, "I don't want to hear that; I do not believe in anything you say," close your mind to truth, and like an ostrich bury your head in a heap of sand. To become a true believer one has to think and explore all realms of thought. Lord Krishna said, "For he who doubts, there is no happiness in this world or in the next world. Doubts came out of ignorance and should be destroyed by the sword of knowledge" (Bhagavad Gita 4:40, 42).

DO YOU HAVE TO BELIEVE IN HINDUISM TO STUDY IT?

Not at all. You can study Hinduism just like you study mathematics, physics or chemistry. You do not even have to believe in a personal or impersonal God. Just have an open mind and be ready to explore new realms of thought. That is all that is required from anyone who wants to study Hinduism.

As far as I am concerned, studying Hinduism is like looking through a giant kaleidoscope. Each time you shake a kaleidoscope, you see a different picture. Similarly, each time you study Hinduism you will come across a different thought.

DADDY, WHAT ATTRACTS YOU TO HINDUISM?

Utmost freedom of thought. That is what attracts me to Hinduism. Where else can you see Krishna, Buddha (who questioned the authority of the Vedas), Adi Sankara (who revolutionized thinking in Hinduism), and Charvaka (who originated a materialistic philosophy) all treated with equal respect? If Sankara and Buddha had been born in some other faith, they would have burned alive. Look at what happened to Socrates and William Tyndale. Look what happened to the Sufi saints when they proclaimed they were God, in tune with the mantra "Aham Brahmasmin" ("I am Brahman" or "I am God"). All were executed for their free thinking.

So in Hinduism, you can argue on any subject and you don't have to accept anything until you are fully convinced of the truth behind it. Again, Hinduism has no monopoly on ideas. Ideas are unwritten laws of the universe; they are open to all who are in the relentless pursuit after truth.

WHAT MAKES HINDUISM REALLY GREAT?

Hinduism is a great banyan tree. On its "sakas" (limbs) one can see the principles of all the great religions of the world. The total surrender Yoga which Jesus Christ spoke of one can see in the Bhagavad Gita. The statement of the Sufis that "I am God" one can see in the Upanishads as "Aham Brahmasmin." The statement of Lao-Tse that everything is Tao can be seen as "Everything is Brahman" in the Upanishads. In Hinduism alone one can see the strange coexistence of an atheist, an agnostic and a theist. When Socrates and the Sufis were persecuted in the West, in India we adored Buddha, who did not recognize the authority of the Vedas, and tolerated Charvaka, who ridiculed the Vedas and attacked the mere existence of God. So let us face it, in Hinduism one can find a religion tailor-made for each of us, whatever be our way of thinking.

Hinduism recognizes the fact that people are on different levels. Matters do not apply or appeal to all persons in the same manner. My mother could go into a trance just by looking at the picture of Lord Krishna. But for you and I, that is unimaginable. I could appreciate and admire the Sanskrit lyrics in the Mahabharata, but for you that may be difficult. That is the reason why Hinduism, which is filled with hundreds of ideas, will appeal to all.

DADDY, WHAT IS THE TRUE HINDU IDEA ABOUT GOD?

Hindus believe in one God expressed in different forms. In a way, that God is beyond any comparison to anything known to mankind. Hindus do not believe that God has human form or any other form as described in mythology or in the biblical Genesis. It won't be wrong to state that God did not make man in His own image as the Old Testament says, but instead man made God in his own image. God is indeed a timeless and formless entity. Just like Allah of Islam, the Tao of Taoism, and Ayin of the Kabbalah have no definition, the God in Hinduism has no definition. In the Kabbalah, the Jewish mysticism, Ayin means "nothing." Ayin is beyond existence. Ayin has no attributes. When Moses asked God, "Who are You?" the answer came from the burning bushes, "I am what I am." That clearly proves that Jehovah ("i am") is not a being with human attributes. The Holy Bible also states that "God is Spirit" (John 4:23-24), and that he who worships Him worships in spirit. Psalms 139:7-10 states that God is a spirit that is everywhere. Luke 24:39 states that spirit does not have flesh and bones. No word or image can express or describe the magnitude of God. Coming back to the Hindu concepts of God, they can be explained further as follows:

1. All came from that one which cannot be defined, called Brahman (monism). Buddhists do not believe in Brahman. They feel that such matters cannot be surely determined.

2. All came from That, so all existence is good and divine (pantheism).
3. There is only one God (monotheism).
4. All of us are Gods. This, of course, is just like saying that if you can analyze one drop of sea water, then you know everything about the entire sea, or that if you know the properties of the electricity within the light bulb, then you know all about the electricity in the entire network.
5. To search for God is like a pinch of salt finding the depth of the ocean. The moment the pinch of salt hits the surface of the ocean, it becomes part and parcel of the ocean. Similarly, a devotee who seeks God becomes part and parcel of That.

WHAT EXACTLY IS THE DIFFERENCE BETWEEN GOD AND US?

It is a tough question to answer since God is beyond all definitions. But to some extent I feel the answer is the same difference between the energy in the light bulb and the energy of the entire network of electric power. The energy in the light bulb is the exact replica of the energy in the network, but light bulb energy is very small unless it constantly links with the network energy. So even though we are indeed God, we do not have the power of God unless we constantly link with the God. That can be achieved only by surrendering the individual will to the will of God. That is more easily said than done.

IS EACH OF US THE CENTER POINT OF THE UNIVERSE?

As far as Hinduism is concerned that idea is true. You and I are the center points of the universe. But that "I" is one. There is no more "you" and "I." There is no more subject and object. One and one only...one "I" which is the universe.

The expanding theory of the universe states that every point in the expanding universe is the center of the universe, and, as per Hinduism, every being in the universe is the focal point from which the universe emerges.

Hinduism also states that every individual is a Sukshma-Jagat, or "minute world." It came from the belief that whatever exists in the universe also exists in the human body. Man is a part and parcel of the universe. The universe and human body are made of identical materials and as such the Hindu saints say that all answers are within. If one can understand the forces within, then one will be able to understand all the forces in nature. In the Jewish Kabbalah, man is viewed as being a microcosm, a minute picture of the universe. The Kabbalah has a belief similar to Hinduism's that man's actions can affect the universe, and that the universe in turn can affect the well being of a man.

DOES HINDUISM STATE THAT ALL TRUTHS ARE ETERNAL?

Let me put it another way. Hindus believe that there are eternal truths and they are open to everyone who seeks them, even if they are ignorant of Hindu scriptures or Hindu ideals. So a true Christian or a true Muslim or a true Jew is automatically a true Hindu. Truths are existing forever. Each prophet found them independently and gave them to the world in his own language. So the so-called word "invention" is not really true. We cannot find out something which is not in nature. A better word would be "discover." Ernst Kapp, the German philosopher, states that all inventions up to the computer are natural extensions of human nature.

IS IT A FACT THAT MANY CALL HINDUISM A PERSONAL RELIGION?

It is indeed true. Hinduism, if at all someone wants to name it a religion with boundaries, is indeed a personal religion. Each Hindu prays and meditates alone. Bhajans (devotional group singing) are part of the modern trend in Hinduism. There is no word "pooja" in Vedic literature. Pooja is a part of the mythological scriptures of Hinduism. Great Rishis used to sit and pray for a common cause and then depart. This praying was known as Yatna. According to Hinduism, each person's religion is unique. He/she is seeking within for all answers, so we have to conclude that Hinduism is a personal religion. A Guru can be a Raja Yogi and his disciple can be a Bhakti Yogi. Everyone follows a unique religion. That is the beauty of Hinduism.

WHAT ARE THE HINDU AIMS OF LIFE?

The Hindu aims of life are popularly known as Purusharthas or human goals. They are Dharma (right conduct), Artha (material gain), Kama (sexual love) and Moksha (salvation). All men try to achieve all four goals in their life.

WHAT DOES HINDUISM HAVE TO SAY ABOUT CREATION?

As per Hinduism, creation has neither beginning nor end. It is a continuous process. Birth and death are part and parcel of creation. Millions of galaxies take birth every day and millions of galaxies destroy themselves every day. Lord Nataraja, the dancing god of India, is the symbol of the cyclic creation and destruction of the universe.

As per this principle, energy can neither be created nor destroyed. Hindus use the word manifestation when they talk about creation. Creation is manifested out of Prakriti, or Nature, and then it goes back into its original source. I do hope now you properly understand the Hindu view of creation.

WHAT EXACTLY IS OUR PROBLEM?

As far as I know there is a rhythm of life, and man's ignorance of this important fact is creating all problems for him. Even the Rig Veda, the first scripture of Hinduism, talks about a cosmic order known as Rta. From alternating currents to everything else, life is cyclic as well as rhythmic. Everything in the world is pulsating. Look at light. Even it is only a form of electromagnetic radiation traveling in various wavelengths. Lao-Tse, the great Chinese mystic, taught that the world moves according to a divine pattern which is reflected in the rhythmic and cyclic movements of nature, and that man's happiness depends upon his capability to understand the rhythmic and orderly nature of the universe. Lord Nataraja, through his cosmic dance, is showing us that the world is in rhythm, involving constant creation and constant annihilation.

All matter, including you and I, has rhythmic movement within it, and our quest should be to create a proper rhythmic harmony within ourselves. Mantra Yoga, Pranayama and other exercises help a man to make his vibrations rhythmic. According to Mantra Yoga, all living things in all states of existence have bodily forms fully attuned to certain frequencies of vibration. Mantra, a system of syllables made with particular frequencies of vibration, is used to change one's vibrational frequency to a better state.

You feel happy when you sit near an ocean because your vibrations try to synchronize with the frequency of the waves. Even in the devotional aspects of all religions where the devotees cry for Krishna, Rama, Jesus or Jehovah, the final accomplishment is rhythm--an understanding of the rhythm of the universe. According to the expanding theory of the universe as well as the contracting theory of the universe, the universe itself is rhythmic--more or less acting like a pulsating heart. Hinduism calls the great rhythm of the universe by the name Spandhanam. Earth and the universe are in an eternal cosmic dance, according to Fritjof Capra and his very famous book, *The Tao of Physics.*

WHAT DO YOU THINK IS THE GREATEST PARADOX IN LIFE?

I feel the mysterious "I" or ego is the greatest paradox in life. We always say "I," "mine," "my son," "my house," "my car," etc., but we do not know the answer to the question "Who am I?" When the soul leaves the body at the time of death, the dead body does not say "I am here," and neither does the departed soul say "I am here outside the body." Yet when body and soul join together, we hear "I" all the time. Don't you think that is a great paradox? The "I" or "ego" feelings make our lives miserable. If I tell you that one thousand houses were demolished by a car bomb in a remote village in the Middle East, then you will shake your head as if nothing happened. But if I tell you that there is a small fire in one of the houses in our street you immediately become panicky. But at the same time, if you increase your sense of ownership from limited to unlimited, you feel free. When you think about your son you are worried about his welfare, but when you think about all the children of the world you have no worry and indeed you are very happy. It is said that a God-realized man sees the "I" as the universe and the universe as "I." So when the limited ego becomes the universal ego, we achieve everlasting happiness.

Of course, to transform the limited ego into the universal ego is not an easy job, but by continued practice of different methods of God-realization we can achieve that Herculean task confronting all of us. According to Ramana Maharshi, "finding the real I" is the supreme goal of a man's life, and his teachings are based on erasing the ego.

WHAT SHOULD A MAN DO TO HAVE A HAPPY LIFE?

If you are looking for a one-line answer from me, then that answer is to be harmonious with nature. Most of a man's problems start when he fights with nature. Man knows very well that he cannot discover or invent anything that is already in nature. Still man tries to fight nature. Going back to nature does not mean living like stone-age human beings. It only means to bring back truth, love and peace in day-to-day life. As I stated before, Lao-Tse said that the world moves in a rhythmic and cyclic pattern, and man's happiness depends upon his capability to understand this rhythmic and orderly nature of the universe. Nature is the basis of Taoism.

Hinduism as per History

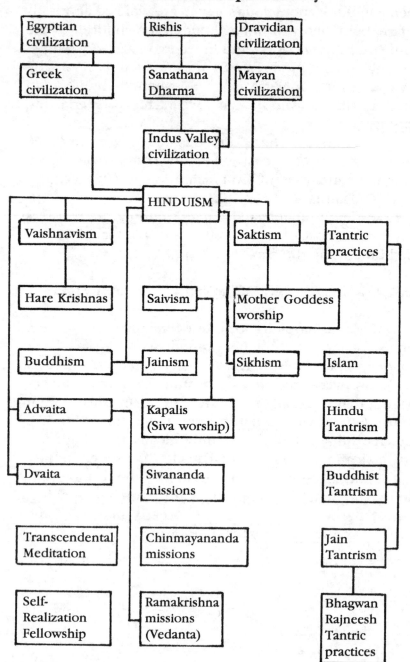

4 ‎
Indology

DADDY, WHAT IS INDOLOGY?

Indology is the study of Indian history, literature, religions and languages by the West. It started with the publication a Dutch translation of poems by the saint Bhatrihari by a Dutch missionary to South India, Roger Abraham, in 1651. Bhatrihari's poems dealt with the customs and religion of the Brahmins. Later, in 1790, an Austrian Roman Catholic priest by the name of Fra Paolino de San Bartolommeo wrote two Sanskrit grammar texts for the use of Christian missionaries in India.

The enthusiasm of the West for India reached its climax after Voltaire referred to the Yajur Veda in his book *Customs and Spirit of Nations* (1759). The man who really caused the development of Indology was none other than the first English Governor-General to India, Warren Hastings (1732-1818). He was indeed lost in the beauty of the Bhagavad Gita and he arranged the first English translation of the Gita into English. He wrote in the preface to this translation (1875) that the Gita would survive when the British dominion should have long since ceased to exist.

Warren Hastings made the Brahmin pandits prepare a condensed text of the Hindu codes and laws based on ancient scriptures. This text, originally written in Sanskrit, was later translated into English and was published in 1776 as *A Code of Gentoo Law* by Nathaniel Halhed.

After Warren Hastings, very many scholars from Europe became fascinated by Hindu scriptures, and they studied Sanskrit and translated many of these scriptures into English. One German scholar, Gundart, came down to Kerala state and wrote a dictionary for the language Malayalam.

Germany is one of the countries in the world where Indology is still popular. Philosophers like Max Muller and scientists like Oppenheimer (father of the atom bomb) were fascinated by Hinduism after studying Indology. When the first atom bomb was exploded in the deserts of New Mexico, a jubilant Oppenheimer greeted the news by chanting Sanskrit verses from the Bhagavad Gita.

It may not be wrong to conclude that even Adolf Hitler was influenced by the Tantric part of Hinduism. From where else did he pick up the swastika and his unique hand gesture which resembled the Hindu Abhaya Mudra? Anyway, that is something for speculation.

5 ஒ
Sruti and Smriti Literature

DADDY, WHAT ARE THE HINDU SCRIPTURES?

Son, the Hindu scriptures can be broadly classified into two groups. One is Sruti ("that which is heard") literature and the other is Smriti ("that which is remembered") literature. Both these literatures are considered as "revelations of God" just like all Biblical literature is considered to be God-inspired.

WHAT ARE THE FOREMOST SACRED BOOKS OF HINDUISM?

They are known as the Vedas, which means "knowledge." There are four Vedas and they claim to teach a man the highest truths that can lead him to God. The first three Vedas are known as the Triple Vedas.

The Rig Veda (Veda of Hymns)consists of 1028 hymns (ten books) to gods like Indra and Agni.

The Yajur Veda (Veda of Liturgy) concerns the knowledge of rites. This Veda is based on the Rig Veda. It contains the rules explaining how to perform all rituals. It consists of prose and verse. This Veda is indeed a priestly handbook, even describing the rules and regulations of how to make an altar. Sacrifice is one of the most important parts of this Veda.

The Sama Veda (Veda of Music) concerns the knowledge of chants. Sama means "melody." The classical Indian music originated from the Sama Veda. This Veda consists of 1549 stanzas. This Veda is also based on the Rig Veda, and stanzas from the Sama Veda were sung by saints when the Soma sacrifice was performed. This Veda is similar to the Psalms of Christianity. To some extent much of this Veda is a repetition of the Rig Veda, sung in a melodious format. Invocations in this Veda are addressed to Soma (moon), Agni (fire) and Indra (the God of Heaven). One of the supplementary treatises of the Sama Veda is the Chandogya Upanishad.

The Atharva Veda contains the knowledge given by Sage Atharvana. It consists of 731 hymns with 6000 verses. Some state that Atharvana did not formulate this Veda but was the chief priest in the ceremonies associated with it. Atharvana, who is mentioned in the Rig Veda, was regarded as the eldest son of Lord Brahma, the God of Creation. The Atharva Veda was also known as the Brahma Veda because it was used as a manual by the chief sacrificial priests and the Brahmins. This contains many magic charms and incantations.

A large number of Upanishads actually originated from the Atharva Veda. Believe it or not, much of Hindu exorcism of devils came from this Veda. Surprisingly, the oldest records on the Vedas do not talk about this Veda. There is no reference to this Veda in the Chandogya Upanishad or the Brahmana texts or the Jatakas or the Bhagavad Gita. This clearly shows that the Atharva Veda was non-existent when the other three Vedas were composed.

WHAT DOES EACH VEDA CONSIST OF?

The Vedas consist mainly of:
1. Samhitas. Basic texts for hymns, formulas and chants.
2. Brahmanas. Directions for performance of rituals.
3. Aranyakas. Contain Mantras and interpretations of rituals.
4. Upanishads. These are a number of texts revealing the ultimate spiritual truths and various suggestions of ways to realize them. The word Upanishad is composed of Upa (near), Ni (down)

and Shad (to sit). An Upanishad is a teaching taught by the Guru when the disciple sits very close so that nobody overhears the teachings.

HOW MANY UPANISHADS ARE THERE?

There are more than 108 books of Upanishads. The thirteen most important Upanishads are: Isa, Kena, Katha, Prasna, Mundaka, Mandukya, Aitareya, Taittirya, Chandogya, Brihad-Aranyaka, Kaushitaki, Shvetasvatara and Maitri. Some of the Upanishads are named after the great sages who are featured in them. Those sages are Mandukya, Shvetasvatara, Kaushitaki and Maitri. Other Upanishads are named after the first word of the work.

We also have eleven minor Yogic Upanishads. The most important among them are Yogatattva, Dhyanabindu, and Nadabindu. Yogatattva consists of all the details about yogic practices. Nadabindu, as the name depicts, deals with the auditory phenomena that accompany certain yogic exercises. Dhyanabindu deals with the syllable AUM and with many mystic revelations.

6 ☙
Rig Veda

WHAT EXACTLY DOES THE RIG VEDA CONSIST OF?

The Rig Veda is the foremost of all Sruti literature. It consists of 1,028 hymns with a total of 10,562 lines which are described in ten books. A hymn has three basic parts. The first part is an exhortation, the second part is the praise of the deity in the form of a prayer, and the third part is a special request. The religion explained in the Rig Veda can be called Brahminism or Vedism. In the Rig Veda we see the Aryans just settling down in the valleys of the Indus River and worshipping all the powers of nature such as air (Vayu), water (Varuna), sun (Surya), moon (Soma) and fire (Agni). The Rig Veda does not seem to be scripture composed during a particular period of time but a scripture composed in stages over several centuries.

One of the most important ideas that came out of the Rig Veda is the cosmic order named Rta. Rta means "cosmic and sacred order," an ultimate and harmonic structure of reality. Later this cosmic order Rta came to be known as Dharma or Sanathana Dharma or "righteousness forever." Dharma became not only the universal law but also the moral law of Hinduism.

Even though in the Rig Veda we see an evolving society praying to all aspects of nature, we also see the birth of very advanced thinking within the society. Just read the so-called Creation Hymn (Rig Veda X, 129, 6-7):

> After all, who knows, and who can say
> From where it all came, and how creation takes
>   place?
> The Gods [powers of nature] themselves came
>   after the creation
> So who knows truly when it happened?

When all creation originated?
He [the Almighty], whether He fashioned it or
   whether He did not,
He Who surveys it all from heaven,
He knows--or maybe even He does not know.

There is no particular author for the Rig Veda. It is the collective work of many great sages. One of the most important sacrifices in the Rig Veda is the Soma sacrifice. Soma is a narcotic beverage prepared from a plant which many think is none other than a mushroom. The Rig Veda does not shed any light on birth rituals but Viveha (marriage) and cremation of the dead are dealt with. Of all the gods described in the Rig Veda, Rudra is the most important. The popular caste system is also referred to in this scripture. There are also references to the transmigration of souls from body to body.

DADDY, WHAT EXACTLY ARE THE TEACHINGS OF THE UPANISHADS?

As I mentioned before, the Upanishads are the last of the Sruti literature. Most of the Upanishads are in the form of dialogues among saints or between gods and saints. The Brihad-Aranyaka and Chandogya Upanishads are the longest Upanishads. Dr. S. Radhakrishnan said, "So numerous are their suggestions of truth, so various are their guesses at God, that almost anybody may seek in them what he wants and find what he seeks, and every school of dogmatics may congratulate itself on finding its own doctrine in the sayings of the Upanishads."
So the Upanishads' teachings are very complex, and their impact on Hinduism is very difficult to assess. The Upanishads actually opened up the free-thinking spirit in religion. They challenged the rationality of gods and sacrificial rites. Most passages in the early Upanishads are

in prose and they are also in question and answer form. Some of the best books about the Upanishads are written by Hume, Dr. S. Radhakrishnan, R.D. Ranade, and Swami Chinmayananda.

One of the most important sages in the Upanishads is Sage Yatnavalkya. Some of the questioners in the Upanishads are women named Maitreyi (the wife of Yatnavalkya) and Gargi (the daughter of the sage Vachaknu).

An ordinary man who reads the Upanishads haphazardly will find them confusing and contradictory. But if one goes through the entire Upanishads in a very orderly fashion, then one will understand the actual meanings conveyed by them. Now let us briefly go through the teachings of some of the main Upanishads.

The Brihad-Aranyaka Upanishad (very popularly known among Western theologians as the Great Forest Book) is one of the earliest and longest Upanishads. One of the greatest teachers of this Upanishad is the sage Yatnavalkya. Yatnavalkya said, "You cannot see the seer of all things; you cannot hear the hearer of all things; you cannot think the thinker of all things; you cannot understand the knower of all things. That which is beyond all comprehension is the self within you."

This Upanishad talks about the self again differently as follows:

When one breathes, one knows him as breath;
When one speaks, one knows him as speech;
When one sees, one knows him as the eye;
When one hears, one knows him as the ear;
When one thinks, one knows him as the mind.

This is the Upanishad which really dissects the aspects of God. It discusses multiple gods and finally states that there is only one God and that is Breath. This Upanishad also explain God as the Brahman--the Absolute Soul. It states that the Atman--the individual soul--is only a reflection of the Brahman. In a dialogue between King Janaka (the father of Princess Sita) and Sage Yatnavalkya, the light of the Brahman is explained in a very interesting manner. According to this, everything in the world has name, form and activity. The Absolute, which is the unmanifest, is the manifestation of these three aspects.

One of the most popular prayers of Hinduism comes from this Upanishad and it is as follows:

> Lead me from the unreal to the real,
> Lead me from darkness to light,
> lead me from death to immortality.
> (OM Shanti, OM Shanti, OM Shanti)

When a devotee sings the prayer this last line is added to the body of the prayer.

The Chandogya Upanishad is another long Upanishad. According to this everything is Brahman. It clearly states that originally there was the Being, and the world manifested out of the Being and not out of the Non-being. This Upanishad argues against the notion that the world came out of Non-being.

The sage Saudilya said, "At the time of death, a knower of Brahman should meditate on 'Thou art imperishable; Thou art the changeless reality: Thou art the source of life.'" In verse 3:14, this Upanishad states, "Verily, the whole world is Brahman. Let one worship it as that from which one came forth, as that into which one will be dissolved, and as that which one breathes."

The Katha Upanishad starts with a story. Once upon a time a Brahmin named Vajasrabasa was sacrificing everything hoping to get some divine favor. In the midst of his sacrifices, one of his sons, Nachiketa, implored his father to sacrifice him to the God of Death, Yama. Finally the father sacrificed his beloved son to Yama. When the boy reached the abode of the God of Death, Yama was perplexed by the act of Nachiketa and asked him to go back to his father. The lively theological conversation that took place between Nachiketa and Yama is what comprises the Katha Upanishad. Yama is explaining the ultimate secrets of the universe and the nature of the Brahman in this beautiful Upanishad.

The Kena Upanishad says that which cannot be expressed in words by which the tongue speaks--know that to be the Brahman. That by which the mind comprehends--know that to be the Brahman. According to this Upanishad Brahman is the ultimate factor of the universe. The sense organs work because of the Brahman. He who says he knows the Brahman does not know the Brahman, for knowing that is to lose the identity of the knower in the Brahman. A devotee who seeks the Brahman merges with the Brahman, like a pinch of salt which tries to find the bottom of the sea becomes one with the sea. Maybe that is the reason why the Chinese mystic Lao-Tse said, "He who knows never tells. He who tells never knew."

The Aitareya Upanishad provides an interesting story of creation. The story goes as follows. First there was Atman. It was alone. Then it created waters. Then it wanted to create gods. So then it created a man. For that man a mouth was given. Out of the mouth, speech and the God of Fire came out. Then it gave man nostrils and out of the nostrils came breath and the God of Air. Then it gave man eyes and out of the eyes came sight and the Sun God. Then it gave the man different limbs and out of them came many other gods. Finally Atman entered the man at the parting of the head and became the "I."

The Prasna Upanishad is an interesting dialogue between the sage Pippilada and his devotees, by name

Sukesha, Gargya, Kousalya, Bhargava and Kabandhi. The discussion starts with Kabandhi's question, "Sir, how did the creatures come into being?"

The Mundaka Upanishad differentiates knowledge into higher and lower knowledge. The higher knowledge is that by which one knows the changeless reality. The lower knowledge is the Vedas.

The Mandukya Upanishad contains the teachings of the sage Mandukya on the four stages of consciousness, which are waking, dreaming, deep sleep (Sushupti) and finally Turiya. The Turiya state alone is real. Atman can be realized only in the Turiya state. The Mandukya Upanishad is the smallest of all the thirteen principal Upanishads.

The Taittirya Upanishad consists of five different ways of explaining the world. According to this Upanishad, the Pancha Boothas or Pancha Tattwas, or the five elements of which all matter is made, themselves originated from one another. For example, Ether (Akasha) is born out of Atman, Air (Vayu) out of Ether, Fire (Agni) out of Air, Water (Jala) out of Fire, and Earth (Prithvi) out of Water.

The Shvetashvatara Upanishad consists of the teachings of the saint Shvetashvatara. Unlike others he taught theism and not the Absolute Brahman. He taught that by meditation one can see God. Max Muller described the Shvetashvatara Upanishad as "the most difficult, and at the same time one of the most interesting works of its kind." Adi Sankaracharya himself regarded this Upanishad as a direct contrast to his own monastic ideas. This Upanishad starts with a lot of theological questions such as "What is the cause of our birth?" and "What sustains our lives?" This Upanishad is very much associated with Saivism and is sometimes referred to as the holy bible of Saivites.

My dear son, please understand that my explanations of these few principal Upanishads are extremely brief and as such you should take time and read several books to get a good grasp of the Upanishads.

7 ॐ
Dharma Sutras

PLEASE TELL ME, WHO WERE THE FIRST LAW-GIVERS OF HINDUISM?

They were the sages Manu, Yatnavalkya, Parasara and Gauthama.

WHAT ARE THE NAMES OF THEIR CODE BOOKS?

Their code books are known as the Dharma Sutras.

WHAT DO THE DHARMA SUTRAS CONSIST OF?

The Dharma Sutras are a part of the Vedangas. They give elaborate details on rules of conduct and duties of men in different stages of life and the rights and duties of kings. They also deal with religious matters such as purification rites and funeral ceremonies. They even deal with the rights and duties of women and judicial matters. They also describe penances for various sins. The most important Dharma Sutra is the Manusmriti or the Code of Manu. It has 2,694 stanzas running into twelve chapters.

The next important of the Dharma Sutras is the Yatnavalkya Smriti. It has 1,013 stanzas. Another important Dharma Sutra is the Gauthama Smriti. The Code of Manu is still very popular among Hindus. The Dharma Sutras exercise everlasting influence on Hinduism. They are the backbone of Hindu ethics and morality. Of course many of the rituals described in the Dharma Sutras are not practiced today. But orthodox members of the Brahmin caste still observe the five daily Dharmas known as Pancha Maha Yajnas.

DADDY, WHAT ARE THE PANCHA MAHA YAJNAS?

The five daily Dharmas observed by the orthodox members of the Brahmin caste are known as the Pancha Maha Yajnas. They are:

1. Deva Yajna--worship of God
2. Brahma Yajna--worship of Lord Brahma
3. Pitri Yajna--worship of ancestors
4. Bhuta Yajna--worship of spirits
5. Nara Yajna--worship of man

All Brahmins still undergo three important ceremonies in their lifetime as dictated by the Dharma Sutras. They are:

1. Upanayana--receiving the holy thread in boyhood. After this ceremony the boy is called a Dwija (twice-born).
2. Viveha--marriage
3. Anthyesthi--funeral rites

8 ?

Code of Manu

DADDY, WHAT IS THE CODE OF MANU?

The Code of Manu is the ethical code written by the sage Manu. Very little is known about Manu. In mythology, he is known as Manu Svayambhuva. The Code of Manu is known as Manusmriti or Manu-Samhita or Manava-Dharmashatra. It is the earliest law book of Hinduism. According to Hindu mythology, Manu dictated his codes in one hundred thousand verses to the sage Brighu, who in turn taught them to the sage Narada. Narada, on his part, reduced the codes to twelve thousand verses. The book of codes was further reduced to eight thousand verses by the sage Markandeya. Believe it or not, another sage, Sumathi, reduced it to four thousand verses. Finally, an unknown saint reduced it to 2,685 verses.

The Code of Manu has twelve chapters and it touches all facets of life such as respectful obedience to parents and teachers (2:225-229), repentance and confessions (11:228-231), performance of sacrifices (3:69-81), the sanctioning of wars (7:87-201), allowed and forbidden foods (5:11,17), and offenses and penances (11:49-266).

One of the most important part of this code (Book 10) is the description of the popular caste system. Manu wrote, "For the growth of the world, Brahman created Brahmanas (Brahmins--the priestly class), Kshatriyas (warriors), Vaishyas (traders) and Shudras (manual workers) from his face, arm, thighs and feet respectively." Manu placed Brahmins in a very exalted position and placed the low-caste in a demeaning position throughout his Code.

Regarding the duties of women (Book 5), Manu wrote that a girl, a young woman or even an aged lady should not do anything independently, even in her own house. She should be protected by her father during childhood, by her husband during her youth, and by her son during her old age. No sacrifice, vow or fast must be done by a woman without her husband. If a woman violates her duties in this world then after her death she will take birth as a jackal. Even beating of one's wife under certain conditions is allowed as per this code.

Book 1 gives a philosophical account of creation. Manu states a very elaborate explanation regarding the creation of the universe. At first the universe existed in the form of darkness, and God created world, light and water, in that order. From water came a golden egg and in that He Himself was born as Lord Brahma (the God of Creation). Then Lord Brahma created a Man and a Woman.

The Code of Manu also refers to the theory of reincarnation. Manu wrote, "Man obtains a life of motionlessness [plants, etc.] as a result of the evil committed by the body, the life of birds and beasts because of the evil committed by the speech, and the life of the lowest born because of the evil committed by the mind."

Books 2, 3, 4, 5 and 6 describe the four stages in a man's life. They are Kaumaram (youth), Garhastyam (married life), Vanaprastham (life of a hermit) and Sanyasam (renunciate's life). During Kaumaram a man is supposed to be 100% Brahmachari (celibate). During the stage of Garhastyam he is supposed to marry a virgin girl from his own caste. When the man's Karma as a householder is completed and when he is aged, he is supposed to take refuge in the forest and lead a hermit's life and finally becomes a Sanyasin. Life as a Sanyasin involves surrender of one's free will to the will of God.

DADDY, IS THERE A STORY IN HINDUISM SIMILAR TO THE BIBLICAL STORY OF NOAH'S ARK?

There is a story in Hinduism almost parallel to the story of Noah's ark. According to the story in one of the early scriptures in Hinduism, namely Satapatha-Brahmana, once when Manu was washing in the sea a fish came into his hands. The fish said, "Rear me, then I will save you from floods." First Manu could not believe himself but later decided to obey the request of the fish. Manu first kept the fish in a jar. When it outgrew the jar, he put it in a pit. Later the fish outgrew the pit and finally became a giant. Then the fish advised him to build a ship and warned him that a flood would destroy the entire world. Manu took the advice of the fish and built a ship. This fish was the first avatar of Lord Vishnu, popularly known as Matsya Avatar. When the floods came, Manu entered the ship. The floods carried the ship to the top of a mountain. The flood carried off all the creatures, and Manu alone survived. After the waters receded, Manu went to the plains. It is said that here he began the work of restarting life for another 4,320,000,000 years (time period of the four Yugas: Krita or Sathya, Treta, Dvapara and Kali). Hindus believe that this story of Manu will be repeated at the beginning of the universe numberless times.

SO THE NAME MANU IS NOT A PERSON'S NAME BUT A TITLE.

You are absolutely correct. The name Manu means the Patriarchal Earth Ruler. Manu comes and goes at the beginning of creation of the universe infinite times. Each Manu lives for a period known as Manvantara (Manu-period). According to one mythological story, a Kalpa (8,640,000,000 human years) consists of fourteen Manu-

58

periods or Manus. The fourteen Manus are: 1. Svayambhuva (Manu the law-giver) 2. Svarochisha 3. Uttama 4. Tamasa 5. Raivata 6. Chakshusha 7. Vaivasvata (the Hindu Noah; the Manu of today) 8. Savarna (yet to come) 9. Daksha-Savarna 10. Brahma-Savarna 11. Dharma-Savarna 12. Rudra-Savarna 13. Rauchya 14. Bhautya. As I said before, all these Manus come and go in never-ending cycles.

DADDY, I KNOW MANU COVERED A LOT OF SUBJECTS. PLEASE TELL ME WHAT INTERESTS YOU MOST IN THE CODE OF MANU.

His concept of time and his statement that the universe undergoes an endless cycle of birth and destruction interest me most. Manu defined time thus: When the eyelids move eighteen times, the time elapsed is called Kashta; thirty Kashtas make one Kala; thirty Kalas make one Muhurta; thirty Muhurtas make a day and a night.

WITH ALL DUE RESPECT TO THE CODE OF MANU, DADDY, DON'T YOU THINK HIS STATEMENTS ABOUT WOMEN ARE OUTRIGHT NONSENSE? HOW ON EARTH COULD HE MAKE A CASTE-SYSTEM WHICH IS AN OUTRIGHT DISGRACE TO HINDUISM? I AM SORRY TO EVEN ACKNOWLEDGE IT AS A PART OF HINDUISM.

I can very well understand your sentiments and I fully agree with your statement. But please understand that through the Code of Manu, you are witnessing an evolving society taking grass roots in the river beds of North India. So much of his code is intended for the society of that period and it has nothing to do with the modern society we live in. Similarly, if you read the Old Testament, especially Exodus, you will see statements regarding the treatment of slaves, etc. We all know that you cannot treat anybody the way they treated slaves during the Old Testament times. As I told you earlier, history is part of every scripture, so much so that we should not hastily judge different statements in them. A society maturing out of dark ages is bound to make many mistakes.

All religions in the world have given man an exalted position and provided woman with a demeaning position. Please understand that at that point in history, women were the weaker sex emotionally as well as physically. Today, nobody would ever even dream of making a statement like that. Remember, the most popular democracy of the world, India, had a woman chief executive, and all of us throughout the world are still proud of the departed Indira Gandhi. People may agree or disagree with her policies but all hats are off to her valor and capabilities. She is, as she wanted to be, the Joan of Arc of India. Please do not forget that Manu, who restricted the freedom of women, also said, "Women are to be honored and adorned by fathers and brothers, by husbands, and also by brothers-in-law, who desire much prosperity. Where women are honored, there the gods rejoice, but where they are not honored, there all rites are fruitless."

Similarly, I have to tell you that the caste system is a disgrace to Hinduism. I don't think anybody with a right mind supports the caste system. It only helps Brahmin domination of the lower castes as well as causing large-scale conversion of Hindus to Islam and Christianity. Please also remember that Buddha did not acknowledge the case system, even of the highest castes in India. So the caste system might have emerged from certain needs, but as time passed, it became a curse on Hinduism rather than a blessing. Gandhi said, "If untouchability is a part of Hinduism, I will discard Hinduism."

Caste System of Ancient India

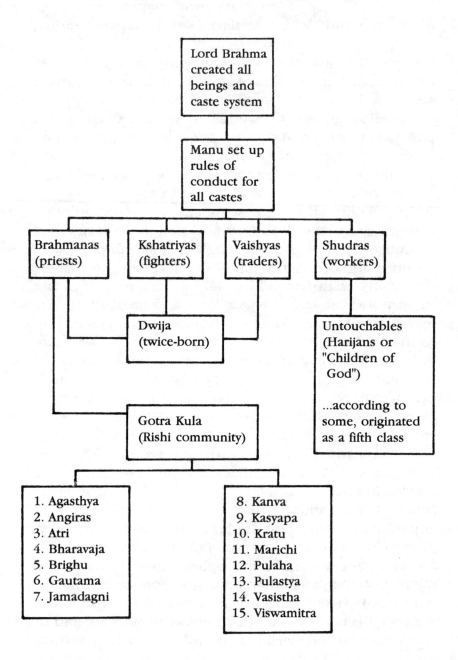

9
Panchatantra and Artha Shastra

WHAT IS THE PANCHATANTRA (FIVE BOOKS)?

It is a collection of stories told by one wise man named Vishnusharman to a few princes to teach them about worldly affairs. Behind each story there is a moral, showing the exact course of action a wise man should undertake. It also teaches the science of statecraft and proper understanding of human nature.

In these stories, human vices are exposed through the characters of animals. The leading parts in the stories are played by two jackals, Karataka and Damanaka. It is said that this famous fable-book of ancient India was written during 200 A.D. One of the very good books on the Panchatantra is a translation by Arthur W. Ryder (University of Chicago Press, 1925). Another good translation was written by Mr. D. Ghosal, named *Thirty-Five Stories From the Panchatantra* (Calcutta, 1925).

DADDY, WHAT IS ARTHA SHASTRA?

Artha Shastra is the code of ethics for kings written by the not-so-saintly prime minister of the Mourya Dynasty, Kautilya or Chanakya. (The literal meaning of Kautilya is "crookedness" or "treachery.") The Artha Shastra is dedicated to Venus and Jupiter, and deals with the Nyaya doctrine and the Atharva Veda. Believe it or not, just like the Dead Sea Scrolls, this scripture was discovered only recently, in 1905.

The book is divided into fifteen parts dealing with a large variety of political and social subjects. Apart from ruling the country properly, this book also teaches an efficient system of espionage. It also teaches different methods of torturing the enemy. It deals with all kind of bodily tortures, like flogging to death, water-tube torture and all kind of mutilation of the organs and limbs. This is indeed the most cynical doctrine known to mankind. It is also the most ferocious criminal code.

DO THE LAWS OF HINDUISM CHANGE FROM TIME TO TIME?

It used to be like that. The great Rishis who guided Hinduism from one age to another made all changes as per the need of the time.

SO DOES THE HINDUISM ALLOW THE INTRODUCTION OF NEW LAWS?

It allows not only the introduction of new laws but also the production of new scriptures. Right now Hindu society has grown very big, and unfortunately most Hindus only know the mythological stories and a few lines from the Bhagavad Gita.

DOES THAT MEAN HINDUISM IS A DEAD RELIGION?

Not at all. Because we do not know most of the scriptures does not mean that we are ignorant of the ideals and codes of Hinduism. Most Hindus practice Hinduism in their day-to-day life. Their family, social and professional lives are reflections of their practice of Hinduism, knowingly or unknowingly. Since we follow the Hindu code of ethics, we have less stain and stress in our lives. I know son, you are very eager to ask me specific questions but let us go through the history and development of Hinduism first.

10 ॐ
Charvaka--The Hindu Materialism

DADDY, IS IT A FACT THAT HINDUISM ONCE HAD A
MATERIALISTIC PHILOSOPHY IN IT?

Yes indeed. Its founder was Charvaka. The most
important book of this system was the Brihaspati Sutra. I
am answering you in the past tense, because as far as I
know this book is not available in India. We only have
quotations from the above book written by other authors
to refute the Charvaka philosophy.

The Charvaka philosophy is known as Nastika
philosophy in Hinduism because this philosophy is
independent of Vedic ideals and principles. It rejected the
existence of God and considered religion as an aberration.

According to this philosophy, the material world is
real and it alone exists; our knowledge of it comes from
sense perception. Matter is made of air, earth, fire and
water. Consciousness is only a function of matter, soul
means body, there is no life after death, there is no God,
the world made itself, pursuit of pleasure is the goal of
man. The Vedas were written by clowns. The Law of
Karma has no basis. This philosophy states, "Enjoy life
while you can, for once cremated, you will never return to
this earth."

I can go on stating different aspects of this
philosophy and they will sound like an atheistic
philosophy of today. To be very frank with you, I feel
much of the statements of this philosophy are like saying
"The earth is flat" and so on without any proper basis at
all. At the same time, the mere existence of this
philosophy in Hinduism is the most important symbol of
Hindu tolerance. In any other religion, apostles of this
type of philosophy would have been crucified or burnt
alive.

As I said earlier, this philosophy is non-existent in India now and almost all of the books on Hinduism do not even mention the mere existence of this philosophy once upon a time. I feel that this philosophy originated due to the rigidity of Hindu orthodoxy in ancient times, and, at the same time, that it died due to the utmost freedom of thought that existed in the later part of Hinduism.

11

Brahma Sutras and Agamas

PLEASE TELL ME, WHAT ARE THE FAMOUS BRAHMA SUTRAS?

The Brahma Sutras are a number of concise statements regarding the whole teachings of the Upanishads. The Brahma Sutras are also known as Vedanta Sutras. They describe in depth the nature of the Brahman.

WHO IS THE AUTHOR OF THE BRAHMA SUTRAS?

Sage Badarayana (Veda Vyasa) is the author of the Brahma Sutras.

WHAT ARE THE AGAMAS?

They are Smriti literature. Agamas means "scriptures." They are a group of literature dealing with the worship of God in many forms and they prescribe detailed courses of discipline for the devotee.

HOW MANY AGAMAS ARE THERE?

Like the Upanishads there are many Agamas. They can be broadly divided into three main groups according to the deity that forms the object of worship--Vishnu, Siva or Sakti. These three groups of Agamas have given rise to the three main branches of Hinduism, mainly Vaishnavism, Saivism and Saktism. The Vaishnava Agamas praise the Almighty as Lord Vishnu. The Saiva Agamas praise the Almighty as Lord Siva. The Sakti Agamas praise the Almighty as the Mother of the Universe. Believe it or not, there are no Agamas on Lord Brahma.

Saivites have 28 Agamas and 108 Upagamas (lesser teachings). Saktiates recognize 77 Agamas. Apart from that, Saktiates have a large number of Tantric texts. Vaishnavites consider the Pancha Ratra Agamas to be the most authoritative of all. Please do not confuse this with the Pancha Tantra work which is nothing but stories. One of the popular books in the Vaishnava Agamas is Vishnu Samhita.

Each Agama consists of four sections: 1. Philosophy 2. Mental discipline 3. Rules for constructing temples 4. Religious practices. All Agamas are based on Sruti.

WHAT ARE THE DIFFERENT METHODS OF GOD-REALIZATION?

There are essentially four methods of God-realization in Hinduism which are broadly known as Yogas or Margas. The word Yoga means "Union with the Divine." Of course the word Yoga is used in so many different ways in Hinduism. In the book Amarakosa, Yoga is given many meanings starting with "nature," "the state of salvation," "determination," "chapter," "creation," "union," "logical view" and even "preparation for war." In the Bhagavad Gita, the word Yoga is used in the beginning of each chapter to designate it. For example, Arjuna Vishada Yoga means "chapter on Arjuna's despondency."

The four Yogas are:

1. Jnana Yoga (or Marga) --the path of knowledge
2. Bhakti Yoga (or Marga) --the path of devotion
3. Karma Yoga (or Marga) --the path of action
4. Raja Yoga (or Marga) --the path based on the practice of Pranayama and thought-control

The different methods or paths are not airtight divisions; instead they merge into each other.

12

Jnana Yoga

WHAT IS JNANA YOGA OR DARSANAS?

Jnana Yoga, or Darsanas, is known as the Hindu philosophy. There are essentially six systems of Jnana Yoga. All of them are based on the Vedas and were developed from the theory of reincarnation. All paths lead to salvation. The six systems of Jnana Yoga are as follows: 1. Samkhya 2. Yoga 3. Mimamsa 4. Vaisheshika 5. Nyaya 6. Vedanta. The Vedanta system is further divided into the Advaita and Dvaita systems.

    1. Samkhya system. It is the most ancient philosophical system in the world. This was founded by the sage Kapila. This system recognizes no personal God. It sees the universe with the forces of Purusha (spirit) and Prakriti (matter).

    2. Yoga system. Yoga is the word derived from the root word "Yuj," meaning "to yoke" or "to join." The Yoga system resembles the Samkhya system. Its ideas are based on dualism (seeing the universe as two--subject and object) and does not talk about a personal God. To some extent it talks about God as an inanimate object with the word "It." Raja Yoga and Hatha Yoga are the most important Yogas.

    3. Mimamsa system. The leading exponents of this branch of philosophy were the sages Kumarila and Prabhakara. The Mimamsa system is based on the avoidance of rebirth. Mimamsa means the start of the Vedas. The actual founder of this system was Sage Jaimini, who was the disciple of Sage Veda Vyasa. Jaimini wrote the book Mimamsa Sutra, which is the most important authority of this system.

    4. Vaisheshika system. This means "particularity." This is the atomic school of Hinduism. It was founded by

the sage Kanada, who wrote the book Vaisheshika Sutra. It teaches that the universe is made of nine elements: earth, water, air, fire, soul, mind, ether, water, and time/space. There is no mention of God in this system. God is mentioned simply as "That."

5. Nyaya system. This system was founded by Sage Gauthama. He wrote the book called Nyaya Sutra. This system is primarily concerned with the logical analysis of the world and its atheistic nature. It resembles the Vaisheshika system.

6. Vedanta system. Vedanta means "end of the Vedas," indicating that this was written based on the Upanishads which came after the Vedas. (The Mimamsa system was actually the start of the Vedas and was based on the Vedic ideology.) The Vedanta system was founded by Sage Badarayana (Veda Vyasa), who wrote the book called Vedanta Sutra or Brahma Sutra. The central doctrine of Vedanta is that God (Brahman) and the individual soul (Atman) are one and the same. According to this system, nothing exists excepts Brahman. The human problem is not sin but ignorance. The ignorance of the true nature of oneself results in the endless cycle of birth and rebirth.

Advaita philosophy and Dvaita philosophy are the two important branches that emerged from the Vedanta system. The greatest exponent of Advaita philosophy was the sage Adi Sankaracharya. Through his commentaries on the Upanishads and Brahma Sutra, Sankara established the Vedanta system. The greatest exponents of the Dvaita philosophy were the sages Ramanuja and Madhava. Sankara's theory of Advaita is that there is only one reality and that is known as the Brahman, whereas Ramanuja and Madhava took the position that reality is two: dependent and independent. God is independent. Matter and soul are dependent upon God and are controlled by God.

13 ❧
Adi Sankara

DADDY, I KNOW YOU ARE VERY MUCH INTERESTED IN ADI SANKARA. I WISH TO KNOW MORE ABOUT HIM.

Yes, my son. I have indeed a hero-worship towards Adi Sankaracharya. He was the founder of the Advaita philosophy. He was a saint with Christ-like powers, but still he is well known for his philosophical approach of interpreting the Vedas. He was a very versatile genius who made his mark on every aspect of Hinduism. He performed his mother's funeral rites and also composed several poems and prayers worshipping gods and goddesses. Still he spoke of Brahman alone. Swami Chinmayananda often says, "Sankara starts where Einstein ends." Such was the knowledge of Sankaracharya.

He was born at Kaladi, about six miles from Always, in the state of Kerala. By the age of eight he had mastered all four Vedas, and by the age of twelve he was well versed in all Hindu scriptures. By the age of sixteen he had completed writing many important books, and at the age of thirty-two he departed from the world. According to Western historians, Sankaracharya lived between 788 and 820 A.D. It is said that when he was eight years old he went to North India and became a disciple of Govinda Bhagavadpada, who was a disciple of Gaudapada. Later Sankara went to Benaras and there Padmapada, Hastamalaka and Totaka became his disciples. According to some, the last days of Sankara were spent in Kanchi, where he departed from his body. According to some, Sankara never died. He just departed from sight. Saivites believe that Sankaracharya is an Avatar of Lord Siva.

During his short sojourn on earth, Sankaracharya wrote many books. He wrote commentaries on the Bhagavad Gita, Upanishads, Brahma Sutra and Vishnu Sahasranama. He wrote two independent manuals named

Upadesasahasri and Vivekachoodamani. He also wrote Adma Bodham and Bhaja Govindam. Of all the devotional poems he wrote, Saundarya Lahari is the best.

He also established four monasteries in different corners of India which are known as Sankaramaths. They are at Sringeri (Mysore), Badrinath (Himalayas), Dwaraka (Gujaret), and Puri (Orissa). The Sankaramath in Kanchi (Tamil Nadu) is a saka (branch) of the Sankaramath at Sringeri.

Just like Jesus Christ, Sankara came not to destroy but to fulfill the spiritual vacuum in India during a particular period in Indian history. Sankaracharya stopped the onslaught of Buddhism on Hindu ideals and restored Hinduism to its past glory. According to him, "The Brahman alone exists; all the rest is Maya or illusion. The individual soul (Jeevatman) is Brahman alone and nothing else. People are bound by endless cycles of reincarnations due to ignorance. Ignorance is the root cause of all problems. Knowledge eradicates and delivers one from bondage."

Sankara also said, "The difference between God and man is a matter of degree. Ultimately they are one and the same being. That which is within the man is called Atman, and that which embraces the universe is known as Brahman. They are one and the same like the space inside a cup and the space outside the cup are one and the same."

Just like the Tao of Taoism, the Allah of Islam and the Ayin of Jewish mysticism, Sankara's Brahman has no qualities, no parts and no consciousness, and is timeless. If you read the writings of Adi Sankara about Brahman and the writings of Lao-Tse on Tao, both sound similar.

Hinduism owes quite a lot to Sankaracharya. His teachings are the true personification of absolute freedom and they are not limited to any particular group in

Hinduism. You should try to read and study all his books in your lifetime.

DADDY, HAS SANKARA EXPLAINED WHY BRAHMAN, WHICH IS COMPLETE IN ITSELF, CREATED THIS PROBLEMATIC AND IMPERFECT WORLD?

I am sorry to state that Adi Sankara had never explained this question in any of his writings. Many Vedantists, including the mystic Aurobindo (1872-1950), have pointed out the problems with Sankara's theories. Why should the Brahman, which is perfect and complete in itself, evolve the great web of Maya or illusion from its own essence? If it is complete why should imperfection come out of it? If Sankara's Brahman transcends all personality feelings, how did it make a creation with consciousness? According to Aurobindo, Sankara could not successfully explain, on his negativistic principles, why the Absolute should descend into the finite. Both the Mahabhagavatam and the Bhagavad Gita address this question in an indirect manner. Both talk about the instrumentality of creation. The Srimad Mahabhagavatam states that it is a Leela (divine play) for God to create things. The Bhagavad Gita, on the other hand, states that it is part of nature to create and procreate. Unluckily, no scripture clearly answers the "why and what" question about creation. Even in Genesis we see an instrumentality of creation, where Elohim transformed into Jehovah ("I Am") and created the universe in six days. In the Vedanta Sutra the word Leela--the Divine Sport--is used to explain creation as the desireless expression of God. Why does God want to express Itself? I don't think we will ever have an answer to your question from anybody on earth with any human capabilities.

Sankara himself states that a question like the one you have raised has no basis, since this material universe is indeed illusion or Maya, just figments of imagination. You and I have problems since we are not able to transcend this great veil of Maya.

Sankara never said that the world is not important. He only pointed out the fact that the world we see is not the real world. The world we see is constantly changing. Sitting in your car, one mile away, the water you saw on the road was momentarily real, but when you came close to that water what you saw became a mirage. The dream burglar who is attacking you is real in the dream. You put up a dream fight with him. But when you wake up, you will say to yourself, "It was only a dream. Sankara says a man will speak similarly about the world the moment he realizes true knowledge.

Whatever may be the criticism on the finer aspects of Sankara's Advaita, I personally feel Advaita philosophy will stay forever. If tomorrow a human being is manufactured, within a lab, without the donations from a male sperm and a female egg, most organized religions in the world will fall. But Sankara's Advaita philosophy alone will be standing tall that day. If Sankara can resurrect himself then, he may shout, "God creates illusion but now man has started doing that himself!" That day only Advaita philosophy can be jubilant; all the rest will crumble.

WHAT IS DVAITA PHILOSOPHY?

This philosophy is the philosophy of duality propagated by Madhava (1197 A.D.), who believed that devotion to God is extremely important. According to him the world is real and there is a difference between man and God. Reality to him is of two kinds, independent and dependent. God is the only independent reality. Matter and self are dependent on and controlled by God. Self is active and is responsible for its own release from countless reincarnations by devotion to God.

Ramanuja, the very first apostle of Dvaita philosophy, was born about 1050 A.D. He was a devotee of Lord Vishnu. He took a middle path between the Advaita and Dvaita philosophies. Sage Ramanuja said that God is not an unqualified principle, as Adi Sankaracharya said, but a very personal God, who can be loved and understood through devotion. He argued that Adi Sankara stood against this devotion to God. But at the same time, Ramanuja believed in the traditional Vedanta position of oneness with the Almighty God. He believed in the principle of Jeevatman (individual soul) and Paramatman (absolute soul) and the merging of Jeevatman in Paramatman for attaining salvation. Both Advaita and Dvaita philosophies prevail in India with equal importance even today.

DADDY, I AM CONFUSED. IF ADVAITA AND DVAITA PHILOSOPHIES ARE DIFFERENT, WHICH ONE IS RIGHT?

As I said earlier, it is normal to be confused sometimes about these philosophies. In fact, both philosophies are one and the same but they differ only according to the level from which we look at them. If I look at you and a robot as a bundle of electrons and protons, then you are both one and the same. But looking at another level, the human being is very much different from any inanimate robot. Both are truths, but they differ in the level of perception. A model's face is very pretty to the naked eye, but it is ugly under a powerful electron microscope. When the level of perception changes the truth derived also changes accordingly.

Look at visible light. Sir Isaac Newton said, "Light travels in straight lines." Albert Einstein, with his quantum theory, proclaimed to the world, "Light moves in wave patterns." Now we study both Newton's and Einstein theories of light and use them both in the development of science.   On one side light is a continuous wave in motion, and on the other side the same light is made up of independent particles in motion. Examining further, it is an electromagnetic radiation in the wavelength range including infrared, visible and ultraviolet rays, with a speed of approximately three hundred million meters per second when it travels in a vacuum.

Without duality-perception action is impossible. We can perceive the world only because it a series of contrasting dualities.   Man can act only in a subjective-objective environment. According to Taoism, the Absolute One becomes two in creation.

The renowned Chinese I Ching, or Book of Changes, sees the universe as Yin and Yang, or male and female. Yin is the physical and emotional force, and Yang is the intelligence and the spiritual force. They are indeed the two aspects of one absolute power, just like the north and south poles of a magnet.   Taoists try to attain a proper balance between the Yin and Yang.

It is said that the earliest champion of the famous binary system, the German genius Gottfried Wilhelm Leibniz, in 1666 laid down the foundation for the modern electronic computer based on the ideas he received from the I Ching on Yin and Yang. According to him, "one" represents God, "zero" represents Void, and from one and zero everything came just like one and zero can explain all mathematical ideas. So within the integrated circuits of the modern computer, one can come across the Advaita and Dvaita systems.

By keeping the microscopic electronic switches in a modern computer's central processor in "on" or "off" positions, representing one and zero, man has indeed created a dream world. All the complex problems of the world an electronic computer sees only as "zero" and "one," as "off" and "on" positions of a large number of switches. It may sound mind-boggling, but it is indeed the truth. I hope from the above examples it is very easy to understand why the Advaita and Dvaita philosophies are equally important to Hindus.

Again, there are no airtight divisions between the philosophies. Adi Sankaracharya himself wrote several devotional poems to different forms of God. Just like Taoism, Adi Sankara did not reject the material world or ordinary life, but asked his devotees to use them to transcend the material world. The doctrine of Maya, on which Sankara wrote volumes, does not state that the world is unreal but that our perception of the world is wrong. Our perception of the world is relative, subject to time, space and causation. The word Maya is usually explained by Hindu saints as "negation" and "so let us stop all actions." That explanation is far from truth and it is against all the teachings of the Bhagavad Gita. The word illusion came from a Latin word meaning "to play the game." So we cannot stop acting until action naturally stops in our life or until we see "inaction in action and action in inaction" as expounded by the Gita.

To some the Advaita philosophy will appeal and to others the Dvaita philosophy according to their individual natures. Personally, I feel both philosophies are part and parcel of one great philosophy, like the north and south poles of a magnet. These two philosophies helped Hinduism to really explore the unknown realms of our lives.

ARE YOU CONCLUDING, DADDY, THAT ADVAITA MAY BE TRUE BUT THAT DVAITA IS THE PRACTICABLE SYSTEM?

I think I explained that already. Anyway, let me explain once again. If you see Advaita and Dvaita philosophies as two different philosophies, then Advaita is the Absolute Truth. But when we live in a world of subjective-objective relationships, we are forced to act under the Dvaita principle. Even Sankara himself did not rule out the Dvaita principle altogether, as his famous "rope and snake" example in his commentary on Gaudapada's Karika shows. The man who saw the rope as a snake in darkness was forced to undergo the mental stress of facing a snake face-to-face. Later, when he found out the snake was actually a rope, he might have thought about his stupidity. But nobody can blame the man for seeing the rope as snake in darkness.

A man experiencing a dream sees a tiger chasing him. In his dream he tries to get away from the tiger. Without even moving an inch in his bed, he feels he ran miles and miles through the thorny forest, but when he suddenly gets up he says to himself, "It was only a dream." The agonizing experience he had in his dream suddenly becomes a mere stupidity when he wakes up. According to Adi Sankara, we will feel the same way about this materialistic world when we wake up from this materialistic dream.

At the same time, all of us have to fight in this world of duality as long as we are seeing the world as dualistic in nature. Shouting or screaming about Advaita will not make one realize oneness with this universe. But along with Sankara, many masters have stated their capability to see the world as Advaita--one entity. Sufi saints are perfect examples. If you search, finally you will reach that state of the Sufis and Adi Sankara.

14 ♌
The Ramayana

WHAT ARE THE FAMOUS EPICS AND WHO WROTE THEM?

The two famous epics or Ithihasas are the Ramayana and the Mahabharata. Sage Valmiki wrote the former and Sage Veda Vyasa, son of Sage Parasara, wrote the latter. The story about Sage Valmiki is in the Uttara, a supplement to the great Ramayana epic.

WHAT IS THE STORY OF VALMIKI?

In the early part of his life, Valmiki was a highway robber without a name. He used to rob travelers to support his wife and children. One day the great saint Narada was passing by and the robber attacked the holy man. Narada asked Valmiki why he was robbing him. "To take care of my family," answered the robber. "When you rob a person, you also incur a lot of sin. Would your family share that sin also?" asked the great master. "I am sure they will," answered the robber. "All right," said the sage. "Why don't you tie me up here, go home, and ask everyone whether they are ready to share your sins along with the money you are bringing home." The robber agreed. He tied the sage against a tree and ran to his simple home. There he accosted all the members of his family with the question, "Will you share my sins?" All the members of his family, including his wife, gave an emphatic "no." For the first time in his life, the robber understood the truth. With tears trickling down his cheeks he ran to Narada and begged for his forgiveness. The sage taught the robber how to worship God. It is said that the robber so engrossed himself in meditation that ants built anthills surrounding him. Finally, after years, a voice came from nowhere asking the meditating robber to get up from his meditation. The voice named him Valmiki, meaning "he that was born in the anthill." This is the story of Valmiki.

WHAT IS THE STORY BEHIND HIS WRITING THE EPIC RAMAYANA?

Once Valmiki was walking through a forest and saw two doves romantically involved with each other. As the sage was engrossed in that pleasant sight, a cruel arrow passed by him and struck the male dove. The female dove went down in remorse and started chirping around the dead companion. Valmiki saw the hunter and called him a wretch, but immediately felt that as a saint he should not have spoken like that. Then a voice from the sky said, "Oh! Valmiki, your words are poetic; don't be distressed. This the right time for you to write the story of Lord Rama." Upon the instructions from that voice from the sky, Valmiki wrote the immortal poem Ramayana, the story of Lord Rama. Valmiki wrote the whole Ramayana as the narration of the crying female dove to him. In the beginning of each chapter, he makes the reader aware of the fact it is a crying bird which is narrating this great story of Lord Rama.

WHAT DOES THE RAMAYANA EPIC CONSIST OF?

In brief, the Ramayana is the story of Lord Rama and Princess Sita. It is a poem with 24,000 couplets. The story in brief is as follows. Once upon a time there was a king named Dasaratha who had three wives, Kausalya, Kaikeyi and Sumitra. Unluckily, Dasaratha had no children through any of the three queens, so he conducted a special sacrifice by the name of Puthra Kameshti Yagam. Out of the fire of the sacrifice came an elixir which all three queens consumed. As a result, Kausalya had a son named Rama, Kaikeyi had a son named Bharata, and Sumitra had two sons named Lakshmana and Shatrugna. Rama and Lakshmana became very fast friends from childhood onwards, and so too did Bharata and Shatrugna.

When the children entered puberty, Rama married Princess Sita, the orphan daughter of the great king Janaka. Thereupon, King Dasaratha thought of renouncing the throne and making Prince Rama the king. The whole country rejoiced at the news, except Kaikeyi and her maid Mandara. Finally the jealousy and plotting of Queen Kaikeyi made Rama give up the kingdom and seek the jungles along with his sweet wife Sita and his beloved brother Lakshmana. In the jungles, poor Sita was kidnaped by Ravana, the demon-king of Sri Lanka. Lord Rama went to rescue her with the aid of the monkey-king Sugreeva and his prime minister Hanuman. In a great battle, Rama annihilated Ravana and his army. Rama, along with Princess Sita, finally returned to the kingdom at Ayodhya.

The Ramayana is a very cherished poem of the Hindus. The holy Deepavali festival is a celebration of the victory of Rama over the demon-king Ravana. Deepavali or Diwali--the Festival of Lights--is celebrated throughout India.

Rama is an Avatar of Lord Vishnu and the Ramayana is a story which projects the Hindu ideals of life. Rama is the perfect man, Sita is the perfect wife and Lakshmana is the perfect brother. There are many versions of the Ramayana. The Hindi version was written by the sage Tulsi Das. The Malayalam version was written by Thuncheth Ezuthachan. The original text of the Ramayana was written in a very stylish Sanskrit language.

15 ❧
Yoga Vasishtha

WHAT IS THE FAMOUS YOGA VASISHTHA?

It is one of the most important works in Hindu philosophy, believed by some to have been written during the seventh century A.D., although since this book emerged from the epic Ramayana many believe that Valmiki wrote this book also. The Yoga Vasishtha contains 29,000 verses. All aspects of Darsanas (Hindu philosophies), right from Samkhya to Vedanta, are intricately woven into the Yoga Vasishtha. The principal figures in this book are Lord Rama and Sage Vasishtha. Just like the Bhagavad Gita, this is a dialogue, this time between Vasishtha and Lord Rama. Vasishtha advises Rama on all aspects of life.

Vasishtha is an important figure in Hinduism. Manu refers to him as one of the exponents of Hinduism. Adi Sankaracharya refers to him as the first sage of the Vedanta school. One of the most important parts of the Yoga Vasishtha is the doctrine of mind. According to this book, when the mind vibrates, the world comes into existence, and when the mind stops vibrating, the world is destroyed.

The language and style of the Yoga Vasishtha is very poetic. It is filled with fantastic stories and very philosophical discourses. Valmiki ends the Yoga Vasishtha with the statement that he who listens to the dialogue between Sage Vasishtha and Lord Rama will be liberated and will attain knowledge of the Brahman.

16 🍃
The Mahabharata

DADDY, WHAT DOES THE MAHABHARATA EPIC DEAL
WITH?

The Mahabharata consists of episodes, stories,
dialogues, discourses and sermons. It contains 110,000
couplets or 220,000 lines in eighteen Parvas or sections.
They are: Adi Parva, Sabha Parva, Vana Parva, Virata Parva,
Udyoga Parva, Bhishma Parva, Drona Parva, Karna Parva,
Salya Parva, Sauptika Parva, Stri Parva, Santi Parva,
Anusasana Parva, Asvamedhika Parva, Ashrama Parva,
Mausala Parva, Mahaprasthanika Parva, Svargarohana Parva.
Apart from these eighteen sections there is a section of
poems in the form of an appendix with 16,375 verses,
which is known as Harivamsa Parva. So in total there are
nineteen Parvas even though some saints do not consider
the last section as an important Parva. The Mahabharata
is thus the longest poem in the world. The Bhagavad Gita
is a part of the Mahabharata.

CAN YOU TELL ME THE ACTUAL STORY OF THE
MAHABHARATA?

It is very difficult to narrate the story of the
Mahabharata in a few words. Anyway, let me try to narrate
it to you in brief. Lord Brahma was born out of the navel
of Lord Vishnu. Atri was Brahma's son. Soma was the son
of Atri. Buddha and Pururavas were the sons of Soma.
Ayus was the son of Pururavas. Yayathi, Dhushyantha,
Bharata, Kuru and Santhanu were born in the lineage of
Ayus.
King Santhanu had a son by Mother Ganges, known
as Gangeya, Devavrata, and popularly known as Bhishma.
After the birth of Bhishma, Mother Ganges separated from
King Santhanu. Santhanu on his part fell in love with a

woman named Sathyavathi (of the fisherman tribe). Sathyavathi's father made Bhishma take a vow of celibacy throughout his life in return for his daughter's hand in marriage to King Santhanu. From Sathyavathi, Santhanu had two children named Chithrangada and Vichitravirya. They married two daughters of the king of Kasi, Ambika and Ambalika. Chithrangada was killed by a Gandharva (celestial being) and Vichitravirya died of an illness. Suddenly the country was left without a ruler. So Queen Sathyavathi summoned her son, Sage Veda Vyasa, to impregnate both the princesses. Princess Ambika gave birth to Dhritarashtra. Princess Ambalika gave birth to a son named Pandu.

Veda Vyasa also impregnated a servant girl who gave birth to Vidura. Pandu, though the younger prince, became the king since his elder brother Dhritarashtra was blind. He married the princesses Kunti and Madri, and from Kunti he had three sons named Yudhishtara (also known as Dharmaputra), Bhima and Arjuna. From Madri he had Nakula and Sahadeva. All five children of Pandu were collectively called the Pandavas.

Dhritarashtra married Princess Gandhari, and had one hundred sons and one daughter. The eldest son's name was Duryodhana and the daughter's name was Dussala. King Pandu had an accidental death, so Dhritarashtra was crowned as the king. But he couldn't rule. He was totally under the influence of his eldest son Duryodhana. When the Pandava brothers came to stay in Hastinapura, the capital, Duryodhana tried to annihilate them in many ways. The feud between the Kauravas (Duryodhana and his ninety-nine brothers) and the Pandavas finally resulted in a fierce battle known as the Mahabharata War. Lord Krishna sided with the Pandavas in the war. In the war all the Kauravas were killed. After the war Yudhishtara became the king. Some years later Lord Krishna, along with his clansmen called the Yadavas, left this world. Immediately after that Yudhishtara and his brothers handed over the kingdom to Pareeshit, Arjuna's grandson, and left for heaven. This in brief is the great Mahabharata epic.

Lord Krishna

17 ❧
Bhagavad Gita

WHAT IS THE NAME OF THE HINDU HOLY BIBLE?

The majority of Hindus consider the Bhagavad Gita as the Hindu holy bible. It is said in one of the Hindu scriptures that if the Upanishads can be considered as cows, the Bhagavad Gita can be considered as milk. Truly, the Bhagavad Gita is the essence of the Vedas. It is indeed a summation of the Upanishads. The Gita is in the form of a conversation between the warrior-prince Arjuna and his charioteer and friend Lord Krishna at the outset of the Mahabharata War. Just before the beginning of the fight, Arjuna refused to fight when he saw that he had to kill his own kinsmen. Krishna advised him in detail on a variety of subjects. At the end, Arjuna took Lord Krishna's advice and fought a very fierce war.

The Bhagavad Gita consists of eighteen chapters and about seven hundred verses. It deals in depth with all the Yogas or ways of God-realization. There are many versions of the Bhagavad Gita available in the market. The very first English translation was done by Charles Wilkins in 1785, with an introduction by Warren Hastings, the British Governor-General of India. But the most popular English translation was done by Sir Edwin Arnold, under the title *The Song Celestial*.

The Gita has an answer to every problem a man may face in his life. The Bhagavad Gita never commands one what to do. Instead, it gives the pros and cons of every issue and the final decision is left to oneself. Throughout the Bhagavad Gita, you will not come across even one line starting with "Thou shalt not."

When Christian scriptures talk about permanent hell for sinners, the Bhagavad Gita proclaims salvation for all in various couplets (4:36, 9:30, 9:32). All of us, whether we believe in God or not, are destined to attain salvation one day. Only the time factor differs for the best and worst among us. The Gita exhorts, "The truth shall set you free."

DADDY, WHY IS THE BHAGAVAD GITA THE MOST IMPORTANT SCRIPTURE OF THE HINDUS?

I think the Bhagavad Gita is the most important scripture of the Hindus because of the variety of subjects discussed in its seven hundred couplets. It advocates selfless actions. It teaches the importance of the annihilation of desire and ego. It teaches the different ways to control the mind and the senses. All the great teachings of Jesus Christ regarding devotion and oneness with God you can see in the Bhagavad Gita. The Gita describes oneness with God in chapters 11, 12, 13, 14 and 18 with lines such as "enters into Me," "attains Me," "abides in Me," "realized Me," "attains Brahman," etc. The beauty of the Bhagavad Gita is that it requires of a man complete change of consciousness rather than mere changes in lifestyle or in outward appearances. Always remember that after the great Bhagavad Gita discourse Arjuna did not become a hermit; instead he fought a very fierce war, annihilating all his enemies.

Most intellectuals go through the Bhagavad Gita at least once in their lifetime. Aldous Huxley wrote, "The Bhagavad Gita is perhaps the most systematic scriptural statement of the perennial philosophy" in his introduction of *The Song of God* by Swami Prabhavananda and Christopher Isherwood. It won the interest and admiration of such intellectuals as Von Humboldt of Germany and Emerson of America. It has influenced thinkers like Hegel and Schopenhauer.

Robert Oppenheimer, the first chairman of the U.S. Atomic Energy Commission, really shocked the world when he quoted a couplet from the Gita (Chapter 11:12) after witnessing the very first atomic explosion test in the state of New Mexico. Later, in a congressional hearing, he said that nuclear bombs reminded him of the Hindu god Lord Vishnu who said, "I am Death, the devourer of all."

I feel the whole story of the Mahabharata with its ferocious war was written by Sage Veda Vyasa to create a proper atmosphere to convey to the world the unwritten laws of the universe. I feel that even Lord Krishna and Arjuna were specially picked by the great sage to provide an authoritative outlook to the ultimate truths he wanted the world to know. For example, if I discuss the U.S. constitution, not even a fly will listen. But if the Supreme Court Chief Justice speaks one line about the U.S. constitution, all of America will listen. If details of the U.S. constitution are discussed by the President and the Chief Justice of the Supreme Court, the whole world will listen. The same analogy is applicable in the narration of the Bhagavad Gita. If it was written as "Veda Vyasa said so," it would not have been read by many, but because it was written as a lively conversation between the great archer of the world, Prince Arjuna, and the greatest teacher of the world, Lord Krishna, at the outset of the great Mahabharata War, the whole world rejoices in reading it.

Legends say that after Veda Vyasa wrote the Mahabharata, the sage Narada compelled him to write the Srimad Bhagavatam Purana with the help of Lord Ganapathi, so that even laymen could understand all the teachings of the Bhagavad Gita in a very devotional format.

DADDY, DO YOU THINK THE TEACHINGS OF THE BHAGAVAD GITA ARE MORE IMPORTANT THAN THE PERSONALITY OF LORD KRISHNA?

It is indeed a very tough question to answer. To a person who believes that Lord Krishna is the Absolute

Personality of the Godhead, Lord Krishna stands equal to or higher than all the teachings of the Bhagavad Gita. But to thousands of intellectuals around the globe, the teachings of the Bhagavad Gita are more important than Lord Krishna since they are ignorant of our mythology. When they read the Gita, they will not visualize the colorful, versatile, playful idol of the Gopis. They study the Gita as they study mathematics or physics or chemistry. In science, the theory of relativity and the laws of action are more important than Einstein or Newton. In the same way, intellectuals read the Gita more as a "basic science" than as something taught by Lord Krishna. In a way, when one thinks deeply, one will be able to find that Lord Krishna is a microcosmic picture of the Infinite.

Lord Krishna showed that "shapeless shape" or "formless form" of himself as Viswaroopa to Arjuna in the eleventh chapter of the Bhagavad Gita. Lord Krishna said, "Arjuna, you cannot see me with your eyes, therefore I am giving you divine sight. Behold my supreme Yoga power" (Chapter 11:18). Then Arjuna saw the entire universe with its many divisions resting together in the body of the God of gods (Chapter 11:34). In the same chapter, from couplets 14 to 31, Arjuna describes that "formless form" in detail. So we have to conclude that the Almighty came down as Lord Krishna and in his own words he will come down again and again in different forms whenever the world needs him. So even though it is normal for you and I to conceive a personal fascination for Lord Krishna, it is better to understand him as the Supreme Power who also came down as Buddha and Christ and Mohammed and other prophets of the world.

All through the Bhagavad Gita, Lord Krishna says "I am the Way" and "Come to Me." In the Holy Bible, Jesus Christ made the same statements a number of times. Lord Krishna and Jesus Christ spoke similarly because both came as the Infinite Power in finite forms. To understand the immortal words of Christ, one needs the Bhagavad Gita and other Hindu scriptures. Without the aid of Hinduism, one may even come to erroneous conclusions when one tries to explain the sayings of Christ. Jesus Christ said, "And if thy right eye offend thee, pluck it out, and cast it from thee, for it is profitable for thee that one of thy members should perish, and not that thy whole body should be cast into hell," and "If thy right hand offend thee, cut it off, and cast it from thee; for it is profitable for thee that one of thy members should perish, and not that thy whole body should be cast into hell" (Matthew 5:29,30, and also read Mark 9:45,46,47). How will one explain this? If you read the Gita, you will see very detailed explanations for what Christ said. In verses 58 to 70 in the second chapter, Lord Krishna says, "All senses (Indriyas) have love affairs with sense objects. Just like a tortoise withdraws its limbs into its shell when it perceives danger, so too wise men withdraw their senses from sense objects when they see that the senses are losing themselves in the sense objects." Without the proper control of the senses, nobody can realize the Absolute Truth. Don't you think with this explanation you can understand the immortal words of Christ better?

Coming back to the Bhagavad Gita, whichever way you look at it, you are following the right way. If you follow the teachings of the Bhagavad Gita in a very logical and mathematical manner, you will achieve salvation, since the Gita contains the unwritten laws of the universe. On the other hand, if you read it with devotion to Lord Krishna and if you follow the Gita on a devotional basis, still you will achieve salvation. Both the intellectual way and the devotional way will lead you to God.

18 ❧
Last Days of Lord Krishna

DADDY, CAN YOU PLEASE TELL ME ABOUT THE LAST
DAYS OF LORD KRISHNA? HOW DID HE DIE?

After the Mahabharata War, Lord Krishna took
Queen Gandhari for a tour of the battlefield of
Kurukshetra to see the dead bodies of her one-hundred
sons. After witnessing the horrible scenes, she cursed
Lord Krishna: "Oh! Krishna, you are the cause of this war.
If you had not participated in it, my children would be
still living today. Krishna, you and your family will perish
in a similar manner." Hearing the curse of Gandhari,
Krishna said, "Thank you, Mother, I eagerly look forward
to that day." Lord Krishna said so because his own family
was becoming a burden to Mother Earth, due to their evil
actions which so warranted extinction.

Lord Krishna went back to his island kingdom,
Dwaraka, after the coronation of Yudhishtara, the first of
the Pandavas. One day as the great Saptha Rishis (seven
ever-living masters) were travelling through Dwaraka, a
few of the Yadava youngsters thought of making fun of the
great seers. They dressed up a sixteen-year old boy as a
pregnant girl and they asked the seers when the girl
would deliver and what would be the sex of the child. In
one voice, the great seers replied, "This girl will deliver a
metal club and the whole Yadava community will perish
by that club." Saying so, the Saptha Rishis vanished into
thin air.

The young Yadavas laughed and laughed not
knowing about the impending danger. Whosoever heard
of a boy delivering a club? After a few hours, lo and
behold! the boy delivered an ugly black metal club. The
frightened youngsters immediately took the club to
Ugrasena, one of the top men of the Yadava clan.
Ugrasena had the club ground into powder and thrown

into the ocean where it became reed pollen. The pollen came back to the shore and became long knife-like grass. One spear-head piece that remained from the club which was thrown into the sea was devoured by a fish. A fisherman by the name of Jaras happened to catch that fish, and when he cut open the fish he was astonished to find a strange metal piece. He presented that piece to a hunter who made the tip of an arrow out of it.

In the meantime, Lord Krishna, knowing everything that had happened, summoned Narada, his greatest devotee, and told him that the time had come for all the Yadavas, including himself, to be destroyed to lighten the burden of Mother Earth. He said that he himself would be killed and that he would go back to Vaikunta as Lord Vishnu. He said that with the annihilation of the Yadavas he had fully accomplished the purpose of his Avatar.

One day the Yadavas held a big celebration on the seashore. Suddenly a feud erupted among them and they started attacking one another with the long knife-like grass. The fight among the Yadavas became so violent that in a matter of a few hours, all the members of the Yadava clan dropped dead on the seashore. After coming to know about the death of the Yadavas, Balarama, the brother of Lord Krishna, jumped into the sea and gave up his life by a special yogic method.

Lord Krishna went to the forest and lay down under a tree. At that time a hunter came along, saw Krishna's toe which he mistook for a rabbit, and struck him with his arrow. The all-knowing and all-powerful Lord Krishna started bleeding profusely. The hunter, seeing the calamity he has caused, prostrated before Lord Krishna and begged for his mercy. Krishna smiled and told him that he had done absolutely nothing wrong and that he (Krishna) was actually obeying the unwritten Karmic law, for in his last life, he had killed the hunter in a cunning manner when the hunter was the monkey-king Bali and

Lord Krishna was the great Lord Rama. Lord Krishna then asked the hunter to go and inform everyone in Dwaraka that he was leaving his body and that Dwaraka would go underwater a few hours after his departure. So saying, Lord Krishna left the physical body and went back to Vaikunta as Lord Vishnu.

After Lord Krishna's departure from earthly life, Dwaraka went under the sea. It is said that Lord Vishnu takes the form of Krishna whenever a devotee worships him with intense faith.

19 &

Puranas and Srimad Bhagavatam

WHAT ARE THE PURANAS?

The Puranas are religious stories which expound truths. Just like the parables told by Jesus Christ, these stories are told to common folk to make them understand the higher truths of life. According to Jesus Christ, the mysteries of the universe are revealed to those who are spiritually awake but to others those mysteries have to be explained in parables. On that note, the Puranas can be called the Vedas of the common folk, for they present all the mysteries through myth and legend.

The word Purana means "ancient." The Puranas always stress devotion to God. Almost all Puranas deal with the creation and destruction of the universe, the genealogy of the gods and saints, and details about the Solar and Lunar dynasties. Some of the them, like the Mahabhagavatam, have descriptions of future events just like the Bible's Revelations.

Among the large number of Puranas, eighteen are called Major Puranas or Mahapuranas. Each of these provides a list of all the eighteen Puranas including itself, but the names on the list in some Puranas vary slightly, so much so that we have a list of twenty Major Puranas. Out of these twenty Puranas, six are addressed to Lord Vishnu, six are addressed to Lord Siva and six are addressed to Lord Brahma.

The Puranas are written in "question and answer" form. They consist principally of stories about Hindu gods and goddesses, supernatural beings, seers and men. The Puranas do not have a specific date of composition, but some say that they date from the sixth century A.D.

DADDY, WHAT ARE THE TWENTY MOST IMPORTANT PURANAS?

The six Puranas addressed to Lord Vishnu are the Vishnu Purana, Narada Purana, Srimad Bhagavata Purana, Garuda Purana, Padma Purana and Varaha Purana.

The six Puranas addressed to Lord Siva are the Matsya Purana, Kurma Purana, Linga Purana, Vayu Purana, Skanda Purana and Agni Purana.

The six Puranas addressed to Lord Brahma are the Brahma Purana, Brahmanda Purana, Brahma-Vaivasvata or Brahma-Vaivarta Purana, Markandeya Purana, Bhavishya Purana and Vamana Purana.

According to many, Siva (or Saiva or Devi-Bhagavata) Purana and Harivamsa Purana are also Major Puranas, even though they do not come under the list of the eighteen Major Puranas.

DADDY, ARE THERE MINOR PURANAS?

Yes indeed. The Minor Puranas are known as Upa Puranas. Believe it or not, there are at least twenty-seven Minor Puranas. They are as follows: Aditya, Ascharya, Ausanasa, Bhaskara (Surya), Devi, Saiva (some call this a Major Purana), Durvasa, Kalika, Kalki, Kapila, Mahesvara, Manava, Marichi, Nandikesvara, Narada, Narasimha, Parasara, Samba, Sanathkumara, Sivadharma, Surya, Suta-Samhita, Usanas, Varuna, Yuga, Vaya and Vrihan. I am very sure that the list I am giving you is not a complete list. There still could be Puranas in Hinduism unknown even to the great apostles of Hindu doctrine.

IS THE SRIMAD BHAGAVATAM A VERY IMPORTANT SCRIPTURE?

It is a very important scripture to Hindus and especially to Hare Krishna devotees. It contains 18,000 stanzas. It has twelve chapters known as Skandas. It was written by the sage Badarayana, also known as Veda Vyasa. The greatest exponent of the Srimad Bhagavatam was the sage Suka, the son of Veda Vyasa. This book was recited to King Pareeshit, the last of the Pandava dynasty, by Suka one week before the foretold death of the king by a serpent bite. Much of the book is a dialogue between King Pareeshit and Sage Suka.

The Srimad Bhagavatam consists of stories of all the Avatars of Lord Vishnu. The tenth chapter of the book deals with the story of Lord Krishna in detail. The last chapter deals exclusively with the Kali Yuga, the present age, and the last Avatar of Lord Vishnu, Kalki. There is also a vivid description of Pralaya, or the Great Deluge, in the last chapter. This book is an authority on Vaishnavism and, as I said before, is the most important scripture of the Hare Krishnas.

According to the Srimad Bhagavatam, the universe and creation came into existence because God willed it to do so as a sport or Leela. A realized devotee sees himself and all beings as part and parcel of God. According to this scripture, there are nine different ways of exhibiting Bhakti, or devotion to God, like listening to stories of God, meditating, serving, and finally self-surrender to the will of God.

Hindu Scriptures

Sruti -- "That which is heard"

1. Vedas: Rig Veda
             Sama Veda
             Yajur Veda
             Atharva Veda
2. Upanishads: 108 Upanishads (see page 43 for 13 most important)

Smriti -- "That which is remembered"

1. Vedangas: Dharma Sutras (Manu Smriti, Gautama Smriti, Yatnavalkya Smriti)
             Jyotisha
             Kalpa
             Siksha
             Chhandas
             Nirukta
             Vyakarana
2. Darsanas: Nyaya
             Vaisheshika
             Samkhya
             Yoga
             Mimamsa
             Vedanta (Advaita and Dvaita systems)
3. Ithihasas: Ramayana
             Mahabharata
4. Puranas: Mahapuranas (see page 98)
             Upapuranas
5. Upavedas: Ayurveda
             Dhanurveda
             Gandharva Veda
             Artha Shastra
6. Agamas: Vaishnava
             Saiva
             Sakti
7. Upangas: logical, ritual form of thought
8. Tantras
9. Charvaka

20 ❧
Thirukural--Holy Bible of Saivites

DADDY, CAN THIRUKURAL BE CONSIDERED A HINDU SCRIPTURE?

It is indeed a great Hindu scripture but it is unknown to Hindus in general since this scripture, unlike others, is written in the Tamil language. It is indeed a part of the Dravidian civilization of South India. Thirukural can be considered as the holy bible of Saivites (people who worship Lord Siva--the Lord of Annihilation). It was written by a weaver named Thiruvalluar during the first century B.C. In Tamil, Thiru means "holy" and Kural means "short" or "brief." This scripture consists of short couplets. In fact, the entire scripture consists of 133 chapters, and each chapter consists of ten couplets. So in total there are 1330 couplets in this sacred literature. Even though Thirukural is considered to be the holy bible of Saivites, the scripture itself is universal in nature. It teaches a man the values of life. In a way it is an enlarged version of the Ten Commandments.

Almost all who come across this scripture will fall in love with it, due to its simplicity and universality of expression of facts. Followers of Jainism love to read it, because it exemplifies the ideals of Ahimsa or non-violence. The Christians in South India like to read it, since many things written in this scripture are similar to the Sermon on the Mount.

The late Dr. Albert Schweitzer called it "one of the grandest achievements of the human mind." I hope you will definitely read this lovable scripture.

21 ॐ
Classical Music

DADDY, IS INDIAN CLASSICAL MUSIC A PART OF
HINDUISM?

Indian music can be broadly divided into two
groups, Hindustani music and Carnatic music. Hindustani
music originated in North India and has been influenced
by Persian and Arabic cultures and also by the Urdu
language. Carnatic (Karnatic) music, on the other hand,
is the music of South India and is known as the classical
music of India.

Carnatic music has its roots in the ancient Hindu
Sama Veda and has absolutely no Persian or Arabic
influences. It is said that this music was originally
composed by Gandharvas (celestial beings), and their
composition was called Gandharva Veda. But we have no
proof of that, since nobody has ever seen a Gandharva
Veda. Anyway, the last six chapters of Natyasastra (written
by the sage Bharata in 300 A.D.) deals with music, and it
is said that some part of the music was written by the
mythological saint Narada.

Carnatic music is very much associated with
devotional songs to deities. Very few instruments are used
in this music and even if instruments are used, they are
used alone and they imitate the singing. The music is
based on the seven letters Sa, Ri, Ga, Ma, Pa, Dha and Ni.
These seven letters are mathematically improvised to make
thousands of tunes named Ragas and cyclic rhythmic
patterns known as Talas. One of the great exponents of
Carnatic music was Swami Thyagaraja (1767-1847) of
Tanjore. His mother tongue was Tamil, but he composed
his songs in Telugu. Most of his songs are devotional
songs to Lord Rama. It is said that Swami Thyagaraja
composed more than 2,000 tunes or Ragas. Lately,
Carnatic music is becoming very popular since Indian

movies have started making film music to the tune of Carnatic music. The present day centers of this music are the states of Kerala, Tamil Nadu, Mysore and Andhra Pradesh.

Hindu Dances

HOW DID THE DANCES OF INDIA ORIGINATE?

Hindu dances originated from the Lord Siva's famous dance, namely Tandava Nirthyam. There are many versions of Tandava Nirthyam. The first one is the most horrendous dance of Lord Siva with his crew after the annihilation of his father-in-law Daksha. Another one is a "dance of death" in which Lord Siva is accompanied by Bhririgi, a skeleton attendant. A third form is popularly known as Nadanta, in which the dancer as a toothless old man desperately dances the vigorous dance of Lord Siva. The last one is the dance of Siva mounting Nandi (his bull), and this dance results in the creation of earth.

The first rules of the Hindu dances were codified by Sage Bharata (not the great King Bharata) between 100 and 300 A.D. His treatise on drama, dance and music was known as Natya Shastra. It is said that he composed the first syllables of Bhava (emotion), Raga (melody), Tala (rhythm) and Rasa (mood). Of course, just like any other Hindu scripture, we have no conclusive proof to show that Bharata wrote the Natya Shastra. It might have been the work of hundreds of saints. Anyway, in some aspects the Natya Shastra resembles Aristotle's *Poetics*.

Hindu dance is closely linked with emotions. It resembles a perfect harmony between classical music and bodily movement. In fact, its objective can be summed up as the creation of different moods in the minds of the spectators. Almost all Hindu dances are performed barefoot. Sometimes in North India the dancers wear tiny slippers. Believe it or not, once upon a time Hindu dances were performed only by Deva Dasis, or "God-servants," who were more or less temple prostitutes, and as such the dancer's profession was looked down upon by the society. But today all dancers are treated with respect and admiration throughout India, and almost every girl tries to learn dancing in India and abroad.

Dance is basically composed of Abhinayana (facial and body expressions), Mudras (hand gestures) and Gati (all forms of footwork).

HOW MANY TYPES OF INDIAN DANCES ARE THERE?

There are four prominent Hindu dances and they are as follows: Bharata Natyam of Tanjore, Kathak of Uttar Pradesh, Kathakali of Kerala and Manipuri of Assam. Of course, there are still a large number of dances like Mohiniyattam of Kerala, Kunchipudi of Andhra and Chhau of Orissa. India is full of folk dances, and even though you may not see an ordinary Indian dancing in his day-to-day life, the tradition of dancing is part and parcel of Hindu culture.

Bharata Natyam actually originated in the temples and was performed by Deva Dasis. It originated in South India and was greatly patronized by the Chola Kings. Legends say that during his exile as a transvestite, Arjuna, the celebrated warrior of the Mahabharata, taught this to the women in the harem of King Virata. Bharata Natyam is a solo dance and its classical poses have been sculptured on the walls of the temple at Chidambaram.

As far we know, there are six types of Bharata Natyam dances:

1. Alaripu. An introductory and short form of Bharata Natyam lasting about five minutes.
2. Jethi-Svaram. More advanced form of dance. A very rhythmic form of footwork and body movements associated with different patterns of music.
3. Varnam. This is the dance which can make the spectator spellbound by its furious tempo. This

is very elaborate and complex, and lasts about one hour.

4. Sadanam. A dance associated with a poem.
5. Padam. Another dance associated with a poem.
6. Tillana. This dance is closely associated with Carnatic music, and most people like Tillana as the best form of Bharata Natyam.

Kathak is dance in a story form. This dance is very popular in Punjab and Uttar Pradesh. It is based on mythological stories about Lord Krishna and his favorite consort Radha. Like Bharata Natyam, this dance was also performed by Deva Dasis in temples of North India. Just like Bharata Natyam, this dance also is a proper combination of Abhinayana, Mudra and Gati.

Kathakali dancing originated in Malabar, Kerala. This dance is more or less in a dance-drama form, narrating mythological stories in dance format. Almost all dancers are men and they are masked to depict the mythological characters they are representing. This dance lasts for ten to twelve hours, usually starting at 7:00 p.m. and ending at 7:00 a.m. It is an all-night show.

Manipuri dancing is usually performed by the hill people residing in Manipur, in the state of Assam. Both men and women take part in this dance accompanied by chorus singers. The costumes of the dancers are very colorful, with girls wearing long, wide skirts. Just like Kathak dancing, Manipuri dancing is centered on Lord Krishna and his girlfriends, the Gopis.

Lord Nataraja, the King of Dance, symbolizes the rhythm of the universe--the perpetual cycle of creation and annihilation. In his very famous book, *The Tao of Physics*, Fritjof Capra explains dance as the most basic and relevant of all forms of expression, and uses such phrases as "the dance of creation and destruction" and "energy dance." So, in a nutshell, the Hindu dances which I have told you about represent the vibration (Spandhanam) in every being and every atom in this universe.

23 ❧
Avatars in Detail

WHAT IS AN AVATAR?

An Avatar is an incarnation of God. When God comes down to earth in any life-form, then we call that an Avatar.

DADDY, WHAT IS THE PURPOSE OF AN AVATAR?

In the Bhagavad Gita it is written, "Whenever there is a decay of Dharma (righteousness) and outbreak of Adharma (non-righteousness), I descend Myself to protect good, to annihilate the wicked and to re-establish Dharma. I am born from age to age."

IS JESUS CHRIST AN AVATAR?

Of course, he is an Avatar like Krishna, Buddha or Mohammed. He came with a mission, delivered a mission, and finally left unattached to anything or to anyone. Avatars are not limited to India. They happen world-wide.

DID CHRIST VISIT INDIA?

There are inscriptions in the Pali language in Tibet about a saint named Isa or Issa. Some believe that Saint Isa was Jesus Christ and that he was in India during the unknown years of Christ. Of course we have no conclusive proof. In fact, I discussed this with the Worldwide Church Of God in Pasadena, California, and they said that Jesus's travels to the East have no Biblical foundation. Nevertheless, what intrigues me most is the similarity between some aspects of Christianity and Buddhism, as well as Hinduism. Of course, all this could be mere coincidence.

DO HINDUS BELIEVE THAT ANOTHER AVATAR WILL COME IN THE FUTURE?

Yes, just like Christians and Moslems, Hindus also believe that. When God comes to earth again, each will see "It" according to individual faith. A Christian may see "It" as a Christ--a man on a white horse" (Revelation 6:1-2), a Hindu may see "It" as Kalki--also "the man on the white horse," and a Moslem may see "It" as Allah.

The Holy Koran tells Moslems that the Last Judgment will come at the end of this age and that Allah will pronounce judgment on everyone. So there are similarities between Hindu, Christian and Moslem beliefs. Christians believe that it could happen within one thousand years, whereas Hindus believe that it will happen only at the end of Kali Yuga--that is, 427,000 years from today.

24 ❧
Avatars of Lord Vishnu

WHAT ARE THE TEN AVATARS OF LORD VISHNU?

Matsya (fish), Kurma (tortoise), Varaha (boar), Narasimha (man-lion), Vamana (dwarf), Parasurama (warrior with an axe), Rama, Krishna, Buddha and Kalki (the man on the white horse). All these Avatars are very important to the Vaishnava movement in India. The Kalki Avatar is yet to come. Hindus believe that the Kalki Avatar will come at the time of Pralaya, the Great Deluge.

WHY DID LORD VISHNU TAKE SO MANY AVATARS?

Each Avatar has a definite purpose. Lord Vishnu came as Matsya the fish to save Sage Manu (Vaivasvata--the seventh Manu) from the floods and to recover the Vedas from a demon's hands. After that episode, things were still in disarray. Devas (gods of heaven) discovered that the divine nectar of immortality had been lost and was at the bottom of the sea. Lord Vishnu helped in its recovery by becoming Kurma the tortoise.

Lord Vishnu took the Avatar of Varaha the boar to kill a demon named Hiranyaksha, who dragged the earth to the bottom of the ocean. Lord Vishnu, after killing the demon, brought the earth back from the bottom of the ocean. After the death of Hiranyaksha, his twin brother Hiranyaksipu became the king of the demons. He made everyone treat him as God. Since Hiranyaksipu had received a boon from Lord Brahma that he could not be killed by either a man or an animal, Lord Vishnu took the form of Narasimha the man-lion and killed him.

Lord Vishnu came as Vamana the dwarf to get rid of the demon-king Mahabali. Unlike any other demon, Mahabali was a very great king. According to mythology, during the reign of Mahabali, the world was like heaven and everyone was praising him in all the three worlds. Lord Vishnu as Vamana tricked Mahabali into promising him that area of land which he could cover in three steps. Mahabali agreed. Vamana then immediately became a giant and took two steps to cover all the three worlds. He did not have a place to put his third step so poor Mahabali requested him to place his third step on his (Mahabali's) head. Then Vamana pushed Mahabali to the third world known as Patala. People in Kerala State still celebrate the reign of Mahabali by a celebration named Onam.

Lord Vishnu came as Parasurama the warrior to save the Brahmin caste from the tyranny of the Kshatriyas. Then he came down as Rama to annihilate Ravana, the demon-king of Sri Lanka. We read the story of Rama at length in the Ramayana epic.

The incarnation of Lord Vishnu as Krishna is the most popular Avatar of all. Even though Hindus consider Buddha as an Avatar, except for an idol of Buddha in every temple Hindus seldom worship Buddha. To some extent, the Hindus' attitude to Buddha is similar to the attitude of Jews to Jesus Christ.

Kalki, as I said before, is an Avatar yet to come to restore earth's purity. You should read the Srimad Bhagavatam to get all details.

ARE THERE MORE AVATARS OF LORD VISHNU?

Of course the ten Avatars of Lord Vishnu which I described to you at length are the principal Avatars of Lord Vishnu. According to the Bhagavata Purana, there are twenty-two incarnations of Lord Vishnu. They consist of the ten incarnations I have already described to you and twelve more incarnations as follows: 1. Sanat Kumara (youth) 2. Sage Narada (exponent of Bhakti and Tantras) 3. Saints Nara and Narayana 4. Sage Kapila (founder of

Samkhya system) 5. Dattareya (the great magician who restored Vedic rites and originated Tantric rites) 6. Yajna (Lord Vishnu is identified as the sacrifice) 7. Rishabha (founder of the pre-Aryan Jain philosophy) 8. King Prithu 9. Dhanvatari (founder of Ayurveda--he came from the ocean of milk holding the divine elixir Amruth) 10. Balarama (came as the brother of Lord Krishna--he is an embodiment of virtues) 11. Sage Veda Vyasa (author of the Mahabharata and the Bhagavata Puranas) 12. Mohini (the enchantress who deprived the demons of the divine elixir Amruth).

There are still more Avatars of Lord Vishnu which are not mentioned in the list above. For example, once upon a time Lord Vishnu happened to lose his head by an accident and he became horse-headed, and therefore known as Hayasirsa. As Hayasirsa, Lord Vishnu went and killed the two demons Madhu and Kaitabha and rescued the Vedas from them.

25 ❧
Ayurveda and Jyotisha

IS AYURVEDA A KIND OF MEDICINE?

Ayurveda is one of the Upavedas of the Atharva Veda. The four popular Upavedas are Ayurveda, Dhanurveda, Gandharveda and Artha Shastra. Ayurveda has its roots in the Atharva Veda. It is said that the original text of Ayurveda, composed by Lord Brahma himself, contained 100,000 verses spread over one thousand chapters and was composed long before the creation of beings (Susruta Samhita 1:1-5). Now, the Atharva Veda only contains six thousand verses, so some call Ayurveda the Fifth Veda.

Ayurveda is not mysticism. It is not voodoo, but a systematic study of the human body, mind and soul. When Western medicine, by its pills and probes, relentlessly searches to isolate and destroy invading organisms, Ayurveda relies on clinical observation-- including the ancient art of diagnosing a patient's ailment by feeling the pulse--to identify the underlying imbalance of nature's three basic forces known as Vata, Pitta and Kapha.

By definition, Vata is responsible for both physical and psychological movement--both muscle tone and moodiness. People dominated by Vata are high-strung, restless, and prone to high blood pressure.

Pitta governs heat and metabolism. People dominated by Pitta are intense, have sharp intellects and are quick to anger. Skin rashes and ulcers may result from too much of this force.

Kapha maintains structure and stability. Kapha types are strong, even-tempered personalities who tend to gain weight easily.

According to Ayurveda, ten different personalities arise by different combination of Vata, Pitta and Kapha forces in the body. By balancing those three forces by meditation, diet, herbal supplements and special exercises, one will achieve perfect health.

The gods of healing in Ayurveda are Dhanvantri, Brihaspati and Indra. The prominent physicians of Ayurveda were Charaka (who lived from 80 to 180 A.D.), Susruta (who lived around 350 A.D.), Vagbhata (610 to 850 A.D) and Madhava (who lived around 1370 A.D.).

ARE ASTROLOGY AND ASTRONOMY INTERCONNECTED?

In Hinduism, the word Jyotisha means both astrology and astronomy. Both were part of the group known as the Vedangas. Hindu historians refute the theory that Hindus inherited their knowledge in astronomy and astrology from the Greeks. According to them, the origins of astronomy and astrology in India date back six thousand years. The earliest Hindu treatises on astronomy are known as Siddhantas. Aryabhata (476-520 A.D.), the Hindu mathematician, was the first who tried to explain the actual cause of eclipses. Another great Hindu astronomer was Varahamihira (505-587 A.D.).

Hindus are always fascinated by astrology. Hindu astrology functions with the realities of Karma, reincarnation, and the inner worlds we occupy at death. As per the legends, the sage Brighu wrote astrological charts giving the horoscope of every person ever born or to be born in this world. The writings of Brighu are popularly known as Brighu Samhita and are available from a few astrologers in India.

Other great treatises in astrology are known as Sathya Samhita, Narada Samhita and Saptarisi Nadi. Saptarisi Nadi consists of twelve books and it was printed in Tamil. Brighu Samhita consists of four books and about ten thousand. The Hindu God of Astrology is Lord Subramaniyan, the son of Lord Siva. Some say that once upon a time astrology was a very well-developed science, but today's astrology is only a skeleton, with most of the valuable knowledge lost due to the practice of utmost secrecy by the learned men of Hindu society.

DO YOU MEAN TO SAY THAT WE SHOULD IGNORE ASTROLOGY ALTOGETHER?

I cannot say so. If the moon can affect the tides in the sea, why can't stars affect the tides in the life of a man? Man is essentially an electromagnetic network. So movements of planets and stars which affect the earth's magnetic field should also affect the magnetic fields of human beings. Nostradamus (1503-1566 A.D.), the French astrologer and physician, indeed predicted many incidents in world history, like the execution of King Charles IX, the rise and fall of Napoleon and Adolf Hitler, and even the assassination of President Kennedy. Some of these could be strange coincidences and some of them could be explained by the theory of probability. However, I will not rule out astrology as a false science without fanatical arguing for and against it.

26 ஜ
Hindu Mathematics

DADDY, IS IT A FACT THAT ANCIENT INDIA DEVELOPED
A VERY HIGH SYSTEM OF MATHEMATICS?

Definitely so. When I say Indian mathematics or
Hindu mathematics, the name that will come up in your
mind is the name Ramanujam, the man who knew infinity.
But believe me, long before Ramanujam, long before the
Arabs, India had great knowledge in mathematics. The
zero was invented by ancient India. So too the decimal
system. Indian or Hindu mathematics was known as the
Sulva Sutra or "cord of verses." It dealt with the
construction of altars and sacrificial places. The formulas
of the Sulva Sutra are empirical in nature. In fact, it is
said that the Sulva Sutra might have been the influence
behind the later development of Greek geometry. Let me
repeat again that of all the things which came out Indian
mathematics, the zero stands out.

Aryabhata, who lived from 476 to 520 A.D., is the
first Hindu mathematician known to the world. His
treatise on the subject is the first Hindu work on pure
mathematics, and consists of thirty-three couplets. He
explained the causes of solar and lunar eclipses. He gave
a rule for the solution of simple intermediate equations
and accurate determination of the value. Believe it or not,
Aryabhata stated the relation of the circumference of a
circle to its diameter.

After Aryabhata, the next great Hindu
mathematician was Brahma-Gupta, who lived from 598 to
660 A.D. His work is known as Brahma-Siddhanta and it
consists of theorems and rules. After Brahma-Gupta, the
next great mathematician was Lalla who in 748 A.D. wrote
a slender treatise on mathematical theory. Mahavira, who
lived in 850 A.D., discussed quadratic equations.

Valuable information regarding Hindu mathematics is found in the Bakshali manuscript discovered in North India in 1881. In this manuscript, a small cross or plus sign is used to represent negative quantities and zero is represented by a dot.

One of the later mathematicians who came to prominence was Bhaskara, who lived from 1114 to 1160 A.D. He is the author of the Bija-Ganita, a work on mathematics, the Siddhanta-Siromani on astronomy, and the Lilavati on algebra. Believe it or not, in his computation of the size of the hydrogen atom, he used differential calculus.

Bhakti Yoga

WHAT IS BHAKTI YOGA?

One of the easiest Yogas or paths to follow or practice is Bhakti Yoga. Bhakti Yoga comes from the root word Bhaj which means "to be attached to." The Bhakti relationship between man and God is described in six different forms:

1. Madhura Bhava - sexual love
2. Kanta Bhava - love of wife for husband
3. Shanta Bhava - love of child for parent
4. Vatsalya Bhava - love of parent for child
5. Sakhya Bhava - friendship
6. Dasya Bhava - affection of servant for his master

One of the great exponents of Bhakti Yoga was Sage Narada. He states in his book the Narada Bhakti Sutra, "A man who loves God has no wants or sorrows. He neither hates nor survives with a zeal for any ends of his own. Through devotion he attains peace and is ever happy in spirit." In the highest aspect of Bhakti Yoga, the devotee goes for "total self-surrender to God." Lord Krishna promises in the Bhagavad Gita that he himself will undertake the burden of the day-to-day problems of a devotee who has dedicated himself to God by surrendering his free will. This promise of God is repeated many times in the Gita, in different slokas. The theme of total surrender of self is often repeated in the Holy Bible too.

WHAT DOES A DEVOTEE ACCOMPLISH WITH BHAKTI YOGA?

Like other yogas, the final goal is salvation. Bhakti also indirectly leads to the total dissolution of the "I" or the ego. According to Hinduism, ego is the cause of all problems.

WHO ARE THE GREAT EXPONENTS OF BHAKTI YOGA?

There are several great saints who practiced Bhakti Yoga in India. A few of the very prominent ones are Lord Chaitanya, Tulsi Das and Meera Devi. Lord Chaitanya and Meera Devi worshipped God as Lord Krishna. Tulsi Das worshiped God as Lord Rama. One of the greatest exponents of Bhakti in modern times is Sri Ramakrishna Paramahamsa. He worshipped God as the Mother Goddess named Kali.

IS BHAKTI YOGA INFERIOR TO OTHER YOGAS?

Hinduism never states that any form of Yoga is superior to others. In fact it looks down upon any effort by zealots who practice Jnana Yoga, Karma Yoga or Raja Yoga to condemn Bhakti Yoga. Throughout Hinduism, one can also see a disciple taking a different path or yoga from his teacher. Sage Ashtavakra, who is an Avadoota (a yogi who travels all the time), was the Guru of King Janaka (who ruled a country), and King Janaka was the Guru of Sage Suka who was indeed a great Bhakti Yogi. Similarly, Sri Ramakrishna Paramahamsa's Guru was Totapuri (an Avadoota) and his disciple was Swami Vivekananda, who was a Raja Yogi.

28 ॐ
Bhakti Schools

DADDY, WHAT ARE THE BHAKTI SCHOOLS OF HINDUISM?

Bhakti, as I have stated before means "devotion to God." But historically, intense devotion to God has been associated with the worship of Lord Vishnu (God of Preservation) or his most popular incarnation, Lord Krishna. The religion associated with the devotion to Vishnu or Krishna is known as Vaishnavism. The Bhakti renaissance happened in India from the 12th through the 16th centuries. There were mainly five Bhakti schools of Vaishnava origin, and all of them argued against the monastic doctrine of Adi Sankara.

1. Ramanuja's school. Ramanuja was born about 1050 A.D. He was the very first to propagate the Vaishnava Bhakti, which was started by devotional mystics of South India called Alvars, in the proper format. He wrote many Vedic texts and established the proper methods of worship.

2. Madhava's school. Madhava (1197-1280 A.D.) was dissatisfied by Sankara's Advaita philosophy. He taught that God is self-dependent and that the world or souls are God-dependent. He established Dvaita or dualistic philosophy. He emphasized five distinctions: 1. between God and the individual soul 2. between God and the inanimate world 3. between the individual soul and the inanimate world 4. between one individual soul and another 5. between one inanimate object and another. Like some Christian teachings, he even said that some individual souls are eternally doomed and cannot hope to get liberation. There are twenty-four major monasteries in India in the Madhava tradition.

3. Nimbarka's school. Nimbarka paved the way for the very popular worship of Radha and Krishna around the 14th century. He was the first to identify the Supreme Brahman as the divine couple "Radha-Krishna." In that respect his ideas resemble the Yin and Yang of Taoism. His philosophy is known as Dvaitavaita, "oneness and difference," a position between Sankara's monism and Madhava's radical dualism. He said that both dualistic and non-dualistic aspects of reality are equally real. Souls and inanimate matter are parts of God, not separate from Him. Devotion to God ultimately brings knowledge, which liberates the soul from future births.

4. Vallabha's school. Vallabha (1479-1531 A.D.) taught pure monism. He taught about Saguna Brahman-- the Brahman with attributes. He saw everything as Lord Krishna. Everything is God and therefore good. He said that souls are one with God, as sparks are with the fire, and contain the qualities of Brahman--eternity, intelligence and bliss. He taught that the Bhakti Marga, the path by which God's grace is gained by devotion, brings liberation. In his school, God is worshipped as the baby Krishna. The image of the child Krishna lifting the Govardhana hill is adored and worshipped by this sect.

5. Chaitanya's school. Chaitanya (1485-1534 A.D.) emphasized the importance of glorifying God's name and chanting it in congregation, called Sankirtan, with devotees. He taught that everything in the world is one and yet different from God--Achintyabhedabheda. In sects associated with Lord Chaitanya, Lord Krishna with his consort Radha is worshipped as the personification of ultimate love. Chaitanya said, "God is everywhere and in everything; and yet God is nowhere and nothing except Himself, to be found in the highest heaven." Chaintanya's philosophy is a strange combination of Sankara's Advaita and Madhava's Dvaita philosophies. The Hare Krishna

movement (ISKON), started by Sadguru Prabhupada, is based on Chaitanya's school of thoughts.

29 ह
Karma Yoga

WHAT IS KARMA YOGA?

The word Karma is derived from the Sanskrit word
Kri, meaning "to do." The word Karma is used in many
senses in Hinduism. Here the meaning of the word Karma
is work. We do Karmas all the time. When we breathe, it
is a Karma. When we think, it is a Karma. The Karmas we
do dictate our past, present and future. According to
Hinduism, all destined duties are good Karmas if they are
duties popularly known as Svadharma.

According to Samkhya philosophy, Karmas are
controlled by three forces: Tamas, Rajas and Sattva. Tamas
represents inactivity. Rajas represents activity. Sattva is
the equilibrium of the two. Karma Yoga involves properly
employing these three factors to do our work better.

As I said earlier, the different paths of
God-realization in Hinduism are not airtight divisions, but
they merge into one another. So Karma Yoga has a lot to
do with Bhakti Yoga and Jnana Yoga. Chapters 3,4, and
5 of the Bhagavad Gita deal with Karma Yoga.

WHAT IS KARMA YOGA IN BRIEF?

Attaining freedom by unselfish actions is known as
Nishkama Karma. Selfish actions retard our goal.
Unselfish actions take us towards our goal. So Karma
Yoga is the system of attaining freedom through selfless
actions. A Karma Yogi may or may not believe in God or
in any religious doctrine. Einstein, Father Damien and
Mother Theresa are some of the Karma Yogis outside
Hinduism.

WHAT DOES THE BHAGAVAD GITA SAY ABOUT KARMA YOGA?

The Gita allots three chapters and 113 verses or slokas to explain Karma Yoga. Some of the important points are:

1. No man will reach a state of actionlessness (Nishkarmata) by shunning actions.
2. Action is the nature of all beings in creation.
3. He who controls his desires of the flesh and does selfless actions is an honorable man.
4. Do actions without seeking profit, because such actions will ensure salvation for you.
5. Look at Me, I am God. There is nothing I have to do in the three worlds. There is nothing in the three worlds I need or I can't get. Still I work all the time.
6. A man should do his duty (Svadharma). A man will meet with disaster if he does someone else's duty. Svadharma, however despicable it may be, is better than someone else's duty.
7. The senses are good. Mind is better than senses. The soul is better than mind.
8. In whatever form a man worships Me, I will make his devotion steadfast in that form. Whatever path a man may take, it will finally lead him to Me.
9. He who performs unattached actions by surrendering them to me will be untouched by sin, just like water drops on a lotus leaf do not wet it.
10. Actions do no taint Me nor do I have any desire for the fruits of actions. He who knows Me in this way, no action is binding on him.

30 ❧
Raja Yoga

WHAT IS RAJA YOGA?

Raja Yoga in essence is a very scientific path of God-realization. In this path, God is more or less treated as pure energy. Sage Patanjali, the author of the Yoga Sutras, was the first to systematize the practices of this technical Yoga.

Patanjali defined Yoga as "Chitta-Vritti-Nirodha." Yoga means "union with the divine" or "salvation." Chitta means "mind." Vritti means "modifications" or "vibrations." Nirodha means "stoppage," "suppression," or "restraint." So according to Sage Patanjali, the union with the Divine or salvation means stoppage of the vibrations, or modifications of the mind. As per Patanjali, modifications of the mind are fivefold and are either painful or non-painful in nature. They are Right Knowledge, Wrong Knowledge, Fancy, Sleep and Memory.

The practice of Raja Yoga dates from the Vedic age. The Bhagavad Gita glorifies and recommends it by starting with the statement, "Raja Yoga, Raja Guhyam (kingly guarded secret), Pavitram (the most purified), Uttamam (the best), Pratyakshavagamam (immediate result giving), Dharmyam Kartum (steadfast to Dharma)..." (Chapter 9:2).

DADDY, WHO IS PATANJALI?

The founder of Raja Yoga, who was supposed to have lived from 240-180 B.C. There is a scholarly debate as to whether he is the same Patanjali, the grammarian who composed the great commentary Mahabhasya to Katayana's critical gloss (Varttika) on Panini's Sanskrit Grammar, or not. Some say that he is none other than the reincarnation of the serpent king Anathan.

WHAT DOES A DEVOTEE ACHIEVE BY PRACTICING RAJA YOGA?

In Raja Yoga, a devotee tries to achieve a state above the mind and in a way tries to achieve a mindless state. It is very difficult to explain it in simple terms. A student of parapsychology may be able to understand the scientific aspect of Raja Yoga better than anyone else. The ordinary man whose consciousness is confined to the lower mind can conceive of only concrete images of objects, which are derived through the sense organs. In a nutshell, for a perfected Raja Yogi, thinking is a voluntary process all the time, unlike most of us who think so many things involuntarily. We think about the pros and cons of every issue, even if we do not want to think about the issue at all. For example, if we decide not to think of monkeys for the next hour, we will be thinking about monkeys for the next hour. That is the way the mind works all the time.

The Patanjali Yoga Sutra consists of 196 slokas. In his book Patanjali never states or mentions that this is the only way for God-realization, but implies that the state of mind which he expounds, as well as God-realization, can be achieved by other religious practices also.

WHAT ARE THE DISCIPLINES AND EXERCISES IN RAJA YOGA?

Raja Yoga mentions eight kinds of disciplines: Yama, Niyama, Asana, Pranayama, Pratyahara, Dharana, Dhyana and Samadhi. Yama means abstinence from all vices. Niyama means observance of purity and contentment. Asana means a posture suitable for meditation. Pranayama consists of prolonged expiration (Rechaka), inspiration (Purakha) and retention (Kumbhaka) of breath. This exercise is supposed to be done only under the proper guidance of a realized master or Guru.   In the Pranayama exercise, the devotee is supposed to control the vital currents in the body. Pratyahara means retraction or withdrawal of the sense-organs from sense-objects.   Dharana means the fixing of mind on any object. Dhyana means meditation.

Samadhi is the final state.   He who meditates ultimately attains Samadhi. In that state, the mind loses its complete identity and assumes a formless state, even though it can assume the form of any object it contemplates on. In Samadhi, the devotee realizes the ultimate truth. Nirvikalpa Samadhi and Savikalpa Samadhi are the two types of Samadhis which devotees attain in their divine pursuit.

31 ❧
Samadhi and the Koshas

WHAT IS SAVIKALPA SAMADHI?

The meaning of Samadhi is "union with God" (Sam - "with;" Adhi - "lord"). Savikalpa Samadhi means "having separateness." So in Savikalpa Samadhi the duality of perception is maintained. The devotee purposefully maintains this separate identity most of the time.

WHAT IS NIRVIKALPA SAMADHI?

Nirvikalpa Samadhi means "having no separateness." In Nirvikalpa Samadhi duality of perception does not exist at all. In that stage, the devotee becomes one with God.

WHAT ARE THE FOUR LEVELS OF CONSCIOUSNESS?

According to Hinduism, there are four levels of consciousness: 1. waking state 2. dreaming state 3. dreamless state, or Sushupti 4. Turiya. The fourth state, Turiya, is a state above the mind and it is the highest level of consciousness. You may never see the Turiya state mentioned in any modern psychology books. It is believed that a realized Yogi enters the Turiya state whenever he meditates.

WHAT IS THE DIFFERENCE BETWEEN JIVANMUKTA AND VIDEHAMUKTA?

Jivanmukta mean "a person who is liberated while living." Videhamukta means "a person who is liberated after death, living in soul." A Jivanmukta lives in the world just like any one of us, but he is not attached to this world.

IS THE BODY AN ASSEMBLY OF MANY SHEATHS?

According to the Tantras, the body is an assemblage of five sheaths or Koshas. They are:

1. Annamaya Kosha (Anna-food; Maya-made of; Kosha-sheath)
2. Pranamaya Kosha (Prana-vital energy)
3. Manomaya Kosha (Mano-mind)
4. Vijnanamaya Kosha (Vijnana-intellect)
5. Anandamaya Kosha (Ananda-bliss)

The five sheaths of the self make the self manifest as Jiva. These are: matter (Prakriti), life (Prana), consciousness (Manas), intelligence (Vijnana) and bliss (Ananda).

What is Occultism?

WHAT ARE SIDDHIS OR OCCULT POWERS?

Powers like clairaudience (hearing sounds which the normal human ear cannot hear), clairvoyance (power of discerning objects not present to the senses), and telepathy (capability of transferring and receiving thoughts) are some of the Siddhis known to mankind. Even the capability of materializing and dematerializing at will is looked upon as a Siddhi. According to Hinduism, a Siddhi is an obstacle in the path of God- realization as it develops unwanted ego in a devotee. So Hinduism looks down upon Siddhis. But some are born with Siddhis, like Christ-like masters and Christ himself. In Jesus Christ and masters like him, Siddhis or occult powers flow out like fragrance out of a rose flower. Christ gave no importance to his powers at all. He did not try to influence the public opinion with his Siddhis. In fact he had an aversion for people who came for his occult powers. "Unless ye see signs and wonders ye can not believe, go to thy home, there thy son liveth" is a symbolic statement of Christ's aversion to Siddhis. All great Hindu saints acted exactly like Jesus Christ.

It is said that some psychic powers of the lower level can be developed by using certain kinds of drugs. But this method of using chemicals to develop Siddhis is the most dangerous method with dire consequences. Again, Hinduism forbids the use of any form of drugs in Yoga practices.

HOW EXACTLY ARE OCCULT POWERS DEVELOPED IN A PERSON?

According to Hinduism, Siddhis are developed in a human being by the rise of Kundalini power or serpent power through the spinal cord. This Kundalini power resides in Muladhara opposite the sexual organ at the bottom of the spinal cord in every human being. It is believed that as a human being evolves spiritually, this power rises up slowly and it goes through the six centers (Chakras) in the spinal cord and finally merges in the topmost point in the brain known as Sahasrara. At that point the person develops Siddhis. So it is believed that artificially stimulating that power from its resting point by chemicals can do serious damage to the body, since the ordinary body is not designed to meet such a tremendous force.

DO MANTRAS HELP TO DEVELOP OCCULT POWERS?

Some Mantras (chants) like Pranava or Gayatri can bring about the unfoldment of consciousness and there is no limit to such unfoldment. These Mantras are the Mantras of the highest order and they develop Siddhis naturally and slowly, so they are always welcome. There are certain Mantras like the Vasikarani Mantra which can be used for a specific objective, in this case to attract or win someone over.

DADDY, DO YOU THINK OCCULTISM IS VERY DANGEROUS?

Almost all who know a little bit of spirituality also talk about occultism, especially about Hindu occultism, in their daily sermons. But nobody tells the audience what exactly occultism is--what part of it is dangerous, and what part of it is good. Hinduism states that occult powers should not be sought. If they come to you, they should come naturally as a by-product of your pursuit of God-realization.

Another point I want to make. Do not attempt to do all types of Hatha Yogic exercises. The Western body is not conditioned to do many of them. You have to under adept supervision to do Yoga exercises.

If someone wants to do Pranayama, the best one is taught by the Self-Realization Fellowship in Los Angeles, California. Their method is known as Kriya Yoga and it is a psychic Pranayama. Their address is available in the book *Autobiography of a Yogi* by Paramahamsa Yogananda at any book store.

It is said that when Alexander the Great conquered parts of North India, he was startled by the depth of Hindu spirituality as well as by Hindu occultism. The actual origin of Hindu occultism can be traced back to the Dravidian civilization in India, long before the arrival of Aryans, at least five thousand years before Jesus Christ.

Hindu theologians consider black magic, spells to injure, and dangerous practices of Yoga as occultism. Normal breathing exercises like the Hamsa method or Kriya Yoga as taught by the Self-Realization Fellowship are not occultism. Of course, all Hindu theologians warn disciples that they should not practice exercises specified in Yoga books without consulting an adept in them. Both the Gheranda-Samhita and the Hatha-Yoga-Pradipika warn about the possibility of contracting diseases by doing strenuous exercises without adept supervision. Sirshasana, the art of standing on one's head, is good only if it is done properly. If it is done improperly, one can have problems such as distressing hallucinations.

IS OCCULTISM SEEN EVERYWHERE IN THE WORLD?

It is found everywhere in the world, including in Hinduism. To those who attack Hinduism as the torch-bearers of occultism, I have only one reply. Please do not use U.S. dollar bills anymore for they also carry the symbols of occultism. Those symbols or emblems consist of the Egyptian pyramid, the Third Eye of the Hindu God of Annihilation Lord Siva (or the all-seeing eye of the Christian churches of England) and the statements "Annuit Coeptis" (meaning "he prospers our undertaking") and "Novus Ordo Seclorum" (meaning "new order of the ages"--the Aquarian age, occurring in astrological terms after the Gold, Silver, Bronze and Iron ages).

It is said that the reverse of the great seal of the U.S.A. depicts the Masonic emblem described above because more than fifty of the signatories of the Declaration of Independence were either Masons or Rosicrucians and were very much concerned with esoteric sciences such as astrology and the Kabbalah. The name Pentagon for the U.S. military headquarters had an occult beginning. Believe it or not, the most powerful laser ray on earth is called "Siva," symbolizing the powerful rays of Lord Siva's third eye, and the word "trident" came from the weapon of Siva. I feel most Hindu mythological names were brought to U.S. defense and space exploration by the German scientists who came to the U.S. after the Second World War. It is likely that they were well-versed in Indology. So one can see the symbols of occultism every where in the world.

You can see the metaphysical aspects of occultism in the Rig Veda and its practical applications in all aspects of Yoga. One scripture which can be called the authority on Hindu occultism is the Atharva Veda, which consists of all kinds of chants and also magic spells. Even one part of the Ayurveda (the Hindu medicine), known as Bhuta-Vidya, deals with diseases caused by spirits.

Once again, Hinduism does not support using occultism for selfish motives and dissuades everyone from meddling with occultism.

Law of Karma and Reincarnation

DADDY, WHAT EXACTLY IS THE LAW OF KARMA?

Hindus believe in life after death. They also believe in the idea, "Whatever a man soweth, that shall he also reap" (Galatians 6:7). That is the basis of Karmic law. To put it in modern scientific terms, Hindus believe that every action has a reaction. There is no such thing as action without any result. Every action, even every thought, produces a reaction. Hindus believe that every thought and every action is weighed on the scales of eternal justice. The Law of Karma is one of "cause and effect." It works in the scientific world as well as the moral world. These unwritten Karmic laws are universal and we can but obey these laws. These laws act in a similar manner in similar circumstances. For instance, whenever you put your hand in fire, you automatically burn your fingers. This happens at all times and at all places, to the newborn as well as to a physicist who might have done ten or fifteen years of research on fire alone. Nobody can get away from the claws of Karmic law, because by nature we all do actions all the time. Even those who sit idle are doing actions with their mind, even though their actions will be fruitless and idiotic. The doctrine of Karma started in the days of the Rig Veda and it is very well explained in the Brihad-Aranyaka Upanishad.

WHAT HAPPENS TO US WHEN WE DIE?

According to Hinduism, the body alone dies, the soul never dies. But the path the soul takes is decided upon by the past actions which are popularly known as Karmas.

The actions of the former body do not die with the body. As I said above, past actions are attached to the soul and they decide the path of the soul's travel. So if you are born rich or poor, it is because of your actions in your previous life. If you are born with disease, that is also the result of your past actions done in past lives. After death, the soul carries a heavy load of Karmas and seeks an ideal body to be born in again. If you lived as a rotten individual in your last life, then the soul will take birth in a home where people will be leading rotten lives. If you lived a pious life, then you will be reborn in an ideal home where both parents will be pious and happy.

According to Hinduism, the soul continues this journey with a heavy load of Karmas from one life to another until it exhausts all Karmas by undergoing pain or pleasure sensations in the body. The different methods of God-realization provide easy ways to put an end to this drama. Then the individual soul, which is popularly known as Jeevatman, will merge with the Absolute Soul or infinite power, popularly known as Paramatman. This merging process is known as salvation.

DADDY, HOW IMPORTANT ARE OUR THOUGHTS?

According to Hinduism, every thought, however insignificant it may be, is counted. Every thought we entertain circles around us. A thought never dies. It may lose its strength in time, but it never dies completely. If you repeatedly think about the same thing, then that thought becomes a power-source. If you repeatedly think that you will get into an accident, then your wish will be fulfilled. You will get into an accident. It was your powerful negative thoughts that resulted in an accident. At the same level, if you develop prosperity thoughts in you, then your life will change dramatically, even if you are a pauper at present.

Believe me, Jesus Christ spoke volumes when he said "Love thy enemy" (Luke 6:27). Here he was teaching people the importance of powerful thoughts of love. The love Christ was speaking of is the love without motive, love that has nothing to do with carnal feelings. It does not even involve touching and kissing. By sending thoughts of love to your enemy, you will become a generator of love. Most probably your enemy may refuse to accept your thoughts of love. In that case, those powerful thoughts of love will come back to you like a boomerang; you will become a fortress of love. Thoughts of hatred work exactly in the same manner. Remember the immortal words of Jesus Christ: "Every...word that men shall speak, they shall give account thereof in the Day of Judgement" (Matthew 12:36).

If you hate someone and you harbor that thought again and again, you will become an embodiment of hate. In the course of time, you will find even your best friend loathing your presence. Knowing the power of vengeful thoughts, Mahatma Gandhi said, "Fight without malice." We have the right to fight injustice without hating the personalities or circumstances involved.

DADDY, HOW CAN YOU SAY THAT THE LAW OF KARMA IS TRUE?

Son, just think, how else can we explain the inequalities around us? A baby is born in the dry deserts of Ethiopia; another baby is born in the luxury of Buckingham Palace. Both are innocent babies. One suffers from malnutrition and diseases, whereas the other grows up in luxury. What a paradox! Son, tell me now, is there another answer?

The laws of Karma and reincarnation indeed answer many questions. They explain the variety of personalities we find in the world, the gap between the good and the bad, the rich and the poor, etc. They explain all kinds of inequalities. They give answers to perplexing questions such as why one person dies young and another old. They may even have an answer to the horrifying deaths of millions belonging to a certain race, during the Second World War. Did they inherit a great mountain of Karmic debt by willfully stating that the punishment or sin of crucifixion of Christ should fall on them and their children and grandchildren?

DO YOU THINK OUR PROBLEMS ARE GOD'S PUNISHMENTS?

No, son. God will never punish us. God has created man near to perfection and has given him the free will to decide whatever he wants. God never interferes in man's decisions. There is no such thing as being cursed (refer to the Bhagavad Gita verses 5:14, 15 and 4:14). We ourselves make our lives miserable or happy. Even in the Bhagavad Gita, Lord Krishna never tries to influence his disciple Arjuna's free will. Lord Krishna, like an advisor, only discusses with Arjuna the various options he could take in his life. Just think, Christ even allowed his apostles to deny him at the hour of crucifixion. So it is stupid to say things like "revenge of God."

IS GOD BOUND BY THE LAW OF KARMA?

Hindus believe that even God is bound by the law of Karma once He takes human form. For example, when God came down as Lord Krishna, he had to be killed by a hunter because he had killed the hunter in his previous life in a very cunning manner. (In his previous life, when God came down as Lord Rama, he killed the monkey-king Bali by attacking him from the rear.) The Yadavas, the blood-relations of Lord Krishna, were also killed since their collective actions warranted their extinction.

Hindus believe that when God came down as Jesus Christ, he took over the Karmas of all his disciples and thousands of devotees around him. Then, to fulfill the law of Karma, he allowed himself to be crucified. Jesus Christ allowed himself to take care of the Karmic debt of his apostles and the devotees surrounding him. Each time he saved someone from death and each time he cured incurable diseases of people, Jesus Christ was voluntarily accepting their Karmic load.

The all-knowing, all-powerful Christ could have easily (with one glance) transformed the whole Roman army into his obedient devotees. Instead he even refused to answer the questions of the Roman governor Pilate. His statements during the Last Supper showed that he was dictating his own fate by crucifixion. He did not have even an iota of hatred towards Judas. Instead he showed compassion and love towards everyone including the Romans who accused him, and allowed himself to be abused, tortured and finally crucified. Why? The only answer is that the all-knowing, all-powerful Christ was obeying the law of Karma, the unwritten law of the universe.

34 ໄ
Science of Reincarnation

DADDY, HOW DID THE CONCEPT OF REINCARNATION
ORIGINATE?

The first mention of reincarnation in world history
is in the Rig Veda, but the ancient Egyptians also believed
in the transmission of souls. Passages in the Egyptian
Book of the Dead imply the possibility of a "second birth."
The Greek historian Herodotus tells us that the ancient
Egyptians believed in an eternal soul, which was separate
from the body. They even thought that people of royal
origin could take any life-form they chose after death. The
Egyptian idea of reincarnation was later adopted by the
Greek philosophers Plato and Aristotle. Plato taught the
existence of an immortal soul that undergoes frequent
rebirths.

Reincarnation is currently a very hot topic all over
the world, especially in the Christian media. Many
Christian theologians call it a "pagan superstition." Some
Christian theologians even say that the theory of
reincarnation is satanic. Millions of people today are
curious about reincarnation, and many believe that they
have lived before. According to a recent survey, one in
four Americans and West Europeans now believe in
reincarnation. Reincarnation is a frequent theme of
movies and novels. Increasing numbers of people around
the world are involved in past-life regression therapy to
discover who they were in previous lives. Reincarnation
is part and parcel of the New Age movement. One can
find it in the teachings of theosophical societies and
psychics such as Jeanne Dixon and the late Edgar Cayce.

WHAT IS REALLY THE SCIENCE OF REINCARNATION?

Let me repeat to you briefly what Lord Krishna told Arjuna about reincarnation. Lord Krishna said, "At the time of death, the body dies but the soul never dies. The soul passes from one body to another after death like a body changing clothes. The soul goes on taking an endless number of bodies, until the soul exhausts all Karmas attached to the soul. This process is known as reincarnation" (Bhagavad Gita 2:22).

To explain further, Hindu saints found out that our lives are neither an accident or chance, nor is God responsible for the inequality among us. According to Hinduism, life is a stream which flows ceaselessly, without beginning or end. All things are part and parcel of this existence. Everything exists life after life, until it has achieved the true knowledge of itself or unity of the individual soul with God. Each of us will have many opportunities to realize our true identity. The doctrine of reincarnation offers hope to all. Nobody is punished forever. The best among us will achieve salvation by one life and the worst among us will achieve salvation by many lives.

WHAT IS SALVATION?

When the individual soul (Jeevatman) exhausts all its Karmas and merges with God the infinite soul (Paramatman), then we say the individual soul has attained salvation.

WILL ALL MEN WHO DIE REINCARNATE AS MEN IN THEIR NEXT LIFE?

Not necessarily so. If a man exhibits beastly character throughout his life, he will reincarnate as a beast. Lord Krishna said, "I make the cruel and vicious persons take birth again and again as ferocious animals" (Bhagavad Gita 16:19). A glutton may take birth as a pig or other lower form of life. The Vedas talk about 8.5 million species of life, right from amoebas to human beings and semi-gods. A man can take any one of these life-forms. Sometimes the soul will also remain in a standstill state for long periods of time without taking any body at all. However, please understand that the soul can get rid of its Karma only if it takes a body. So for attaining salvation, the soul is bound to reincarnate.

DADDY, DID KRISHNA SAY THAT A PERSON'S NEXT LIFE IS DECIDED BY HIS THOUGHTS AT THE TIME OF HIS DEATH?

Of course, Lord Krishna said that whatever form one thinks of during the time of death, one will attain that form. But at the same time, you know very well that a man who has beastly ideas throughout his life is unlikely to think of God during the time of death. Only God-fearing people can think of God during the time of death; others will think of a multitude of things but not about God (Bhagavad Gita 8:5, 6).

WHAT HAPPENS TO A MAN WHO WAS VERY GOOD THROUGHOUT HIS LIFE BUT ENDED UP AS A ROTTEN HUMAN BEING AT THE TIME OF HIS DEATH?

As I told you before, when a man dies his soul takes with it the sum total of good and bad Karmas. If the sum total of his actions is bad, he will go for a worse life-form. So it is the sum total of Karma that decides the travel route of the soul. One or two bad actions alone do not determine the soul's new destination (Bhagavad Gita 6:40-43).

CAN WE CONCLUDE THAT IF A SICK OR RETARDED CHILD IS BORN, THE PARENTS AND THE CHILD ARE EQUALLY RESPONSIBLE?

As per the law of Karma, the parents are destined to have a sick child to worry about and the child is destined to be born with sickness. But understand, both the parents and the child can make life better by new good positive actions.

HOW WILL ONE KNOW WHICH ACTION IS GOOD?

The most important part of any action is the motive behind it. If the motive is bad, then the best action is poisonous. For example, let us say that you are helping a poor innocent young girl to come up in her life. But if you are doing it with the intention of exploiting her at some future time, then your action is vicious and bad. But if your intentions are strictly humanitarian, then your action is a virtuous action indeed. The surgeon and the soldier do diagonally opposite actions. One saves life and the other takes it away, but the motives of both actions are very good. So both actions are good.

DADDY, WHAT HAPPENS TO SOMEONE WHO COMMITS SUICIDE?

As per Hinduism such an action will condemn the soul for thousands of years, and it will be forced to start life all over again from the lowest level of the evolutionary ladder. The soul will have to wait countless years to finally take a human body again. Sometimes the soul will remain in a standstill condition, becoming a ghost without taking a body, as per the Mahabhagavatam.

DOES THE REINCARNATION THEORY TALLY WITH DARWIN'S THEORY OF EVOLUTION?

It not only agrees, but goes one step further by saying that the soul of a man can even go back on the ladder of evolution and take the body of an amoeba.

It may be a mere coincidence, but at the same time it is very interesting to note that the ten Avatars of Lord Vishnu are curiously complying with Darwin's theory of evolution. First Lord Vishnu came as Matsya (fish--living in water). Then he came as Kurma (tortoise--living in water and on land), then as Varaha (boar--living on land only, an animal), then as Narasimha (man-lion, a combination of man and beast). Next he came as Vamana (child or dwarf), then Parasurama (ferocious fighter born to kill the Kshatriyas), then Rama (a king with all the problems of an ordinary human being), then Krishna (the super-human, in a way the superman beyond any comparison with anyone else), then Buddha (the silent one, a realized master) and finally is still to come as Kalki (the destroyer to annihilate creation, so that the process of recreation can be started all over again). As I said before, this could be a strange coincidence, or mythology may have been written based on in-depth knowledge of seers into human reproduction and development of a human being within the womb, where the fetus undergoes timely transformation in tune with Darwin's theory of evolution. One theory states that an embryo of a fish, an embryo of a pig and an embryo of a human being are all exactly alike. Only timely transformation makes one a fish, another a pig and another a human being. (refer to the embryonic recapitulation theory of Ernest Haeckel, 1860. Of course, this theory is disputed by many.)

IF KARMA IS THE CAUSE OF REINCARNATION, THEN WHY WAS I BORN IN THE FIRST PLACE, WHEN I SHOULD NOT HAVE HAD ANY KARMA?

I could answer that you were an amoeba first and then from that life you slowly evolved by thousands of reincarnations to a human being, but your next question will then be, "How did I take birth as an amoeba?" I do not want to speculate. No scriptures talk about it. The Bhagavad Gita says, "Creation came out of food which came out of the rains which came out of Yajna. Yajna came out of Karmas, which came out of Nature, which, finally, came out of the Infinite." This answer shows the instrumentality of creation. It shows that our birth is purely instrumental and our desire for salvation is also purely instrumental. As long as you experience pleasure or pain, you are forced to correct the path you are traveling along and go above those experiences. When you go above those experiences, you are automatically a realized soul. I am sure that if you contemplate on the above question, you will one day find the answer, but once you know the answer, you will be unable to express it in words for anyone else. Remember Prince Siddhartha renounced the world to find answers to old age and disease and finally became the Buddha, the Silent One. When his devotees questioned him for answers to old age and disease, he told them to follow the eightfold path and that would lead them to truth and provide all answers.

DOES GOD CREATE KARMA?

The best answer you can find is in the Bhagavad Gita. In verse 5:14, Lord Krishna says, "God does not create Karma or activities for beings, nor does He induce people to act, nor does He create fruits of actions. It is the nature that creates actions." In verse 5:15, Lord

Krishna says, "God does not assume anyone's sinful or pious actions. True knowledge is covered by ignorance."

DADDY, DO YOU THINK PEOPLE IN ETHIOPIA ARE CURSED AND THAT IS THE REASON WHY THEY SUFFER TODAY?

Please do not think that even in you wildest dreams. God cannot curse anyone. The Vedanta Sutra states, "God neither hates nor loves anyone, though He appears to do so." As I told you before, God has given us free will and our fate is decided by our own actions and our own thoughts. Each moment of our life we are doing things which decide our fate. Our past actions in our last life determine the trajectory of travel of the soul in the present.

So, as per the Hindu law of Karma, people who have done bad Karmas in their past life take birth in bitter conditions in this life. Unluckily, many souls whose past lives' Karmas were very bad are born together in the deserts of Ethiopia, but they are not destined to suffer forever. They should on their part help themselves to come out of this terrible condition. We on our part should help them to do so. It is our duty to do everything in our power to wipe out starvation and misery from Ethiopia. By serving them we are actually bettering our own fate, for even the best among us may have an abundance of past bad Karmas. So remember the words of Christ, "Judge not, that ye be not judged" (Matthew 7:1). The only thing we can do for the poor and the sick is to help them come out of all miseries, and by doing so, we make our present and future lives better. The Hindu law of Karma explains all the problems we see in our lives.

DADDY, I KNOW THAT THE LAW OF KARMA IS BASED ON REINCARNATION. IS THE SCIENCE OF REINCARNATION REAL?

I have to admit to you in all honesty that we do not have any corroborative scientific evidence to prove the science or theory of reincarnation. Many books have been written on this subject and some of them narrate stories told by people under hypnotic suggestions.

Unluckily, most of these books are written by zealots who are carried away with the idea of reincarnation. Therefore I cannot point out to you concrete evidence, but at the same time, I want to say that there is a mystery regarding death and reincarnation and unless and until someone proves to the world that reincarnation science is false, this age-old scientific idea is here to stay. Please tell me, are there better theories to explain the problems in the world than the theory of Karma and the science of reincarnation? There are even statements in the Bible pointing out the science of reincarnation. Christ said, "But I say unto you, that Elias is come already, and they knew him not" (Matthew 17:12) and "Then the disciples understood that he spake unto them of John the Baptist" (Matthew 17:13). Through those lines Christ is declaring to the world that the beheaded John the Baptist was the reincarnation of Elias. As a proof of existence of the soul, Christ said, "And fear not them which kill the body, but are not able to kill the soul" (Matthew 10:28).

DID EARLY CHRISTIANITY BELIEVE IN REINCARNATION?

Early Christian theologians such as Saint Augustine of Hippo were very much influenced by the Greek philosophy of Plato and Aristotle. Until 553 A.D., the Christian Church had an uncanny fascination with reincarnation. Justin Martyr (100-165 A.D.), founder of the first Christian school in Rome, wrote in his *Dialogue With Trypho* that the soul inhabits a succession of bodies, but that it cannot remember its previous lives. Another Christian theologian, Origen, tried to incorporate much of the beliefs of Greeks and Hindus into Christianity. Those ideas became so controversial that in the sixth century they were officially condemned in the second council of Constantinople as anathema. The teachings of Origen on reincarnation were thus expunged from Church doctrine, never to return.

WHY DO YOU THINK THE EARLY CHRISTIAN CHURCH WENT AGAINST THE REINCARNATION THEORY?

The only reason I can think of is the fear of Roman, Greek and Hindu ideas taking over Christian doctrines. Theologians like Saint Augustine of Hippo, Origen and Tertullian were closely associated with Platonism. Some of the Roman pagan festivals became Christian festivals in the early days of the Church. Apart from that, Gnosticism, with its Eastern ideas of God, tried to take over Christianity. Gnostics, like Hindus, believed in an impersonal God--a nameless, unknowable being called the "Abyss." Gnostics also taught that redemption from sin does not involve the death of Jesus Christ. Redemption is simply each person's effort to secure emancipation from flesh. Gnostics believed in spiritual discovery like Hindus and Buddhists, and differentiated themselves from other Christians by their claim to possess "gnosis" or knowledge secretly revealed to them by an unknown God. Like Hindus, they believed that man is part and parcel of God, a divine spark, and that achieving true knowledge is the ultimate goal of a human being. So early Christianity could not tolerate all those ideas that had Roman, Greek

154

or Hindu origin. That is the reason why in Christianity reincarnation is a taboo today.

DID JESUS CHRIST SUPPORT THE THEORY OF REINCARNATION?

Other than the words Jesus spoke about John the Baptist mentioned above, there is no evidence in the Bible we read today one way or another. Christ neither supported or condemned the theory of reincarnation, even though it was in the minds of the apostles, King Herod and the Pharisees.

WHY DO YOU THINK CHRIST DIED ON THE CROSS?

According to Hinduism, Christ died on the cross to take care of the Karmic debt of all the apostles and all the devotees around him. Hindus do not believe that Christ took care of the Karmic debt of all of humanity. If he had indeed done this, then there would have been no sickness or poverty in the world. A child is born in the luxury of Buckingham Palace and another is born in the deserts of Ethiopia. One child lives in luxury and the other suffers from malnutrition and all kinds of diseases. If indeed Christ had taken care of all Karmas, those paradoxes would not have been seen in the world. Only by the law of Karma can we explain them.

DO YOU BELIEVE IN THE CONCEPT THAT THOSE WHO SURRENDER THEIR INDIVIDUAL WILL TO THE WILL OF JESUS CHRIST WILL HAVE NO SIN?

That is indeed true as far as Hindu beliefs are concerned. The Bhagavad Gita very clearly states that those who surrender their personal wills to the will of the Almighty (in this case, in the form of Jesus Christ) will have no Karmic debt. In the Gita (Chapter 18:66) Lord Krishna says, "If a man gives up all material and religious activities and surrenders his will to Me, then I will save him from all Karmic debts and so-called sins." This surrendering oneself to God is very well explained in other Hindu devotional scriptures as well. The problem is that only a very few have the capacity to practice this method of God-realization, maybe one in a million. Man by nature wants to do everything as his ego dictates, and it is very difficult for him to surrender his will to the divine will of, for example, Jesus Christ or Lord Krishna.

Remember, even the great apostles, who saw Jesus face to face and witnessed countless miracles, had problems in surrendering their wills to him. Even Peter failed to believe in Christ fully when Christ asked him to walk on water. At the end, Peter even lied to save himself at the hour of crucifixion. On the part of Saint Thomas, he doubted the true divine nature of Christ even after his resurrection. Now you know how difficult it is for ordinary people to surrender their wills to an Almighty they cannot see, hear or touch. Once again, this surrender is more easily said than done.

DADDY, DO YOU IMPLY THAT THE REINCARNATION THEORY IS SUPERIOR TO THE RESURRECTION THEORY?

No, I will never say that. As far as I am concerned, both reincarnation and resurrection are just theories, since both lack scientific evidence to corroborate their concepts. Reincarnation theory fails to explain the reason or reasons for the "first birth." On the other side, the resurrection of Jesus Christ is a part and parcel of the New Testament and Christian faith. The Catholic Encyclopedia states that the New Testament writings are primarily documents of faith written by believers for believers. So from that we have to conclude that both reincarnation and resurrection are belief systems, backed by God-inspired scriptures of Hinduism and Christianity respectively.

Most Christians believe that the ultimate destiny of human beings is either joyful life with God forever in heaven or eternal pain and despair in hell, whereas the reincarnation theory states, "Salvation is for all; only the time factor differs between the best and the worst of us. The best will achieve salvation with one life, whereas the worst will achieve salvation by many lives." Christians view time as linear, with a definite beginning and a definite end, whereas Hindus believe that time is cyclic, an endless repetition of events.

35 ॐ
AUM--The Word and Sound

WHAT IS AUM (OM)?

The sacred syllable AUM (OM) stands for the Absolute. It is uttered at the beginning and the end of most Hindu prayers. Sage Manu said that the monosyllable AUM means "earth," "sky," and "heaven." AUM is considered as the very essence of the Vedas. Some say that "A" represents the waking state, "U" represents the sleep state (Nidra), "M" represents the deep sleep state (Sushupti) and the combination AUM represents total consciousness. The Katha Upanishad says, "The word which all the Vedas and all austerities declare, and desiring which men lead a life of chastity--the word I will tell you briefly. This syllable is indeed Brahman; this syllable is indeed the Supreme." The Mandukya Upanishad says, "AUM--This syllable stands for the whole world." The past, the present, the future, everything is just the syllable AUM. Even threefold time too is just AUM."

Sage Patanjali who wrote the Yoga Sutra speaks of God as "AUM." He wrote, "Meditate on AUM to actually contact Ishwara (God). AUM is His symbol." In the Christian Bible, AUM is mentioned as the Word. "In the beginning was the Word, and the Word was with God, and the Word was God." The exact parallel line in the Rig Veda reads, "In the beginning was Brahman, with whom was the Word [AUM], and the Word was truly the Supreme Brahman." The word AUM, Christian "Amen" and Mohammedan "Amin" all represent one and the same. In the Upanishads, AUM has been described as Pranava.

PLEASE TELL ME HOW TO CHANT AUM.

Son, so much is written about AUM in all scriptures of Hinduism. Many people think that they can simply chant AUM with their human voices. The fact of the matter is that since the AUM sound has a very high or low rate of vibration, it cannot be uttered by the human voice. The cosmic sound AUM is not perceptible to the senses, but it can be experienced in very deep meditation. Almost all mystics of the East and West have attested to the real experience of the cosmic sound. Saint Francis of Assisi, for example, described it as a music so sweet and so beautiful that had it lasted a moment longer, he would have lost himself in it completely. The right way of chanting AUM is mental chanting and superconscious chanting. AUM should be chanted with proper Pratyahara (internalization of the attention) and Pranayama (life-force control and proper withdrawing of senses from sense objects). It is said that he who knows God as the cosmic sound finds himself free of all miseries and death.

ARE YOU SAYING THAT THE "WORD" THAT IS MENTIONED IN THE HOLY BIBLE IS NONE OTHER THAN AUM OR BRAHMAN IN THE HINDU SCRIPTURES?

Please see for yourself the similarity between the statements in the Rig Veda and in the Bible regarding the "Word." How much they are similar! The Vedas (3000 B.C.) state, "Prajapati Vai Idam Agre Aseet (In the beginning was Prajapati, the Brahman), Tasya Vag Dvitiya Aseet (with Whom was the Word), Vag Vai Parama Brahma (and the Word was verily the Supreme Brahman)." John 1:1 (50-100 A.D.) states, "In the beginning was the Word, and the Word was with God, and the Word was God."

36 &
Mantras and Mantra Yoga

WHAT IS MANTRA YOGA?

Mantra Yoga originated from the Vedas and Tantras. This Yoga brings about changes in material consciousness by the agency of sound. Of course, the "sound" Mantra Yoga is referring to is a mysterious sound which you cannot hear by the human ear.

From modern science, we know three important facts: 1. Matter is an expression of energy. 2. This energy vibrates at different frequencies in different types of matter. 3. Our sense organs can only receive sensations made in a very limited frequency range. For example, we can hear only the sound produced in a limited frequency range--anything above this range is called ultrasound and any sound below it is called infrasound. Of course, by no means can one conclude that the sound in Mantra Yoga belongs to one of the categories above. We could say that Mantra Yoga is based on the vibratory aspect of energy and its modifications into varied matter. Mantras are used to bring about substantial results as well as the unification and unfolding of consciousness. Mantra Yoga as such is not a special Yoga; instead it is widely used by devotees belonging to all other Yogas for spiritual upliftment and unfolding of consciousness.

WHAT IS A MANTRA AND WHY IS IT SO IMPORTANT?

"Mantra" combines two root words--Man, "to think," and Tra, "instrumentality." In brief, Mantra means "thought-form." A Mantra is a magic incantation or spell. Most of the important Mantras come from the Tantras. In Hinduism, deities are represented by Mantras and each deity is associated with a particular Mantra. It is said that the power of the Mantra brings down the deity to enter an image and then the image comes "alive." All Hindu Mantras are made of letters of the Sanskrit alphabet. It is believed that each letter has the potency of infinite power and when several of these letters are properly grouped into a Mantra, then that Mantra contributes to create a special effect. According to the power of the Mantras, they are grouped into male, female and neutral types. The Mantras that end in "Hum" or "Phat" are called masculine Mantras, those that end in "Svaha" are called feminine Mantras, and those that end in "Namah" are called neutral Mantras. There are fifty-two letters in the Sanskrit alphabet, so there are fifty-two elements of power which are available for producing Mantras in many different combinations. Of course nobody can say that only sounds produced by the Sanskrit alphabet can become Mantras. The only point to state here is that Hindu Mantras are made by the ancient scientists of the Vedic age, the Rishis, and an in-depth evaluation took place before accepting any word combinations as Mantras. There is an endless number of mantras in Hinduism.

WHAT ARE THE RIGHT METHODS OF CHANTING MANTRAS?

To begin with, a Mantra should be given to a devotee by a Guru if the fullest benefit is to be derived from it. Of course one can pick up any Mantra and start chanting it, and as long as the person has faith in that Mantra he will receive some positive results. Japa is the best known technique in Mantra Yoga, in which a Mantra is repeated constantly, first audibly by the human voice and then silently and mentally. As a devotee continues chanting his favorite Mantra, he will notice changes in his consciousness. But it is not necessary to see any changes in his physical body. There are several types of Mantras, among which Pranava and Gayatri are the most popular.

Just as a seed grows into a particular kind of tree according to the type of seed, so too is the effect of each Mantra.

The Mantra Hare Krishna devotees chant is, "Hare Krishna, Hare Krishna, Krishna, Krishna, Hare Hare; Hare Rama, Hare Rama, Rama, Rama, Hare Hare." This Mantra is specifically used to free one from Karma or bondage according to the Srimad Mahabhagavatam. "OM Namah Shivaha" is a very popular Mantra of South India. Another popular Mantra is, "Sree Ram, Jaya Ram, Jaya Jaya Ram; Sree Ram, Jaya Ram, Jaya Jaya Ram."

There are very many Mantras in Hinduism. There are even Mantras like the Vasikarani Mantra to attract the opposite sex. "OM Mani Padme Hum" is a great Buddhist Mantra, which refers to the "jewel in the lotus of the heart." In Judaism, "Baruch Attah Adonai" means "Blessed art Thou, O Lord our God." For a Christian, the very name of Jesus is a great Mantra. In the Catholic tradition, "Hail Mary" is used as a very powerful Mantra. "Bismillah Ir-Rahman Ir-Rahim" is a beautiful Muslim Mantra meaning "In the name of Allah, the merciful, the compassionate."

AUM -- The Word and Sound

DADDY, WHAT IS THE GAYATRI MANTRA?

The Gayatri and Pranava (AUM or OM) Mantras are the most popular Mantras of Hinduism. The Gayatri Mantra originated from the Hindu Rig Veda (III, 62:10). Some call this Mantra the Savitri Mantra since it contains the word Savitri. Legends say that this Mantra was the composition of the South Indian Sage Vishwamitra, who was a Kshatriya by birth and who was finally elevated to the Brahmana state because of his intense Tapas and devotion to Hinduism.

Like any other Mantra, to get the proper effects, this Mantra should be accepted from a Guru. If one is going to chant this Mantra, one should follow the Devanagiri script. Please do not follow the English version I have given below. According to Hinduism, a Mantra chanted with mistakes in it is worse than chanting no Mantra at all.

Personally I feel that like all other Mantras, this great Mantra is of Tantric origin and that may be why it has locked within itself unexplainable powers.

The Gayatri Mantra reads approximately as follows:

OM
bhur bhúvah sváh
tát Savitúr várenyam
bhárgo devásya dhimahi
dhíyo yó nah prachodáyāt

According to Hinduism this Mantra is not translatable, and writing any erroneous translation to this Mantra is considered by many Hindus as blasphemy. However, so that you may appreciate its meaning, here is an approximate translation: "OM! Glory to Savitri, the excellent, the effulgence of the Divine, let us meditate

upon it. May it inspire us with understanding, who is
Gayatri."

As per the legends, Gayatri (or Savitri) is the second
wife of Lord Brahma (the first wife is Saraswathi, the
Goddess of Knowledge). It is said that once Saraswathi
was missing for an important function at Brahma's palace
so Brahma hurriedly married a girl from a non-Aryan tribe
as a substitute for Saraswathi in the function, and that girl
was Savitri. I do not know how many Hindu theologians
will agree with the authenticity of this legend.

Usually the Gayatri Mantra is given to a teenager of
Brahmin origin during the Upanayana ceremony, when the
teenager becomes a Dwija or one of the "twice-born." The
Upanayana ceremony originated from the Dharma Sutras
of Hinduism. After the Upanayana ceremony, the Dwija
is supposed to repeat the Mantra every morning and
evening and also on other important occasions.

It is said that the syllables of this great Mantra are
the summation of all four Vedas. The Vishwamitra Tantra
states, "The twenty-four syllables of Gayatri are her twenty-
four Saktis or powers. The mode of worship should be
according to the form of Sakti."

Even Sage Vasishtha, who had bitter fights with
Vishwamitra, praised this Mantra, stating that even fools,
criminals and the mentally retarded can attain benefits
from the power of the Gayatri Mantra. This Mantra has
been promoted by almost all Hindu saints, including
Advaitists like Adi Sankara.

Transcendental Meditation

WHAT IS "TM" OR TRANSCENDENTAL MEDITATION?

TM was started by Maharshi Mahesh Yogi in 1956. It is essentially the Mantra Yoga which Maharshi revived and introduced to the world. TM promised a drugless, stressless state of mind with inner peace and knowledge. Many of TM's meditation techniques are guarded secrets, but the procedure is very simple and straightforward. First go and meet the Maharshi or one of his selected instructors. The instructor will ask you questions about your health, feelings, education and marital status. After listening to your answers, the teacher will advise you to chant a special Mantra. As you may know, there are several Mantras, so you may be given a particular Mantra that will help you the most. After receiving the Mantra, you must mentally chant the Mantra for twenty minutes each morning and evening. As a result, your stress problems will vanish and you will be a better person according to the Maharshi. TM definitely has a lot of positive aspects.

TM also received a lot of negative publicity. Its secrecy and special attraction to it for celebrities make it look like a phony "celebrity religion." But as per the Maharshi, "TM is not a religion, but a science." Whatever the critics may say, TM has saved many lives from spiritual decline.

IS TM THE ONLY RIGHT METHOD OF MEDITATION?

I do not think even advocates of TM make such a claim. Maharshi Mahesh Yogi indeed revolutionized the whole concept of meditation. He made it very simple and lovable by all. He indeed took meditation out of all religious dogmas and presented it to the world on a silver platter, but at the same time nobody can say that TM is the only right method of meditation. If that was the only method, Lord Krishna would not have resorted to eighteen chapters and seven hundred verses of advice to Arjuna explaining different methods of meditation and paths of God-realization. TM will suit some, but for some it may not suit at all. For some, very rigid, ritualistic and highly ascetic Hare Krishna methods may suit well. For some, Mr. J. Krishnamurti's intellectual methods of seeking truth may be the answer. Please also understand that some of the claims of TM have been questioned by many, including Prabhupada (of the Hare Krishna movement) and Krishnamurti. Krishnamurti has gone to the extent of saying that repetition of "OM" or even "Coca Cola" will have the same effect on the mind. Anyway, my idea is not to belittle the great gift of Maharshi to the world. I just want to tell you that there are so many ways of right meditation.

39 ?🙠
What is Meditation?

DADDY, WHAT IS MEDITATION?

The word meditation originated from the Latin word "meditari" with the Latin root "mederi," meaning "to heal." So meditation is "the science of healing"--the science of healing of all physical and mental ailments. There are thousands of books on meditation and thousands of definitions on the state or result of meditation. Hinduism itself talks about twenty different levels of consciousness or mental stages. So, to put it very mildly, meditation is the art of making the mind still. To explain it in layman's terms, by meditation one enters a state of mind where there are no thoughts.

DADDY, WHAT IS MIND?

That is another tough question to answer. Mind also has thousands of definitions and if you read them all you will be more confused than ever before. The easiest definition would be: Mind is a space in which thoughts repose. So if we say the mind has become still, it means the mind has entered a thought-less state.

DADDY, WHY IS IT SO DIFFICULT TO MEDITATE?

To begin with, people confuse themselves with all kinds of definitions on meditation and attach unnecessary spiritual dogmas to it. Some even give undue importance to the whole idea of meditation with a very snobbish outlook. People proudly say, "I was meditating for the last four hours." So what? Did you ever hear anyone say that he/she was sleeping for the last eight hours, hence the whole world should salute them? All those things, as I said above, are hindrances to proper meditation. So the first thing is to understand that meditation is as natural as sleep (Sushupti) and it is a vital exercise required of all human beings from cradle to grave.

The art of meditation itself is grossly misunderstood by many people. Many Yogis make controlling the mind a prerequisite for meditation instead of saying a controlled mind is the result or fruit of meditation. Trying to willfully control the mind is like attempting to control the activities of a monkey running around the forest. Nobody can fight the mind and win. The mind is a very powerful force. The only thing anyone can do is to tame it by proper methods. Even Krishna acknowledges the power of the mind and tells a bewildered Arjuna, "Doubtless, oh great warrior, the mind is difficult to subdue. It is restless all the time but oh! son of Kunti, the mind can be conquered by repeated exercises and dispassion to sensual objects" (Bhagavad Gita 6:34).

SO WHAT ARE THE RIGHT WAYS OF MEDITATION?

There are so many ways of meditation, some of them direct and some of them indirect. One is to watch the thoughts that come to the mind without in any way controlling or trying to participate in those thoughts. This method may sound difficult but when you start practicing it, many of the questions you now have will vanish altogether. Pranayama and Mantra Japa are indirect ways of watching the mind.

DADDY, DO YOU MEAN TO SAY THAT I HAVE JUST TO MEDITATE AND DO NOT HAVE TO BE CONCERNED WITH THE "DO'S AND DON'TS" OF HINDUISM?

The "do's and dont's" you have mentioned are known as Yama-Niyamas. I have no intention to belittle their importance. I feel people generally deal with religion with the intention of changing everything overnight. In fact they do act exactly like they are trying to make a perfect vacuum. But there is no such thing as a perfect vacuum. However, it is easy to replace one form of gas with another gas in an airtight chamber. That is the idea on which I am basing my theory. We should first earnestly start meditation exercises and be less harsh on ourselves with "do's and dont's." That does not mean we should tolerate uncontrolled emotions. For example, if you are watching TV for six to seven hours daily, then try to reduce it to one or two hours and watch it constructively. If you have the habit of eating every now and then, try to change it to three times daily, and so on. Changes should be made without giving the mind a chance to fight back with force. Remember Lord Krishna said, "Yoga is not for those who do not eat at all nor for those who eat like a glutton. Yoga is not for those who do not sleep and those who sleep night and day." We are not living in the Himalayas but in cities where thousands of sensual objects pop up every now and then to stimulate our senses. Moderation is the name of the game.

WHAT REALLY HAPPENS DURING MEDITATION?

Science has still to explore this topic. The only thing we know so far is that during meditation the body gets relaxed and there is a change in the brain's electrical waves. The parapsychological departments throughout the world are conducting a lot of experiments on the results of meditation, but so far nobody has come up with any except that during meditation the brain makes alpha waves and sometimes even theta and delta waves. The brain is a mass of electrical circuits constantly sending messages back and forth between different centers of the brain, and as such it will takes years before we know what exactly happens during meditation.

40 ह
Brain Waves and Biofeedback

WHAT ARE ALPHA, THETA AND DELTA WAVES?

Well, let me explain everything from the start. The brain generates a small amount of measurable electricity. Right now doctors pick up this electricity by the use of a machine called the electroencephalograph. The electricity so picked up is amplified and displayed in visual form by a pen tracing a jagged line across a moving graph paper. Doctors call these brain wave graphs. According to variations in frequency, scientists have named the four basic brain waves alpha, beta, delta (one to four cycles per second) and theta (four to seven cycles per second). The fastest of them all is beta, with thirteen or more vibrations per second, a wave-pattern associated with an awakened or active condition. Alpha waves (seven to thirteen vibrations per second) prevail in the brain during the advanced state of relaxation. The discovery of alpha waves really rocked the scientific community and resulted in the development of the biofeedback system.

WHAT IS THE SO-CALLED BIOFEEDBACK SYSTEM?

When scientists found out about the different types of brain waves, they thought brain waves were beyond the control of human beings. Then they accidentally discovered that people could consciously put themselves into the alpha brain wave state. This was indeed a revolutionary discovery in the scientific world. Then a number of scientists started experimenting with people, making them consciously produce alpha waves. This method of a person consciously producing alpha waves by actually knowing the type of brain waves his brain is producing beforehand is known as biofeedback. To state elaborately, first the person is hooked up to an electroencephalograph machine. Each time the alpha wave appears the machine makes a sound. The person will then try to keep the tone going continuously by making alpha waves, and this is known as biofeedback. Most people found that they actually felt relaxed in the alpha wave state. Then some people started stating that they found the underlying principle behind Yoga meditation.

ARE BIOFEEDBACK AND MEDITATION ONE AND THE SAME?

The biofeedback system is very important and it helps quite a large number of people to relax properly. But it cannot be compared with meditation. Scientists have found that some meditators go from alpha to theta and sometimes even to delta waves during meditation. Again, nobody can make a machine like the electroencephalograph a judge to compare biofeedback and meditation. That machine only gives a gross measurement of brain activity. It has no capability to go deeper into the "why" and "how" of the brain waves. Of course, the EEG is used in the proper diagnosis of illnesses like epilepsy and other cases of brain damage. Nowadays it is widely used to determine whether a person is alive or dead. But science only knows that stoppage of electrical activity in the brain means death. It does not know how to inject or stimulate electrical activity in a stopped or dead brain. So we still have to go a long way to know more about the brain and brain waves. How can science explain the capability of a Yogi who can remain fully awake and yet shut himself out entirely from the external world? This capability of some Yogis is fully validated by some parapsychological research centers. Let me repeat that by no means can one pronounce judgment on meditation or even compare biofeedback and meditation with such an instrument as the EEG. It measures electrical activity on the surface of brain and as such provides only a very crude measurement of electrical activity within the brain. Plato's *Republic* and Aldous Huxley's *Brave New World* are governed by brain stimulation. Scientists around the world are doing a lot of experiments on Yogis, and we can only hope that one day they may discover very valuable points about meditation.

Hippocrates (400 B.C.) said, "Men ought to know that from the brain and from the brain only arise our pleasures, joys, laughter and jests as well as our sorrows, pains, griefs and tears."

41 ॐ
Brain Electrical Impulses and Samadhi

DADDY, DO YOU THINK THAT SAMADHI AND OTHER MENTAL STAGES ACHIEVED BY MEDITATION ARE ACTUALLY THE RESULT OF THE ACCIDENTAL SWITCHING ON OF CERTAIN CELLS IN THE BRAIN?

We do not know that yet. The brain has proved to be the most complex organ in the human body. It is irreplaceable and, as I said before, today death is defined as "brain death" or "the absence of the electrical activity in the brain." The brain has been estimated to contain 10,000,000,000,000 cells. Ninety percent of these are glia. The rest are neurons. Thinking and feeling are purely electro-chemical activities in the brain cells. Scientists have also found that the reverse is equally true. That means if brain cells are properly subjected to chemicals (drugs) or electrical impulses, the brain will generate "thinking and feeling" phenomena. This may seem to you as a page out of a Frankenstein novel, but believe or not, a lot of experiments are being conducted on that today. Electrical stimulation of the brain is indeed a well-known idea. Scientists have found that they can affect the brain by transmitting electrical impulses into it from outside to electrodes implanted in different parts of the brain. Stimulation of various parts of the brain has been reported to reduce or increase aggression in animals. Delgardo of Spain exhibited this by a breath-taking experiment. He planted electrodes in the brain of a bull and allowed the vicious animal to charge at him, in the presence of spectators in a bull ring. When the bull came very close to him Delgardo transmitted a signal to the implanted electrodes and to the amazement of everyone, the charging bull became a docile bull. Of course, even scientists will admit that by no means can one compare a bull's brain or a monkey's brain to a human brain. The animal brain reacts only to instincts and it does not have the thinking capability which we have. It is a very well-known fact that scientists still do not know the actual use of some parts of the human brain, which still remains very much an enigma to the scientific world. However, some Hindu scriptures, like Raja Yoga, state that pleasure and pain are in the brain.

So I agree with you that there is a good possibility that the results of meditation may be the result of the accidental switching on of certain unknown cells in the brain. A Yogi will explain to you that different aspects of Samadhi are achieved due to the result of the awakening of Kundalini power within the body, but science still has no idea about the existence of such vital powers within the body. Anyway, one thing is very certain--some of the strange experiences like having the sensation of going out of the body are even experienced by people who have taken certain hallucinogenic drugs. But in ordinary people such sensations are painful, dangerous and violent, whereas in a Yogi the same sensations are smooth and peaceful. We may have more understanding of different levels of Samadhi as parapsychology progresses in its research. By finding out the true meaning of meditation, science may one day prove to the world the religious concept that we are all only bionic robots of an unknown entity, which most of us like to call God. We have a long way to go. We may one day understand the true meaning of the authoritative statement of Lord Krishna to his disciple, "Nimitta Matram Bhava," or "Be an instrument" (Bhagavad Gita 11:33) and the statement of God to Adam, "Dust thou art, and unto dust shalt thou return" (Genesis 3:19). According to the Mahabhagavatam, all this creation is only a Leela (child-play) for that Supreme Power. We may finally find out that we have nothing to do but to obey the unwritten laws of the universe, since we are mere instruments of this Supreme Power.

DO YOU THINK MEDITATION CAN HAVE ILL EFFECTS
ON CERTAIN PEOPLE?

Meditation as such is positive. It has no inherent
negative effects. But if someone uses depression as a form
of meditation, he/she will get into a lot of trouble. Some
use drugs to help them during meditation. That too is
against the basic principles of meditation. Both Hindu
and Buddhist meditation methods strictly forbid the use of
drugs in any form. In some Hindu meditation techniques
even stimulants like tea and coffee are prohibited. Some
think meditation is devilish and a form of black magic.
Some think meditation is a form of brainwashing. Those
ideologies are far from the truth. People do many things
out of fear of losing life but when they are sure that they
will not lose their life, they come to their senses.

The last but not the least accusation against
meditation is that it makes people dull. But surprisingly,
almost all those who meditate are better persons in their
lives and in their professions. All the studies conducted
by the TM authorities prove this to be true. To repeat, as
long as people do not use meditation as a form of
brooding or for the development of hatred or venomous
thoughts, there cannot be any problem at all. Something
that has lasted for ages must have something intrinsically
good in it.

SOME CHRISTIAN THEOLOGIANS STATE THAT IN
EASTERN MEDITATION THE MIND IS TREATED AS AN
ENEMY OF THE SPIRIT, AND IT INVOLVES SHUTTING
DOWN THE MIND. IS THAT TRUE?

That is far from the truth. Eastern meditation
involves the stoppage of all mental activities resulting from
the activity of the senses in sensual objects and the
bringing forth of the true self or Atman. According to

Hinduism, the Atman is deluded by thousands of thoughts, and by meditation one will slowly "know thyself." Remember, Jesus Christ said "The kingdom is within," and by Eastern meditation one is trying to achieving that. By Eastern meditation, one's limited ego becomes the universal ego. For example, instead of caring and loving one's own children, one will start loving children all over the world.

Some Christian theologians ask their parishioners to meditate on God. The problem with such a meditation is that it involves concentrating on a God with name and form. When the mind picks anything with name and form, it becomes restless instead of becoming calm. Unless one transcends name and form, meditation is impossible.

Pranayama

WHAT IS PRANAYAMA?

Pranayama plays a very important role in Raja Yoga. There is no proper definition for Prana. Prana does not mean "breath" or "thought." Some say it means "vital currents" in the body. Ayama means "restraint." So, Pranayama means the restraint of vital currents in the body. Some define Prana as the link between absolute consciousness and the mind and body. The intimate relationship that exists amongst Prana, mind, thought and breath is utilized by different schools of Yoga. In some parts of Raja Yoga, Chitta Vritti, or mental vibrations, are controlled by will power, and Prana indirectly comes under the control of the mind.

ARE BREATH AND PRANA ONE AND THE SAME THING?

Breath is not Prana, but sages have found a direct connection between the two. Sage Patanjali says in the Yoga Sutra, "Regulation of breath control or control of Prana is the stoppage of inhalation and exhalation." In the Bhagavad Gita, Lord Krishna explains Pranayama in a very elaborate way. Some offer Prana (outgoing breath) in Apana (incoming breath) and Apana in Prana, restraining the passage of Prana and Apana, absorbed in Pranayama. The Gita gives an image of two snakes, both devouring each other and attaining a stage of nothingness in the above simile. Anyway, the first step in Pranayama is rhythmic breathing.

PLEASE EXPLAIN THE ACTUAL PRANAYAMA EXERCISES TO ME.

By controlling the motions of the lungs and respiratory organs, one can indirectly control the Prana that is vibrating inside all of us. Some practice a kind of Pranayama called Purakha (filling in). Some practice a kind of Pranayama called Rechaka (emptying). Some practice Kumbhaka, where the breath is held in the body. Usually the practice of Pranayama is a combination of Puraka, Kumbhaka and Rechaka methods. There are several types of Pranayama. Basically they are divided into Adhama, Madhyama and Uttama. This division is according to the time difference in the Purakha (filling in) period. The ratio of time between Purakha, Kumbhaka and Rechaka in all these three methods is 1:4:2. Sagarbha Pranayama is that Pranayama which is done along with the Japa of a Mantra like the Gayatri or Pranava (AUM). Kriya Yoga is the best Pranayama method, taught by Hindu saints. Rhythmic breathing is the balancing act between the Purakha, Kumbhaka and Rechaka stages.

ARE DEEP-BREATHING EXERCISES FORMS OF PRANAYAMA?

Deep-breathing exercises are not Pranayama. Those exercises can be done by anyone at any time. Pranayama should be practiced under the guidance of a very competent Guru. Pranayama should not be done by reading a book or listening to a narration. The body has to be conditioned to accept the power that is generated within it by the control of Prana. Proper dietary control is also necessary to achieve better results. Usually Pranayama is practiced by the aspirant sitting in Padmasana (lotus posture). It can also be practiced in Shavasana (dead-body posture).

WHAT IS HAMSA OR BABY PRANAYAMA?

This is the easiest of all types of Pranayama. It can be done by anyone, anywhere and under any conditions. Hamsa means "swan." It signifies that this method is as pure and as tranquil as a swan. In this method, the aspirant watches the incoming breath (which makes the sound Ham) and the outgoing breath (which makes the sound Sa) without controlling the breathing activity in any manner. In this method, one indirectly chants the Mantra "Sah Aham," meaning "He is I." There are no negative effects to the body. It helps in relaxation and annihilation of stress in the body. The first result of this method will be dreamless sleep or Sushupti.

DADDY, ARE BREATHING EXERCISES THE MONOPOLY OF HINDUISM?

Absolutely not. In the Chinese religion Taoism, there is a breathing exercise known as T-ai-si or embryonic respiration. The Chinese practice this breathing exercise for long life and it has no spiritual value. In some ways, Taoism resembles Hindu Hatha Yoga.

Control of breathing was also practiced by the Sufis. The technique of Dhikr resembles some of the Hindu breathing exercises. Even in Christianity there are some evidences of using breathing for spiritual enlightenment. Breath plays an important role in Genesis (2:7).

43 ❧
Kriya Yoga and Hatha Yoga

WHAT IS KRIYA YOGA?

Kriya Yoga is a very advanced form of Pranayama taught by Yogis in India. Kriya Yoga can be called "psychic Pranayama." One of the greatest exponents of Kriya Yoga in modern times was the late Swami Paramahamsa Yogananda. According to Swami Yogananda, by practicing Kriya Yoga one attains Cosmic Consciousness.

WHAT ARE HATHA YOGA AND ASANAS?

Hatha Yoga is a Yoga of Asanas, or Yoga postures, practiced for radiant health and longevity. In a way, by practicing Hatha Yoga one can make one's conditioned to meditate on God. Asanas help to loosen muscles and joints. They also promote the free flow of energy throughout the body. The Yoga postures are also good for different internal organs and glands. It has been found that bodily postures can affect mental attitudes, and mental attitudes can develop pain or pleasure in the body. By changing the pattern of breathing, one can actually change one's mental attitudes. Yoga postures are very valuable aids in the development of positive attitudes in man.

Relaxation is the most important result of practicing Asanas. Asanas should never be done under strenuous conditions. Those who practice Asanas regularly follow very strict moral, ethical and dietary codes. There are several types of Asanas and they should be done only under the direct supervision of a very able teacher.

WHAT ARE THE DIFFERENT TYPES OF ASANAS PRACTICED BY YOGIS IN INDIA TODAY?

Some of the most important Asanas practiced by Yogis throughout the world are as follows:

1. Shirshasana--standing on the head
2. Sarvangasana--standing on the shoulders
3. Chakrasana--a circular pose of the body
4. Dhanurasana--body bent like a bow
5. Halasana--body at a 90° degree angle
6. Janushirasana--head touching the knee
7. Garudaasana--body twisted like a bird
8. Padahastasana--body twisted like a jackknife
9. Sasangasana--body bent like a hare
10. Sukhasana--sitting in easy pose
11. Vajrasana--sitting in firm pose
12. Siddhasana--sitting in perfect pose
13. Kukkutasana--sitting like a hen
14. Padmasana--lotus pose
15. Shavasana--lying down like a corpse

Most Yogis sit in Padmasana or Siddhasana when they meditate on God. Some even meditate lying down in Shavasana. There are still a lot more Asanas. All these Asanas are practiced after bath, prayers and deep breathing exercises under the guidance of an able teacher.

44 ৯৯
Ashtanga Yoga and Laya Yoga

WHAT IS ASHTANGA YOGA?

Ashtanga Yoga literally means "the Yoga with eight limbs." This is the Yoga Patanjali explains in his book the Yoga Sutra. Of course this Yoga is none other than the Raja Yoga I explained before. The eight limbs of Yoga are:
1. Yama (consisting of truthfulness, non-stealing, celibacy and non-violence)
2. Niyama (consisting of purity of mind, contentment, penance, study of scriptures and meditation on God)
3. Asanas (postures)
4. Pranayama (control of Prana)
5. Pratyahara (withdrawal of the sense organs from sense objects)
6. Dharana (fixation of the mind on any object)
7. Dhyana (meditation)
8. Samadhi (final state of realization)

WHAT IS LAYA YOGA?

The Yoga which concentrates on the awakening of the Kundalini power is known as Laya Yoga. That is why some call it by the name Kundalini Yoga. This awakening of Kundalini is achieved by meditation on the Chakras in a proper order, under the guidance of a very competent Guru. It is said that premature awakening of Kundalini is extremely dangerous and as such extreme caution is maintained about this Yoga in Hinduism. It is said that certain drugs are capable of sudden awakening of the Kundalini or Serpent power, and that is the reason why Hinduism forbids the use of drugs to help in meditation.

45 ❧
Easiest Form of Meditation

DADDY, WHAT DO YOU THINK IS THE EASIEST AND
SAFEST METHOD OF MEDITATION?

Son, so far as I am concerned, Hamsa or the
method popularly known as Baby Pranayama is the easiest
and safest method of all. It has been found that those
animals which take long durations of breath (the time for
one cycle of inhalation and exhalation) live long lives,
whereas those which take short durations of breath live
short lives. It is also interesting to note that a person's
health and character are very much a reflection of his
breath pattern. Generally people who take short breaths
are weak, nervous and very undependable, whereas those
who take longer and deeper breaths are usually
trustworthy, happy people. When a person gets agitated,
his breath pattern changes rapidly, as he takes shorter and
shorter breaths. When a person develops sublime
thoughts within himself, he takes longer and longer
breaths. Thousands of years ago, the Rishis, the great
scientists of Hinduism, found out that there are vital
currents in the body called "Prana." They also found that
there is a close relationship between breath and Prana,
Prana and thought, and thought and mind. In brief, they
discovered that Prana is interconnected with the whole
body mechanism, and they created the system of exercises
called Pranayama.

As I told you before, Pranayama is the most
scientific method of controlling vital currents in the body.
Pranayama has to be practiced only under the guidance of
a very capable Guru and it is associated with a lot of "do's
and don'ts," or Yama-Niyamas.

Hamsa literally means swan--the beautiful white
birds that swim in silent lakes. In Hinduism, the swan
also symbolizes purity and tranquility. In this method,

one indirectly chants the Mantra "Sah-Aham," meaning "He is I." It is also worth noticing that when a man inhales he makes the noise "Ham" or "Aham." When a man exhales he makes the noise "Sa" or "Sah."

Now coming back to the main point, the Hamsa method is the method of watching the incoming and outgoing breaths (inhalation and exhalation) without interfering with the rhythm of breathing. The method is very simple. You may sit or stand or lie down in whatever position you like. You can do it at any time of the day or night. You can do this at any place. You can do it for as long as you like. Prior to following this method, if it helps, then you may do deep breathing exercises to induce "rhythmic breathing" in your system for five or ten minutes.

Now let me elaborate on the actual Hamsa method: Just watch your inhalation and exhalation without interfering with the process of breathing, without even trying to control chest or nostril movements. Do not even try to change the rhythm of breathing. Just say to yourself, "I am just going to watch my breathing--I am going to enjoy myself watching my breathing--I am going to enjoy enjoying myself watch my breath." That is all.

The first result will be that you will fall asleep during this exercise. According to Hinduism, sleep is a hindrance to meditation. But I feel people should be happy if they fall asleep during this exercise since many have to take high doses of sleeping pills to fall asleep. Once you have transcended sleep, in the next stage you will start going into a new mental condition without any thought at all. In this mental state, you will also find your breath pattern slowing down considerably. In this state of mind, you will start enjoying peace and happiness to which you were not accustomed before. Of course, at first you will have this enjoyable mental state for a few minutes only.   As time goes on, this mental state will last for several minutes and finally for hours.

This exercise will immediately reduce stress conditions in you. Stress is the mental condition one has as a result of involuntary thinking. This method will also help you to face difficult situations in life.   One thing worth mentioning about this exercise is that it has no negative effects at all.

The scientific explanation of this method is very simple.   In stress and high emotional stages, your breath-pattern is very erratic and you exhibit a tendency to take shorter and shorter breaths. But when you practice this exercise you will be able to develop rhythmic breathing like an alternating sinusoidal wave. Since there is a very close connection between breath, brain waves, thought and mind, we are indirectly controlling thought, brain waves and mind by directly watching the involuntary breaths. If you look deeper into this method, you will also see that due to its practice, your breath is slowing down since you are trying to make involuntary breathing a voluntary action in the body. During the practice of this method, your brain-waves will change into alpha waves initially. This method is very simple, and believe it or not, we are all doing this at least once every day. Surprisingly, breath is the last thing we are aware of when we go to sleep every day. To repeat, this exercise has no negative effect at all, and even though you may or may not fully agree with some of my scientific interpretations, I think you should try this method of meditation.

The Chakras

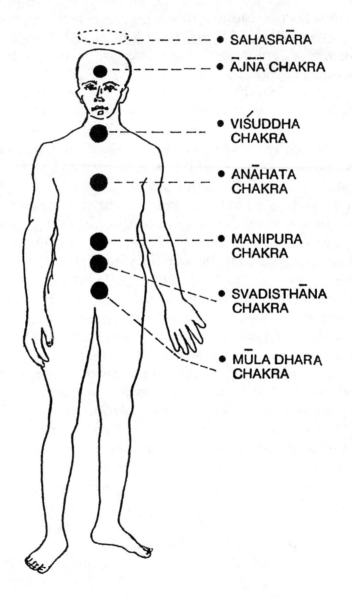

- SAHASRĀRA
- ĀJÑĀ CHAKRA
- VIŚUDDHA CHAKRA
- ANĀHATA CHAKRA
- MANIPURA CHAKRA
- SVADISTHĀNA CHAKRA
- MŪLA DHARA CHAKRA

46 ક્ષ
Tantras, Chakras and Kundalini Power

WHAT ARE TANTRAS?

The Tantras are a branch of Hinduism. Most Tantra literature is still kept a secret and the real meaning of much that is known is still an enigma. Most Hindus, including great scholars, generally do not discuss the Tantras.

The Sanskrit word Tantra means "to expand." Unlike the rest of Hinduism, part of Tantrism believes in the enjoyment of material life. No one knows exactly when Tantrism started or which saints started it. Evidence show that Tantrism existed during the Vedic age. Even Sankara mentions its existence in his book Saundarya Lahari. There are about one hundred and eight books on Tantras. Tantrism and Saktism are almost one and the same. In Tantrism, the deity is Siva-Sakti, a combination of Lord Siva and his consort Parvati. It is a system of practices used for spiritual upliftment. The best part of Tantrism is its knowledge about the vast untapped Kundalini energy in the human body. Tantrism also researched into alchemy (chemistry), astrology, astronomy, palmistry, cosmology and even atomic theory. Mantras are the gift of the Tantras to Hinduism and the world. Yantras, the geometrical figures and sketches associated with Mantras, are also equally important gifts of Tantrism to humanity.

WHAT ARE THE IMPORTANT NERVES AS PER THE TANTRAS?

As per the Tantras the three important nerves, Sushumna, Ida and Pingala, start from Muladhara Chakra, the base of the spinal column. Sushumna is the most important of all nerves, or Nadis, and is invisible and subtle. It runs through the central channel of the spinal column and extends to the topmost point of the head. Ida and Pingala run parallel to Sushumna on the left and right sides of the spine respectively. Ida and Pingala meet Sushumna at Ajna Chakra, the point situated between the eyebrows. They then separate again and flow through the left and right nostrils respectively.

WHAT ARE THE CHAKRAS?

Along Sushumna, there are seven psychic centers starting with Muladhara Chakra. They cannot be seen with the naked eye. They are believed to look like lotus flowers with different colors, and each controls a sense organ's activity.

1. Muladhara Chakra (at the base of the spine) has four petals and controls smell.
2. Svadishthana Chakra (at the base of the genitals) has six petals and controls taste.
3. Manipura Chakra (opposite the navel) has ten petals and controls sight.
4. Anahata Chakra (at the level of the heart) has twelve petals and controls touch.
5. Visuddha Chakra (at the medulla oblongata in the throat) has sixteen petals and controls hearing.
6. Ajna Chakra (between the eyebrows) has two petals and controls the mind.
7. Sahasrara Chakra (located above the topmost point of the head) has one thousand petals. Here the Yogi attains Cosmic Consciousness.

WHAT IS KUNDALINI POWER?

According to Tantric literature, there is a very mysterious and powerful force in the human body called Kundalini power or serpent power. It is lying like a serpent in a coiled or inactive form at the base of the spine at the Muladhara Chakra. (The three important nerves of the human body, Sushumna, Ida and Pingala, also originate from the same point.) As per the Tantras, since this mighty force remains dormant throughout one's lifetime, most people are unaware of its existence. It is believed that as a person evolves spiritually by meditation or Pranayama exercises, this power slowly rises up through the Sushumna nerve. This rise of the Kundalini power is known as the awakening of the Kundalini.

This power rises slowly and steadily and does not shoot up in a straight line. When it passes through each psychic center, the person will have complete control of one of the sense organs. For example, if it reaches Manipura Chakra opposite the navel, the person will have complete control of sight. No Samadhi (union with God) is possible without the awakening of this power. It is said that the Kundalini power passes along the six Chakras and eventually is united with Sahasrara at the crown of the head. When that happens the person attains cosmic consciousness, the highest form of realization.

WHY DON'T HINDUS DISCUSS TANTRISM?

The only reason I can think of is due to the erotic nature of some parts of the Tantric literature. Unhappily, the Tantras also deal with black magic and sexo-yogic exercises between male and female devotees. As per Tantrism, such an act will help both devotees to explore their senses rather than be subdued by them, and to actually make use of their sexual energy for spiritual upliftment. The woman devotee who takes part in these erotic exercises is considered a Sakti (Mother Goddess).

Apart from what I have discussed above, in many Tantric practices devotees follow the "Five M's." They are Madya (wine), Mamsa (meat), Matsya (fish), Mudra (parched rice) and Maithuna (sexual union). During the performance of certain Tantric rituals, devotees even resort to the use of drugs and chemicals.

One of the Tantric practices is known as the Chakra Pooja, or "circle worship." In this ritual an equal number of men and women meet at midnight in a chosen place such as a graveyard and engage in "holy intercourse." This sexual union is very elaborate, starting with acts of "body worship." Many of the erotic paintings and sculptures of India are depictions of Chakra Pooja activities. Even though most religions, including Hinduism (as per the Code of Manu), forbid sexual intercourse during menstruation, Tantrics encourage it with the belief that during this period a woman's vital energies are at their peak. There are Mudras or hand gestures unique to Tantrism, mostly symbolizing sexual activities. Even the AUM symbol is seem by many Tantrics as a mystic symbol emphasizing the union of the male and female. Tantrism has its counterpart in Jainism as well as in Buddhism, which has four schools of Tantra.

All these erotic rituals are against the basic fundamentals of Hinduism. Now you know exactly the reason why many Hindu scholars do not want to discuss the Tantras. At the same time, anyone may wonder why scriptures which gave us the knowledge of Kundalini power in the body, Mantras, and Yantras also resort to wine and sex.

The existence of Tantrism in India is another example of Hindu tolerance. In any other religion, a thinking process like Tantrism would have been suppressed by violent force.

47

Sivalinga, Yantra and Mandala

IS SIVALINGA A PART OF THE TANTRAS?

It is a part of Tantrism. Today you will never see a Hindu temple without a Sivalinga standing in a Yoni. According to the Siva Purana, it represents the space in which the universe creates and annihilates itself again and again. As per the Tantras, it represents the phallus and yoni--a representation of the male and female attributes of God. It also represents the creative principle of life.

Sivalingas may be Chala (movable) or Achala (immovable). The Chala Lingas may be kept on a shrine or in a house or can be prepared temporarily out of clay or dough or rice. The Achala Lingas are the ones installed in temples. They are made up of stones. The lowest part of the Sivalinga is called Brahmabhaga and represents Lord Brahma. The octagonal middle part is called Vishnubhaga and represents Lord Vishnu. The projecting cylindrical part is called Rudrabhaga, to which the worship, called Poojabhaga, is offered.

WHAT IS A YANTRA?

A Yantra is a geometrical figure like (in its simplest form) a dot (Bindu) or an inverted triangle. There are very complicated figures, symmetrical and non-symmetrical, which fall under the name Yantra. All these figures are based on certain mathematical forms and certain methods. Yantras represent deities like Siva, Vishnu, Ganesha, Krishna and especially Mother Goddess Sakti. Mantra and Yantra are very much interconnected. Thought is expressed in subtle form as a Mantra and the same thought is expressed in pictorial form as a Yantra. Believe it or not, there are more than nine hundred Yantras. One of the most important Yantras is Sri Yantra, or Navayoni Chakra, representing both Siva and Sakti. You will see this Yantra exhibited in Sakti temples.

WHAT IS A MANDALA?

Mandala means "circle." It is actually the most complicated form of Yantra. It comes in all shapes and it is very artistic in nature. In Hinduism, Mandalas are used as aids to meditation. The beauty of Hindu temples lie in the number of Mandalas carved on the stones of the temple walls. A Mandala consists of a center and lines and circles placed geometrically around the center. The center usually is a dot (Bindu).

You can see Mandalas even in Buddhist Viharas. Behind each Mandala there are volumes of thoughts. Sometimes looking at a Mandala is like looking through a kaleidoscope.

WHAT IS SRI CHAKRA?

This is indeed one of the most powerful Yantras of Hinduism, which is used by Saktiates, or devotees of Sakti the Mother Goddess, in their worship. Sri Chakra is the symbol of the Lalitha aspect of the Divine Mother. It consists of a dot (Bindu) at the center, surrounded by nine triangles (Trikona) of which five have their apexes downward and the other four upward. The mutual intersection of these nine triangles results in forty-three triangles in total. This is surrounded by two concentric circles of eight lotus petals and sixteen lotus petals. This again is surrounded by three more concentric circles. Finally on the outskirts, there is a square (Chaturasra) of three lines, the lines one inside the other, opening out in the middle of each side as four portals.

48

Salagrama, Kumari Pooja, Mudra and Nyasa

WHAT IS SALAGRAMA?

It is a smooth stone said to be the natural form (Swaroopa) of Lord Vishnu. In fact, the word "Salagrama" is one of the names of Lord Vishnu. This smooth stone is found mainly at the bottom of the Gandaki River in Nepal. The stone picked from the river is worshipped as it is, without consecrational ceremony. Still, icons are permitted to be carved out of the Salagrama stones, as are the idols of Badrinath Temple. The worship of a Salagrama is not associated with any type of Pooja. Even the chanting of Mantras and the sacred water are not necessary. The very presence of a Salagrama in a home is supposed to bring all prosperity. According to some Puranas, all sins, including Brahmahatya (killing of a Brahmin) die instantly with the worship of Salagramas. In the Padma Purana, Lord Vishnu tells Lord Siva, "Oh! Siva, I reside always in the Salagrama stone." Hindu Puranas mention about nineteen different types of Salagramas (Mahabharata, Vana Parva, 84:123, 124, 125).

WHAT IS KUMARI POOJA?

It is a ceremony associated with the Tantras. In this ceremony, a twelve-year old girl from a Brahmin family is installed on a Pita (a stool), dressed up like the image of Sakti, and worshipped accordingly. This ceremony is mostly conducted in the state of Bengal.

WHAT IS A MUDRA?

A Mudra is a very artistic representation of holding the hands and fingers to indicate a particular meaning. Most of the gestures are finger-postures. They are intended to evoke in the mind divine powers as well as to intensify one's concentration. All Hindu deities exhibit some form of Mudra. The most important Mudras are the Yoni Mudra, Padma Mudra, Gada Mudra, Matsya Mudra, Tattva Mudra, Sankha Mudra and Abhaya Mudra. Most Hindu deities, including Lord Nataraja, show Abhaya Mudra, meaning "Fear not, I will protect you." The Yoni Mudra is a Sakti Yantra performed to invoke the power of the Goddess in the Sadhaka (spiritual seeker).

WHAT IS A NYASA?

"Nyasa" means "placing or marking," but this is actually a "touching." In this ritual, various awareness points of the body are touched by the fingertips and palm of the right hand. By doing so, the body is awakened from its dormancy as per the Tantras. The most popular Nyasa is known as Sadanga Nyasa.

49 ?

Kama Sutra

WHAT IS KAMA SUTRA?

Kama means the "desire for sexual gratification." As per mythology, Kama Deva (the God of Love) is a god with a bow and arrow, and when he strikes someone with his arrow, that person will develop sexual desires in him. The legends say that Lord Siva burned Kama Deva to ashes with the fire of his third eye for trying to arouse passion in him for Princess Parvati. Lord Siva later gave life to Kama Deva, who thus became Ananga (bodiless).

The most important Kama literature is the Kama Sutra, written by Sage Vatsyayana around the fourth century A.D. The book describes the daily routine of an ordinary man. It also describes picnics, drinking parties, games, etc.

The book elaborately discusses the art of making love. All things one can imagine about sex are described in this book. The author has gone to the extent of categorizing different forms of embraces, kisses and types of women. The intention of the author may be to teach a man how to woo a woman to become his bride, but his writings are much against the fundamental ideas of Hinduism. Hindus do not even acknowledge this book as part of Hinduism since this book can lead to spiritual decline rather than help man in his married life.

Abhaya Mudra

Nyasa Ritual

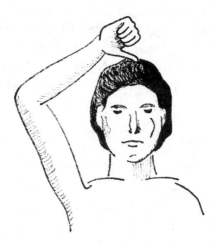

50 ॐ
Who is a Guru?

WHO IS A GURU?

The word Guru is so widely used nowadays to the extent that we may even call someone a "Guru of Wall Street." Most people think that "teacher" is the meaning of the word Guru. But in Hinduism, Guru means God Himself.

Only God-realized masters can be called Gurus. Only they have the right to demand unquestioned devotion and surrender of the free will of their followers. One of the essential qualities of a true Guru is omnipresence.

The majority of the so-called Gurus are merely teachers. No one becomes a Guru by merely studying philosophy and religion and no one can be called a Guru merely because he/she may be an adept in verbal acrobatics.

DADDY, DOES ONE HAVE TO SEARCH FOR A GURU?

There is no need for an aspirant to fanatically search for a Guru. Sage Narada states that all over the world there are hundreds of Gurus, many of them living in spirit, constantly searching for worthy disciples. So Gurus are easy to get, but it is very difficult to get faithful and obedient disciples. If one seeks truth, hundreds of Gurus will come and knock at one's door to deliver it. Swami Vivekananda did not pick his Guru; instead Sri Ramakrishna picked Vivekananda as his disciple.

DO YOU MEAN TO SAY THAT THERE IS A LACK OF FAITHFUL DISCIPLES?

Remember, son, out of the thousands that surrounded him, Jesus Christ chose only twelve disciples, and they were just fishermen without any theological knowledge. He did not pick any learned men of the day. There are also instances in the Bible where Jesus rebukes his disciples for want of enough faith. This again proves the fact that the faithful and obedient disciple is a rare commodity and not the Guru.

Again, as per Hinduism, there are seven living masters, known as Saptha Rishis, who take care of the world forever. They guide us constantly in our spiritual aspirations. So there is no need to crave for a Guru. What an aspirant has to follow is righteousness and truth alone.

Both the Jewish Kabbalah and the Rosicrucians also believe in seven god-men who live in the east. This belief in the seven Gurus was popularized by Madame Helena Blavatsky, the founder of the Theosophical Society, when she wrote the book named *Isis Unveiled*. According to Blavatsky, all those masters normally reside in Tibet but travel around the world in different bodies.

A true Guru is a divine gift to man. No one can become a Guru by self-proclamation. Sage Ashtavakra, who is one of the seven ever-living masters of the world, was the Guru of King Janaka, and the disciple of the materialistic King Janaka was Sage Suka, the great exponent of Bhakti Yoga. What that shows is that different Gurus exhibit different qualities even though they succeed one another.

If we change our consciousness, if we desire God through devotion and by selfless actions, a Guru will definitely come to us. That Guru need not necessarily come in body; he/she can come in spirit also.

HOW WILL ONE DIFFERENTIATE TRUE GURUS FROM PHONY GURUS?

It is indeed very difficult to differentiate a true Guru from the multitude of teachers around us. Unluckily, there are very many phony Gurus in the world today. An aspirant should be extremely careful in attaching his/her own spiritual aspirations to such phony Gurus, because that could bring about destruction of one's own spiritual life. As such it is better for anyone to pick a Guru who is living in spirit rather than living in the body (flesh). The Guru-disciple relationship is a very special relationship in Hinduism and once that relationship is made, there is no breaking away from it. Who is a true Guru? A person who gets agitated and becomes restless and who exhibits emotions is definitely not a Guru. Unless someone is a great seeker of truth, he or she will not be able to recognize a true Guru, even if that Guru comes to him/her. Christ-like masters can pass you by a thousand times, but if you are not communicating on their wavelength, you will never recognize them. All of us are like tiny portable transistor radios, and until we tune our spiritual urge properly, we cannot hope to contact Christ-like masters. They are close to each of us, but yet they cannot come to us, since we are not functioning on their wavelength. Again, you should know that a Guru need not necessarily come in orange or kavi robes; he/she can come in any form and in any kind of clothes, even in a three-piece suit.

ARE KNOWLEDGE AND REALIZATION ONE AND THE SAME?

Hinduism very clearly states the differences between both words. Thousands know about God and scriptures, but one in a billion realizes God. At the same time, history has shown that scriptural knowledge is not a must for God-realization. Hinduism also believes that anyone who seeks the absolute truth will ultimately realize God.

That search for truth need not necessarily be in tune with Hinduism; it can be through any other true religion. It could be through self-dedicated Karma or duty that one undertakes. For example, the souls of people like Albert Einstein, Mahatma Gandhi, Father Damien and Mother Teresa may be closer to God-realization than thousands of so-called Gurus parading around the world. It is difficult for anyone to say who has attained realization and who has not. A man in kavi (ochre) robes may sometimes be inferior to a man who sells drugs at New York's Times Square. With our intelligence we cannot differentiate "who is who." Only God-realized masters can do that. Christ did not go after the learned men of the day, but the understanding souls of the day, who were on a pedestal as far as evolution is concerned. By virtue of Karma, they were just fishermen, a very low caste of the time. Just think, Sage Veda Vyasa himself was a son of a woman belonging to the tribe of fishermen, and Sage Valmiki was a savage, robbing people in the jungles.

51 ❧
Idol Worship

DADDY, DOES HINDUISM ENCOURAGE THE WORSHIP OF IDOLS?

To begin with, Hindu scriptures do not recommend the worship of an idol as God. As the German philosopher Max Muller said, "The religion of the Vedas knows no idols." In fact, scriptures very clearly state that an idol is not a substitute for God, but only a means of making the mind think about God. An idol in a temple is exactly like a cross in a church. Both help men to focus their devotion on God.

Again, Hinduism very clearly states that mental worship is far superior to worship of images, but all worship starts with images. Ordinary people cannot conceive anything without a form. In every religion, God with some form is worshipped. Hinduism has the courage to admit it to the world.

In Raja Yoga, the scientific part of Hinduism, God is looked upon somewhat as pure energy. In that part of Hinduism, there is no mention of God with form. In the Upanishads, God has been described or explained as Neti-Neti, meaning "Not this-not this." Even the Bhagavad Gita states, "Fools not knowing My unalterable transcendental nature think that I, the unmanifested, am equipped with a manifested form."

So even though God is timeless and formless, there is absolutely nothing wrong in worshipping Him with form. In fact many saints, including the late Sri Ramakrishna Paramahamsa, believe that the concept of a personal God (Ishta Devata) is very useful in self-purification.

Lord Nataraja

52 ꙮ
Gods of Hinduism

PLEASE TELL ME ABOUT ALL THE GODS IN HINDUISM.

As per the Christian Bible, everything came from the Word, and the Word was God. Similarly, we in Hinduism believe that everything came from Brahman, and Brahman is God. The vibratory aspect of Brahman is called AUM or OM. So Hindus say that AUM is God. From AUM came the Mother God and the Godhead that is divided into three which is popularly known as the Trinity. They are Brahma (God of Creation), Vishnu (God of Preservation) and Siva (God of Annihilation).

When any of these three gods takes human or any other form, we call that an Avatar. Vishnu's popular Avatars are Rama and Krishna. Vishnu has ten Avatars altogether. They are: Fish, Tortoise, Boar, Narasimha (man-lion), Vamana (dwarf), Parasurama, Rama, Krishna, Buddha and Kalki. The Kalki Avatar is yet to come. It will come at the end of Kali Yuga, when the whole world undergoes floods.

Siva, meaning "the auspicious one," is a personification of destruction including the destruction of ego. He is usually represented as having the River Ganges running through his matted locks and wearing snakes around his neck.

Consorts of all these gods are known as goddesses. They are Saraswathi (the wife of Brahma as well as the Goddess of Knowledge), Lakshmi (the wife of Vishnu and the Goddess of Prosperity), and Parvati (the wife of Siva and the Goddess of Power).

WHO ARE THE OTHER GODS OF HINDUISM?

Since Hinduism evolved as a slowly-developed thinking process, it has a large number of gods. Many of them represent powers of nature like Vayu (Air), Varuna (Water), Agni (Fire), and Aditya (Sun), and there are also other semi-gods like Ananta (Serpent God), Hanuman (Monkey God), Indra (God of Heaven) and Yama (God of Death).

Lord Siva has two sons, and both are gods. Subramaniyan is the second son and he is the God of Astrology. Ganapathi or Ganesha is his first son, who has the face of an elephant and is described as "he who removes all obstacles." Siva actually has two more sons. One is Hanuman and the other is Sri Ayyappan. Hanuman is also known as the son of Vayu, since Parvati, the consort of Siva, transferred her pregnancy to the womb of the consort of Vayu, who delivered Hanuman.

Krishna, the Avatar of Vishnu, is worshipped throughout India in many ways. The actual meaning of Krishna is "the dark one." Krishna's popular consort's name is Radha.

Buddha, even though an Avatar of Vishnu, is not worshipped much among Hindus. Kali, the Mother God, is worshipped very much in the state of Bengal. The most popular devotee of Kali is Sri Ramakrishna Paramahamsa. The notorious tribes of India, the Thugs, also worshipped Kali, and due to their extreme fanaticism and killing of people as sacrifices to Goddess Kali, they were exterminated by the British rulers of India.

DADDY, WHY DO HINDUS WORSHIP SO MANY GODS?

According to the point of view of a Hindu, all gods are but various representations of the one true God. Hinduism repeatedly states that there is only one God. The Vedas call Him Brahman. The Upanishads explain Him by the Neti-Neti ("Not this-not this") method. Sometimes God is referred to as That, an inanimate object, since no human description can ever do justice to His magnitude. The Rig Veda says, "God or Truth is one, only men describe it in different ways."

Now coming back to your main question of so many gods, it is quite simple to explain. Ordinary human beings can only grasp a god in human form and they resort to different forms of worship for different deities, even though they are all actually worshipping one God.

To elaborate further, let us take your mother as an example. You look at her as your beloved mother who takes care of you; I look at her as my partner in life, with whom I share everything; her father looks at her as a little girl who still has a lot to learn. See now, there is only one person, but three of us are seeing that person from three different angles. All three of us are right in seeing her differently, although there is only one person. So even if you worship hundreds of gods, you are actually worshipping one Supreme Being, one God.

Of course, it is difficult for Westerners to digest that ideology easily, even though the "trinity" aspect of God in Christianity is somewhat similar to the multiple gods of Hinduism. Trinity in Christianity is one God expressed as three different forms; God the father, God the son, and God the Holy Spirit. Early Christians had no concept of the Trinity. In fact, the Catholic Encyclopedia states that the doctrine of the Trinity was not taught in the Old Testament. The Triune God was mentioned in the New Testament, and that too only in one place in the four gospels, in Matthew 28:19. Jehovah's Witnesses do not believe in the Trinity. The Nicaean Council (325 A.D.) was actually called by Emperor Constantine to elevate Jesus Christ to the second position of the Trinity, thus killing the teachings of the priest Arius, which stated that Christ is a created being, not a creator, and that Jesus Christ is inferior in divinity to his father.

DADDY, ARE DIFFERENT DIRECTIONS OF SPACE PROTECTED BY DIFFERENT GODS IN HINDUISM?

In Hinduism, some deities are symbolically considered the rulers or protectors of certain directions of space. The Upanishads and the Puranas differ slightly in the configuration of deities who rule the different directions. Anyway, the most up-to-date list is as follows:

The eastern direction is protected by Indra, God of Heaven. The western direction is protected by Varuna, God of Waters. The northern direction is protected by Kubera, God of Wealth. The southern direction is protected by Yama, God of Death. The northeast is protected by Soma, God of the Moon, the northwest by Vayu, God of Air, the southeast by Agni, God of Fire, and the southwest by Surya, the Sun God.

I AM CURIOUS. DID YOU COVER THE COMPLETE LIST OF GODS IN HINDUISM?

I don't think I could ever give you a complete list of all the gods in Hinduism. Some say that there are at least thirty-three crores (330 million) gods in Hinduism. Even some saints are considered as gods. Again, many of the gods worshipped by Hindus have different names in the Vedas. For example, Lord Siva is known as Rudra in the Vedas. The act of worshipping so many gods at the same time is no problem for Hindus, since they believe that all forms are manifestations of the one God or Power.

ARE THERE ANY MINOR GODS IN HINDUISM?

Yes, there are a large number of minor gods in Hinduism. They are mostly Gandharvas (celestial beings), Apsaras (celestial females), Devas (attendants of the God of Heaven) and Nagas (snakes). All attendants of Lord

Siva are also considered as minor Gods. Apart from that, many departed saints are also worshipped as minor gods.

PLEASE TELL ME MORE ABOUT THE NAGAS.

It is said that the Nagas are children of a saint named Kashyapa. According to the Varaha Purana, they occupy the three lower worlds, namely Patala, Atala and Sutala. Of all the Nagas, three are most prominent. They are Vasuki, Sesha (Ananta) and Takshaka. Vasuki is the snake we see crawling around the neck of Lord Siva, and in mythology it helped as a rope to churn the ocean of milk. Sesha or Ananta has one-thousand heads and it is on this snake that Lord Vishnu sleeps in Vaikunta. Takshaka always gets into trouble and is very vicious. It tried to annihilate Arjuna, the great hero of the Mahabharata, and at the end of the Mahabharata War it managed to kill King Pareeshit, the last heir of the Pandavas. The Nagas are worshipped in many Hindu temples along with the major and minor gods.

DADDY, ARE THERE REFERENCES TO WORSHIP OF MULTIPLE GODS IN THE UPANISHADS?

The Upanishads have maintained the existence of one God known as Brahman. The only reference to multiple gods in the Upanishads comes from a conversation in the Brihad-Aranyaka Upanishad between a devotee named Vidagdha Sakalya and Sage Yatnavalkya. The lively conversation is as follows:

"How many gods are there, Yatnavalkya?"

"Three thousand three hundred and six," replied Yatnavalkya.

"Yes, but just how many gods are there, Yatnavalkya?"

"Thirty-three," answered Yatnavalkya.

"Yes, but just how many gods are there, Yatnavalkya?"

"Six," said the great saint.

"Yes, but just how many gods are there, Yatnavalkya?"

"Three."

"Yes, but just how many gods are there, Yatnavalkya?"

"Two."

"Yes, but just how many gods are there, Yatnavalkya?"

"One and a half."

"Yes, but just how many gods are there, Yatnavalkya?"

"One," answered the great teacher of Hinduism.

This conversation makes us conclude that even though there are many gods, in reality there is only one. One God appears in a thousand different forms to devotees according to the way they perceive that Supreme Power.

WHO IS NATARAJA?

He is the dancing god of India, who is actually Lord Siva. Nataraja is very important to the West. You may have seen Nataraja statues even in some James Bond movies. Nata means "dance," and Raja means "king." Lord Siva is supposed to be dancing over the demon Apasmara, or Ignorance--the ego, who makes us forget who we really are. Nataraja brings about the destruction of the ego.

He is also the visible symbol of the rhythm of the universe. He is encircled by a ring of flames, symbolizing the vital processes of universal creation. The Mudras, hand-expressions of the deity, represent different activities. In one hand, Lord Nataraja holds a drum, the symbol of speech, and his second hand shows the Abhaya Mudra

("Fear not-I will protect you"). In the palm of his third hand he has a tongue of fire as a symbol of destruction, and the fourth hand points downward to his uplifted foot. It symbolizes the salvation of the devotee.

IN WHAT OTHER FORMS DO HINDUS WORSHIP LORD SIVA?

Hindus worship Lord Siva as Sivalinga (phallus and yoni), as Nataraja (dancer), as Dakshinamurthi (a meditating ascetic), as Kalyanasundara (the husband of Parvati), as Tripurantaka (destroyer of demons like Tripura), as Ardhanarishwara (half-woman God), as Bhairava (the destroyer), as Maheshwara (the Lord of Knowledge), and as Hara (the remover of death). Among them Sivalinga is the most common form of image of Lord Siva one will see in most Hindu temples.

WHO IS NANDI?

It is a bull of milk-white or snow-white color and is the vehicle of Lord Siva. Another name for this bull is Vrushabha. Its neck is thick and its horns are as hard as diamonds. You will see Nandi outside every Siva temple. It is the guardian of all four-legged animals. Nandi is a symbol of Jeevatman or the individual soul, pulled back from God due to animal tendencies but attracted to God by His divine grace.

DO HINDUS WORSHIP LORD BRAHMA?

It may be surprising to you to hear that Hindus generally do not worship Lord Brahma. The liberation of the soul is connected with Lord Vishnu and Lord Siva, and that may be the reason why Lord Brahma is not worshipped by Hindus. Of course there are representations of Lord Brahma in most temples, and his name is repeated in most rituals. The Skanda Purana gives a number of reasons why Lord Brahma is not worshipped like Lord Vishnu and Lord Siva. One of the reasons is that he was cursed by Lord Siva never to be worshipped by mortals since Lord Brahma once lied to Lord Siva. There is one temple of Lord Brahma in Rajasthan and one in Orissa.

53 ൠ
Kali and Human Sacrifice

DADDY, WHO IS KALI?

Kali is the Mother Goddess--the symbol of terror and death outside, but inwardly loving and compassionate. Her devotees worship her as the primal energy or pure consciousness. Sri Ramakrishna Paramahamsa was the greatest devotee of Kali in modern times. Kali is black in color and she is also the consort of Lord Siva. She is usually depicted wearing a necklace of human skulls. In two of her hands she holds a sword and a dagger, and in the other two she holds severed heads which are dripping blood. Kali is also associated with the left-handed swastika.

Kali's picture is the most horrendous picture of all deities in India. It is said that the Mother Goddess took this horrendous form to kill a demon named Mahishasura, since he could not be killed by a man or a beast.

Just like Bhairava is the terror aspect of Lord Siva, Kali is the terror aspect of Sakti or Parvati, the consort of Lord Siva. Another name for Kali is Durga. According to legends, Kali or Durga took birth to kill Mahishasura, who had a boon from Lord Brahma that neither man or woman or animal could kill him. Since this black goddess is nothing but divine energy, she easily slew the Asura. She later killed the Asuras Sumbha, Nisumbha and Vitunda. Then she killed an Asura by the name of Raktavija by drinking his blood, since each drop had the potential to become a demon like himself if it fell on earth. Finally her blood-spilling spree ended at the request of Siva after the killing of a demon named Tripurasura.

Kali is worshipped in Bengal, especially in Calcutta. Kali worship is also associated with Tantrism. In fact, most of the devotees of Kali are also adepts in Tantrism.

IS IT A FACT THAT HUMAN SACRIFICES WERE PERFORMED IN FRONT OF HER?

Unluckily, during the early stages of Hinduism, that might be a fact. Anyway, no codes on human sacrifices are in any of the Hindu scriptures. But a tribe named the Thugs used to do human sacrifices until 1800. The British government in India finally eradicated the whole tribe, including women and children. I am one hundred percent sure that no human sacrifices are performed in any Hindu temples today.

Human sacrifices are there in the history of all religions. In the Old Testament, one witnesses a God who was constantly angry and who enjoyed human miseries. He demanded and sanctioned human sacrifices. Of course, one witnesses a very compassionate God in the New Testament. As far as the Bible is concerned, Jesus Christ is the sacrificial lamb for the sins of humankind. Today's Christianity abhors the very word sacrifice and it condemns all blood-letting sacrifices.

Abraham was ready to sacrifice his son in the Old Testament, and in the Katha Upanishad the son of Vajasrabasa volunteered to be sacrificed to Yama, the God of Death. In the New Testament, time and time again, Christ was referred to as a lamb of the altar. Again, references to the flesh of Christ and blood of Christ during the Last Supper show that human sacrifices were prevalent even during the time of Christ. The prevalence of human sacrifice is the only reason why the omnipotent Christ used words like blood and flesh to indicate the magnanimity of his teachings. If Christ was born today, he would use words like DNA and electro-magneticism to explain subtle matters to mankind.

IS IT A FACT THAT ANIMAL SACRIFICES ARE STILL DONE IN CALCUTTA?

Unluckily, that is a fact as far as extremely few temples of India are concerned. But the majority of Hindus abhor such acts. Blood and blood products are not at all allowed in the vast majority of Hindu temples. None of the Hindu temples in the U.S.A. allow blood in any form, even as meat products. People who have wounds and women during their monthly period are not allowed to enter the temple. Most Hindus are also vegetarians.

Swami Sri Ramakrishna Paramahamsa was one of the greatest devotees of Kali. Let nobody forget that Ramakrishna was the personification of compassion and love in Hinduism and he did not even hurt an ant in his life. Another great devotee of Kali was Kalidasa, the famous poet who wrote poetry books such as Shakuntala, Vikramorvasi, Maghaduta, Rahuvamsa, Ritu-Samhara and Kumara-Sambhava. So to conclude that all those who worship Kali also indulge in animal sacrifice would be a very erroneous conclusion.

Once again, none of the Hindu temples built in the U.S.A. allow any kind of meat or alcohol in the temple premises. Ask a Hindu about animal sacrifice and he/she will look at you with total dismay and disgust.

Just like you, I pray that all animal sacrifices will come to an end throughout the world. In the true spirit of Buddha, Mahavira and Jesus Christ, all animal sacrifices should be stopped. We have no right to kill animals for the so-called spiritual betterment of ourselves.

WHO ARE THUGS?

Thugs were a horrible tribe who worshipped Kali by the name of Bhavani and sacrificed human beings to the goddess. According to the writings of Chinese traveler Hiuen Tsang, Thugs existed in the seventh century A.D.

Thugs never offered disabled human beings to the goddess. Before anybody was sacrificed they would remove his clothes and examine his body completely. If there were no physical deficiencies, the person was sacrificed by strangulation. Women were lucky with the Thugs, who believed the goddess does not like women. Thugs slowly killed their victims so that, according to them, the goddess could come down and enjoy their agony.

Thugs, according to history, flourished in Uttar Pradesh and Central India. It is said that some of the activities of the Thugs are depicted on the walls of the caves of Ellora.

The British authorities allowed the Thugs to have their way for some time, but exterminated them by 1861. It is said that one of the Thugs' victims happened to be a British officer, and that made Britain exterminate these gangs to the last woman and child. Thanks to the British, the last Thug was hanged in 1882. Now, luckily for India, you can come across the word thug only in the dictionary.

Rationality of Worship of Many Gods

DADDY, WITH ALL HONESTY, HOW COULD ANYONE
SUPPORT THE WORSHIP OF MANY GODS?

Son, even Adi Sankaracharya, the great apostle of
Advaita philosophy, did not look down upon the practice
of worshipping many gods. To begin with, people are at
different stages of understanding the truth. To common
people who understand only mythology, it is very difficult
to realize the fact that there is only one God. Let us take
electric energy, for example. I can explain it to you easily
with the aid of the electron theory, whereas my mother
understands it with a statement that "electricity flows like
water." The same subject, but my mother and I
understand it in two different ways even though we both
have the same results by using electric energy.

Again, Lord Krishna has promised that even if you
worship a thousand forms of God, through all those forms
you are actually worshiping Him--not Krishna the Avatar,
but Krishna the Almighty. When you pray to Jesus Christ,
you are not praying to Christ the man, but to Christ the
spirit, the Almighty.

Finally, by the Hindu code of ethics, Yogis are
warned against tampering with people's beliefs. As per
Hinduism, if a person has steadfast faith in his ideals, he
will ultimately find the truth. So however insignificant his
method of worship may be, the truth will finally come to
him.

The Hindu worship of semi-gods is also somewhat
like the Catholic worship of patron saints. Catholics
worship saints like Saint Jude, Saint Anthony and Saint
Sophia to take care of different problems. Hindus worship
Ganesha for the removal of obstacles, Lakshmi for
prosperity, etc.

DADDY, NOW THAT YOU HAVE PROVED TO ME WHAT IT
IS TO WORSHIP MANY GODS, WHAT PROBLEMS DO YOU
SEE IN THE WORSHIP OF MULTIPLE GODS?

As I said before, it is quite all right to worship many
gods, but one thing devotees have to worry about is the
feeling that one form of God is superior to another, or the
feeling that one's personal god (Ishta Devata) is greater
than one's neighbor's god. In devotion to God, one is
supposed to dissolve the "I-ness," or erase the ego.
Instead, if one develops ego by fighting for his god, then
the whole basis of Bhakti Yoga is totally lost. Ego is ego
in whatever form it comes out, and it is better on the part
of a devotee to recognize it from its start and eradicate it.

Remember, the fighting between Vaishnavites and
Saivites only helped in the downfall of Hinduism until
finally Adi Sankaracharya had to come and raise Hinduism
to its present glory. So you can have a personal god but
try to see your personal god in all forms of God. You
should be able to worship in a Christian church, a Jewish
synagogue, a Muslim mosque or a Buddhist vihara and see
your personal God in all those places of worship. By
doing so, you will be able to establish the oneness of God
as well as eradicate your ego which is a stumbling block
in your spiritual progress.

55 ॐ
Hindu Temple Construction

HOW ARE HINDU TEMPLES CONSTRUCTED?

To begin with, many Hindus believe that only saints like Adi Sankaracharya have the capability to consecrate temples. In fact, as per history, almost all prominent Hindu temples are consecrated by great saints and constructed by Hindu kings. The actual construction and consecration of a temple is done as per the Silpa Shastra, the Hindu architectural book. The process of construction and consecration of a temple is very elaborate. To begin with, temples are constructed on a site that is Shubha (beautiful and auspicious), in the neighborhood of a river. Under all circumstances, temples should be built only in very congenial surroundings. Their erection is considered a reintegration of Prajapati (first man of creation, like Adam), enabling him to continue his creative activity. Two of the most important ritual sequences associated with the construction and consecration of any Hindu temple are Pratishta (installation of icons) and Kumbha-Abhishekam (temple dedication). The Pratishta is the process by which icons are endowed with divinity.

The cosmic pillar is an important part of a Hindu temple. It is supposed to be the communication channel between mortals and gods. In modern times, one of the finest temples in the world is the Sri Venkateswara Temple in Pittsburgh, Pennsylvania, and the construction and consecration of this temple are preserved in a very descriptive documentary film.

DADDY, HOW ARE THE IDOLS MADE?

Idol-making is also a very elaborate process. They are made out of special wood, as well as from special stones. When they are made out of wood, the tree is cut on an auspicious day and time as per astrological calculations. The artisan who makes the idol is known as a Silpi. Prior to making the idol, the Silpi undergoes ritualistic purification and prays to the gods for help. It is said that he meditates and mentally visualizes the idol prior to starting the work. After the idol is made, it is purified by water, darbha grass, honey and ghee (liquefied butter). Then by a special Nyasa ritual (touching ceremony) the deity is invoked in the idol. Finally, by a special Mantra, Prana or "breath of life" is infused into the idol. Now the idol-making is complete. Of course my description is very brief and the actual ceremony is very elaborate and colorful.

WHAT IS GARBHA GRIHA?

It is the innermost chamber of a temple, where the idol is consecrated. The word meaning of Garbha Griha is "the home of pregnancy" which actually means a womb. Some temples have several enclosures; they are supposed to represent the human body which is supposed to have five Koshas or sheaths. The outermost enclosure represents Annamaya Kosha (sheath made of food) and the deity residing in the Garbha Griha represents the Atman or soul.

DADDY, I WANT TO ASK YOU A LOT OF QUESTIONS ABOUT MYTHOLOGY. CAN YOU ANSWER THEM ALL?

Son, to begin with, I want to caution you that mythology, as the word's meaning goes, is the "logic of myth." So there could be instances where certain things contradict themselves in mythology. When someone looks at Hinduism, he should look at the Bhagavad Gita, Upanishads, and Raja Yoga and then ask questions regarding them. Anyway, I shall try to explain to you mythological concepts as clearly as I can.

SINCE HINDUISM ADVOCATES MONOGAMY, THEN WHY DID LORD KRISHNA HAVE 16,008 WIVES?

To begin with, Lord Krishna is God in the flesh, not an ordinary human being. Secondly, Sage Narada himself felt that Krishna was a polygamist. One day Narada went to the 16,008 houses, and he saw Krishna performing household duties in every house. From that observation, he came to the conclusion that Krishna is a polygamist, and the Supreme Being.

There is also another explanation about Krishna and his wives, most of whom are Gopis. The love of the Gopis for Krishna symbolizes the craving of Jeevatman, the individual soul, to merge with Paramatman the Absolute Soul. Here the Gopis represent Jeevatman and Krishna represents Paramatman. To an ordinary man who reads the songs of Swami Jayadeva it will sound like an exaggeration, but actually they are symbolic of the Jeevatman-Paramatman union.

DADDY, YOU EXPLAINED TO ME THAT NON-VIOLENCE IS THE HIGHEST INDIAN VIRTUE. WHY, THEN, DO ALL

THE HINDU GODS CARRY WEAPONS AND KILL SO MANY DEMONS?

Ahimsa Paramo Dharmah--"Non-violence is the highest virtue"--is written for the ordinary man. Of course, Mahatma Gandhi used it effectively as a weapon against the British in India. But gods act on a different plane altogether. Their actions are not motivated by anger, greed or selfishness. They act in a very mathematical and logical manner. Just look at the way Lord Rama killed the demon Ravana. Rama did that without any kind of anger. He could have transformed Ravana, but Ravana was looking forward to death at the hands of Rama so that he could achieve salvation. To give you another example, let us say you put your hand in fire. You get burned. You cry with pain, but the fire did not have any particular desire to hurt you. It is in its nature to burn. Gods act in the same way. When they kill a demon, they do that without anger. They could convert the demon, but still they prefer to kill, because the demon's actions warrant pain for his body in this world. Here we go back to the law of Karma again. Remember the crucifixion of Christ. A person who can distribute seven loaves of bread to thousands could have easily converted all his enemies. Still Christ chose to suffer the agony on the cross. Why? To obey the law of Karma which requires pleasure and pain for the body.

DADDY, WHY ARE YOU SO HESITANT TO ANSWER MY QUESTIONS ABOUT MYTHOLOGY?

Son, you know very well that it is very difficult to answer questions on mythology using logic and reason. For example, how on earth can anybody explain Lord Ganapathi, the elephant-headed god, using a tiny mouse as his vehicle? How can anybody explain the ten heads of

Ravana and the one-thousand heads of the serpent Ananta? Science still cannot tackle the problem of Siamese twins, let alone ten or one-thousand heads on one body. It is indeed funny to hear people criticize Lord Rama for giving up his beloved consort Princess Sita. They know that by no means are they going to get any satisfactory answers on that question, but still this type of criticism of mythology lingers on. Mythological stories may have been written with very high ideological meanings, but unluckily with our very limited knowledge we cannot understand them.

With the aid of modern science we may be able to understand things like Brahmastra (as nuclear missiles), Krishna's Sudarshana Chakra (as a kind of strategic defense initiative weapon with great offensive capabilities like the SDI), the story of the birth of Lord Hanuman, where Goddess Parvati transferred her pregnancy to the wife of the God of Air (as surrogate motherhood), the four sons of Queen Kunti Devi (as test-tube babies), the one hundred sons of Queen Gandhari (she did not use a test-tube, she used big earthenware pots), Pushpaka Vimana (as a helicopter), and so on. Of course, all these are speculations and as such we are all better of using mythology to understand the unwritten laws of the universe. Arguing on mythological stories is the erroneous act of all and as such all arguments should be avoided.

Gods of Hinduism

Brahman
(undefinable, timeless reality - immovable, inconceivable, unborn)

AUM or OM
(vibratory aspect of Brahman - the "Word" of the Bible)

Trimurthi or Trinity
Brahma - creation / Vishnu - preservation / Siva - annihilation

Mother Goddess
Saraswathi - knowledge / Lakshmi - wealth / Parvati - power

Gods of Nature
Surya (sun) / Soma (moon) / Vayu (air) / Agni (fire)
Varuna (water) / Indra or Devendra (heaven)

Kubera - god of wealth
Garuda - god of birds
Himavan - god of mountains
Anathan - god of snakes
Ganges - goddess of rivers
Hanuman - monkey god
Nandi - god of four-legged animals
Kshetrapalas, Dvarapalas, Gramadevatas - gods of fields, gates, villages
Children of Siva - Ganapathi (elephant god), Subramaniyan
Aditi - Rig Vedic goddess; incarnated as Devaki, mother of Krishna
Prithvi, Dyaus - Rig Vedic goddess of earth, god of sky
Scriptural deities - Abhasvaras, Adityas, Anilas, Ganas, Guhyakas,
  Rudras, Valakhilyas, Vasus, Vinayakas, others as in Puranas
All Avatars of Vishnu, Siva, Mother Goddess
Ayyappan - joint Avatar of Vishnu and Siva
Rishis, wives of Rishis
Nagas - Vasuki, Sesha or Ananta, Takshaka
Gandharvas - celestial beings
Apsaras - celestial females (Urvasi, Menaka, etc.)
Planetary gods
Bhairavas, Bhairavis - servants of Siva
Yoginis (attendants of Durga), Dakinis (female imps), Grahis (witches)
Departed saints
Prophets

The Cow and Hindus

WHY IS THE COW SO IMPORTANT TO HINDUS?

When the Aryans settled in India, the cow was the only animal they had domesticated. In the Vedic age, cows were a real blessing to the community. Cows provided them with milk, meat, butter and yogurt. The dead cow's skin was used to make shelters and clothing.

So the community in the Vedic age was really indebted to the cow in many ways. This later made them regard the cow with devotion. Mythology speaks about a celestial cow named Kamadhenu which could grant and fulfill any wish. Lord Krishna was a cowherd and he spent most of his childhood and youth taking care of cows. As time passed, cows were looked upon as a symbol of motherhood. Even in the writings of Sage Manu there are specific references to cows, and he forbids the slaughtering of cows. The Rig Veda (6:28) reads, "Cows are God; they seem to me to be Indra, the God of Heaven." Hindu society, especially the Brahmin caste, is supposed to be vegetarian. To fanatic Hindus, cows are still everything. Of course the majority of Hindus still avoid consuming beef, but they do not look down upon any person who consumes beef. Anyway, among the fanatic masses in India, the slaughtering of cows will be a very controversial issue for years to come.

DADDY, WHAT IS THE TRUE STORY BEHIND VEGETARIANISM IN HINDUISM?

Son, I have thought and read quite a lot about this issue. In fact, you will be surprised to know that abstaining from meat is more a Buddhist and Jainist idea than a Hindu idea. Even the Bhagavad Gita contains no specific injunction against eating meat. The cows mentioned in the Rig Veda as "aghnya," or not for killing, are milking cows. The Rig Veda does not preclude the slaughter of bulls and cows on a variety of religious occasions. Aitareya Brahmana talks about sacrificing oxen to the gods. In the Griha Sutras, the sacrifice of cows is associated with many religious ceremonies. Even Manu, who was against meat-eating in most of his codes, stated, "One may eat meat when it has been sprinkled with water while mantras are recited, when Brahmins desire for one to do that, when one is engaged in performing a rite as per the law, and when one's life is in danger" (Manusmriti 5:27). In the Ramayana, Sage Agasthya ate a ram so that he could annihilate the demon Vatapi. In the Mahabharata it is stated that in the palace of Rantideva, about two thousand cows were killed every day to feed the Brahmins. Meat of all sorts appears during the wedding of Panjali in the Mahabharata.

I feel that, as per the Puranas written after the birth of Buddhism and Jainism, Hindus are forbidden from the consumption of any meat or meat products. With the problems of heart diseases and cholesterol all over the world, we should propagate vegetarianism and abandon meat altogether.

Status of Women in Hinduism

WHY DO HINDU WOMEN WEAR A DOT ON THEIR FOREHEADS?

Actually, all Hindus, especially those who belong to the Brahmin caste, are supposed to wear dots on their foreheads. The dot is supposed to be at the meeting point of the two eyes to protect that important point. The important point is known as the "spiritual eye" or "third eye" or Ajna Chakra. There is a lot of discussion about this center in books relating to Kundalini power (Tantric literature). These dots are made of herbal (turmeric) powder or sandalwood paste.

Only a person who meditates on this point is supposed to see light. Hindus believe that Jesus Christ was referring to this point when he said, "If therefore thine eye be single, thy whole body shall be full of light" (Matthew 6:22). In India Vaishnavites wear this dot in an elongated form, starting from the center between the eyes and going to the topmost point on the head, known as Sahasrara, to smoothen and protect the whole path of the flow of Kundalini power, which I have explained before. Anyway, in India as time went on women kept up the system of wearing dots, and a red dot of herbal powders meant that the woman was a respectably married lady. Widows are not supposed to wear any dot. No particular attributes can be given to this system today. Some women even go for different colors of paint to match the color of the saris they wear!

HOW ARE WOMEN TREATED IN HINDUISM?

In Hinduism, on one side woman is the object of worship of saints and seers, and on the other side she is looked down upon and depicted as the cause of all problems in the world. All religions of the world, including Hinduism and Christianity, have looked down upon women through their scriptures and their respective mythologies. Look at Christian Genesis; woman (Eve) is described as the root cause of the fall of man. Christ's mother Mary is considered as "the immaculate conception," but surprisingly, she never became one of the apostles. What religions taught mankind is repeated in the thinking pattern of the world. The American constitution still reads, "All men are equal," and not "All men and women are equal."

In ancient India, after the Aryans settled on the banks of the River Indus they established a social system in which father, instead of mother, became the head of the family. In fact in the whole of India, it is only among the Nair community of Kerala that women are the head of the family and have property rites. Throughout ancient history, women were obliged to abide by laws made by men. Women in fact obeyed laws made by men for women. However, it is also true that Vedic society had a number of women in key positions and that certain austerities could not be performed by men without their wives. In fact, according to legends, Lord Brahma was forced to take up a girl named Savitri as his consort for a special worship.

Just as it is in the four-fold caste system, the Code of Manu is the starting point of making women inferior to men. Even the Bhagavad Gita indirectly states that women, Vaishyas and Shudras are sinful births (Chapter 9:32). Manu very emphatically stated, "Women do not deserve liberty." The Vedas are full of prayers for the birth of a son. Believe it or not, there are ceremonies and prayers in Hinduism which try to prevent the birth of a baby girl. For example, one can read in the Brihad-Aranyaka Upanishad elaborate ceremonials for the birth of a son. Some of the wedding blessings start with "Be the mother of males." If one scans the length and breadth of Hinduism, one finds repeated examples of male domination.

It is not clear whether this was done to protect women, since they were the weaker sex, or to make them objects of enjoyment. Anyway, what one sees in ancient Hinduism is an exact repetition of the history of the Jews in the Old Testament. In that book, women were obliged to obey the laws which were made for them by men. The same is seen in Hinduism. So we have to look at ancient Hinduism as a part and parcel of the history of a maturing civilization coming out of the dark ages, when men were indeed the dominant figures.

Manu declared that for a woman, marriage was "for all time, irrevocable and unquestionable." He forbade divorce and remarriage. But by the Hindu Marriage Act of 1955, all Hindus are allowed to marry as well as divorce as they please.

On the positive side, Manu also asked society to worship woman, because she is the "light of the house." Hinduism believes that a woman who devotes her entire life to the well-being of her husband is a Pativrata and is endowed with numerous powers usually attained by sages.

In Hinduism, Saraswathi is the Goddess of Knowledge, Lakshmi is the Goddess of Wealth, and Parvati is the Goddess of Power. At the same time, they are the consorts of Brahma, Vishnu and Siva respectively. The Mother Goddess comes before the Trinity of Brahma, Vishnu and Siva. So in mythology and in Sruti literature, women are held in very high esteem. In the Brihad-Aranyaka Upanishad, one of the persons asking grilling questions to Sage Yatnavalkya is none other than a female saint named Gargi. The Saka Agamas or Tantras glorify the Supreme as the Mother of the Universe under one of the names and forms of Devi. In the Tantras, the female aspirant is looked upon as an embodiment of Sakti and she is worshipped through rituals like Kumari Pooja (virgin worship) and Sakti Upasana (goddess worship).

Hinduism has had several women mystics like Andal of Tamil Nadu, Mahadevi of Karnataka, Lalla of Kashmir, Chellachi of Sri Lanka, Karaikal of Tamil Nadu, Mirabai of Rajasthan, Janabai of Maharashtra, Auvaiyar of Tamil Nadu and Muktabai of Maharashtra. At present Amritanandamayi of Kerala is well known in the U.S.A.

Believe it or not, there have been communities in India throughout history where women have played important roles in the society. For example, within the Nair community in Kerala, all property rites are only for the women in the family. In that system, the mother is always the "head of the house."

Among Saktiates, women are always treated with great respect. When Saktiates talk about gods, they name them as female-male combinations, such as Lakshmi-Narayan, Gauri-Sankar and Radha-Krishna. Mythology also shows that women were allowed to have more than one husband. One of our very respected mythological women, Panchali, was married to the five Pandava brothers. The Atharva Veda says that a woman can even marry after having ten husbands. Another respected woman of India, the mythological Tara, who came out of the ocean of milk, married Bali the monkey-king, and after his death married his brother Sugreeva. The fisherwoman Sathyavathi had a son by Saint Parasara, and later she married King Santhanu and had two more sons.

One of the questioners in the Brihad-Aranyaka Upanishad is the young lady saint Gargi. Another lady saint of the Upanishads is Maitreyi, the wife of Sage Yatnavalkya. Mythology talks only with respect about the three consorts of Brahma, Vishnu, and Siva and countless ladies like Ahalya, Anasuya (the wife of Sage Atri), Savitri, Arundhati (the wife of Sage Vasishtha) and Shakuntala. Even mythology does not look down upon dancing girls of heaven like Urvasi and Menaka, who got into all sorts of problems time and time again. The women who surrendered themselves to the will of their husbands were called Pativrata and it is said that even gods can't match their power. It is said that Brahma, Vishnu and Siva were at their wits' end when they tried to tempt Anasuya, the beautiful wife of Sage Atri. In the Ramayana, Princess Sita is looked upon as a great power. It is said Rama asked Sita to go behind the fire (or jump into the fire) so that Ravana might fall in love with the Maya Sita (illusory Sita). It is possible Ravana would not have fallen in love with the real Sita. Who wants to kiss the sun or fire? The real Sita might have been something hard for Ravana to love. Ravana could never even physically touch Maya Sita. He only carried the earth on which Sita was standing back to his island kingdom. It is said that the only way Ravana could have attained Maya Sita would have been if she willed it so. After the annihilation of Ravana, Maya Sita jumped into the fire and the real Sita came back. That is the reason one sees Sita jumping into fire twice in the Ramayana. Many do not understand this aspect of the Ramayana, and unnecessarily blame Lord Rama for male domination and humiliation of Sita.

As far as I am concerned, the most demeaning things to women that happened in Hinduism were child marriage and the Deva Dasi system. There was a time (not anymore--child marriage is now a criminal offense in India) where all girls under twelve were given in marriage to men twice and thrice their own age. From the Ramayana we learn that Lord Rama was sixteen when he married Sita, and Sita was only six at that time.

In the Brahma Purana it is written that a girl who is four is ready for marriage. Believe it or not, there are passages in the Mahabharata referring to marriage at birth. The custom of marrying an unborn child was common once upon a time. A man would marry an unborn embryo and if the fetus turned out to be a baby girl, he would marry her. Child marriages were stopped in 1929 by the Sarda Act, under which no male is allowed to marry under eighteen and no female is allowed to marry under fourteen.

Of all the things that crept into Hinduism, the Deva Dasi (servant or slave of God) system is the worst. The Deva Dasi system was set up initially somewhat like the Christian nuns, where girls from good families were donated to God for taking care of temples. This was later misused by temple priests as well as by royalty.

They used these young girls as temple prostitutes. The Padma and Bhavishya Puranas talk about the Deva Dasi system, but they never expected something exactly like a Christian nun, and the system finally degenerated to the level of Times Square. A girl was donated to the temple at the age of seven or eight. The girl was immediately married to the deity, which was usually Lord Krishna. Later the temple priest or someone in the royalty would make her lose her virginity. In the crudest form, she was forced to lose her virginity by a small Sivalinga. After that, the girl was trained in erotic dancing, usually depicting the romantic interlude between Lord Krishna and his consort Radha. Until India got independence, the profession of a dancer was considered to be the profession of a prostitute. It was demeaning for girls of any respectable family to study any kind of classical dancing in India. Of course, all that has been changed now. Indians at present look at dancing as a very respectable profession.

When a Deva Dasi girl became a woman and later became very old, she was allowed to wander around the country leading a life of prostitution. The Artha Shastra even talks about using prostitution as a means of revenue for the state. Thanks to Hindu reformers, Buddhism, Jainism, Christian missionaries and the British government, the Deva Dasi system is completely eradicated in India today.

Right now in India, compared even to countries like the U.S.A., women have better respect in social life as well as in professional life. In India, women have equal wages with men in all types of professions. A lady doctor gets the same salary a male doctor gets, and a lady engineer gets the same salary a male engineer gets.

Sati--The Most Horrendous Act

WHAT IS SATI AND DOES IT HAVE ANY HINDU
SCRIPTURAL BACKING?

Sati is the most horrendous act of widows killing
themselves by jumping into the funeral pyre of their dead
husbands, sometimes willfully and sometimes forcefully by
others. Sati is a very ancient ritual which existed among
the Rajput tribes of Northwestern India. Sati was
abolished by the British in 1829. Sati has absolutely no
Hindu scriptural backing. No Hindu scripture even
remotely mentions it. Saying that Sati is a part of
Hinduism is exactly like saying that the bloody Spanish
Inquisition of Mexico in 1483 and the Salem witch hunt of
1692 are part and parcel of Christianity. The Spanish
destruction of Mayan temples and killing of millions of
Mexicans has nothing to do with the true Christianity
Jesus preached. The Salem witch hunt had nothing to do
with true Christianity. It stood against all cardinal
principles of Christianity. Similarly, Sati had nothing to do
with Hinduism. It stood against all cardinal principles of
Hinduism. There is nothing in the Vedas to show that
they had sanctioned this act. In fact, according to the
funeral hymns of the Rig Veda, after a ceremony of the
widow sleeping next to the corpse of the dead husband,
she was allowed to marry the dead man's brother.

There are no incidents in the vast Hindu mythology
in tune with Sati. For example, in the Ramayana, when
Lord Rama's father King Dasaratha died, none of his three
wives killed themselves, nor did the monkey-king Bali's
wife kill herself when Bali got killed, nor did Mandhodhari
kill herself when her husband Ravana got killed.

There are no acts of Sati anywhere in the
Mahabharata, the longest epic poem of the world. None
of the wives of the one hundred slain sons of King

Dhartharashtra committed Sati. The only incident one can quote is the suicide of all the wives of Lord Krishna when this Avatar of Vishnu left earth. Here they committed suicide not because Krishna was their husband, but because he was the Almighty.

The acts of the wives of Lord Krishna have no connection with Sati. Some state that the word is derived from Sati the wife of Siva, who committed suicide since her father King Daksha insulted her. But the fact of the matter is, what Sati did has no connection with the horrendous act of Sati. The only act in the whole of the Mahabharata parallel to Sati is the act of Madri, wife of King Pandu, who killed herself in the funeral pyre of Pandu. Here again Madri acted out of contempt for herself, since due to a curse from a saint, Madri's love-making to Pandu had caused his death. Again, to prove the point that Madri's act was not Sati, we should know that Pandu's second wife, Kunti, did not kill herself and lived a very long life.

WHERE DID SATI COME FROM? IS IT A CUSTOM PRACTICED THROUGHOUT INDIA?

Let me answer the second part of the question first. Sati was outlawed in India in 1829 by the British government after a Hindu theologian, Raja Rammohan Roy, worked day and night for it. So for all practical purposes, you will not hear about Sati in India today.

Sati, according to leading Hindu theologians, had its roots in ancient Greece. Pyre sacrifices similar to Sati were prevalent among the Germans, Slavs and other races besides the Greeks. Most probably the practice of Sati came to India during the year 1 A.D. through the Kushans, a Central Asian race which ruled over the northwestern part of India. Sati was never practiced anywhere in South India. Even in North India, it was practiced mostly among the warrior tribes called Rajputs who were descendants of the Kushans, Sakas and Parthians.

The Rajputs were very fanatical Hindu warrior tribes, who were constantly in battle with Muslims as well as among themselves. It is likely that the Rajputs had a lot of young widows who posed serious ethical and moral problems to a monogamous society. Instead of allowing, like Muslims, men to have more than one wife, the Rajputs had an easy solution of taking care of unwanted widows by Sati. That is the only logical conclusion one can derive, looking at the most horrendous practice of Sati.

60 ﷼
Hygiene and Aura

WHY DON'T HINDUS KISS AND HUG LIKE OTHERS?

Of course, the question of hygiene and fear of getting diseases has a lot to do with it. Apart from that, like anywhere else in the world, we are also concerned with such simple actions finally leading to incest.

Apart from all that, there is also an occult theory behind not touching one another. According to this theory, everyone has an aura; in brief, every creature (including plants) has an aura. This aura is more or less like the corona surrounding a high-tension electric overhead line. It is said that the auras of Christ and masters like him were visible to the naked eye. The aura of a man is the summation of his thoughts, actions and past Karmas. It is said, for example, that if the person whom we are embracing has powerful depressive thoughts, it can badly affect our own aura. Similarly, our aura will be benefitted if we embrace a person with powerful positive thoughts. At the same time, embracing amongst the two sexes is equally dangerous, even for God-realized masters, for even they may fall under the mighty power of sexual attraction.

So, whichever way you look at it, embracing and kissing are not good acts to follow as a routine when meeting anyone in our day-to-day life, even if such acts are motivated by very noble thoughts. Again, it is wrong to believe that affection can be expressed only by physical touch.

PLEASE TELL ME MORE ABOUT THE AURAS.

Modern science has not come out with any specific proof about the aura's existence. At the same time, it is coming to the conclusion that our brain is a small electric generator and our thinking and actions are just electric impulses.

Anyway, going back to the question of aura, it is believed that the fingertips are one point through which this powerful aura can be discharged. That is the reason why, when God-realized masters bless you, they bless you by touching the topmost point of your head, which is a powerful center known as Sahasrara in the books relating to Kundalini power. To protect themselves from losing power from the aura, Hindus show the Namaste sign (touching the fingertips of both hands), during which they keep the aura in a close-circuited position like the power of two magnets that are kept intact by spacers short-circuiting their poles.

In Christianity, this power of the aura is known as virtue. When Jesus Christ was dragging the cross to the place of his crucifixion, a leper happened to touch him and Christ said, "Virtue has gone out of me, who touched me?" Then after seeing the leper turned into a healthy woman, Christ said, "Thy faith made thee whole." Here it is the power from the aura of Christ that transformed the woman, who could receive the power only because of her intense faith.

DADDY, WHAT IS NAMASTE?

Namaste is the most popular Hindu greeting, performed by pressing the two hands together and holding them near the heart with the head gently bowed as one says, "Namaste." The gesture of holding both hands together is called the Anjali Mudra. There is a great symbolism behind this greeting. Both hands depict a duality like the Yin and Yang or positive and negative forces, and bringing the hands together to a Hindu affirms the singleness or Advaita in the world. The whole act communicates, "You and I are one. I salute, honor and worship the God within you." It also means, "I prostrate myself before you who is the mirror-image of me, with body, mind and soul."

In Sanskrit, the word Namas means "to bow in reverential salutation." Te means "to you." So Namaste in a nutshell means "I bow to you." This greeting makes a Hindu remind himself that God is everywhere and in every human being we meet anywhere at any time.

Namaste
"I bow to the God within you"

Ashrama Dharmas and Non-Violence

DADDY, WHAT ARE ASHRAMAS AND ASHRAMA DHARMA?

As I have told you before, in Hinduism a man has to undergo four stages in his life. They are Brahmachari or Kaumaram (bachelor student), Garhastyam (married householder), Vanaprastham (hermit) and Sanyasam (wandering renunciate). These four stages are collectively known as Ashramas. In each state, the man is supposed to work hard to attain salvation. During the state of Brahmachari, the celibate student receives instruction about scriptures, and learns self-control and prepares himself for life's responsibilities.   In the Garhastyam Ashrama the man gets married to a virgin girl from his caste and takes up a vocation.   He leads a married householder's life as per the instructions of the Dharma Sutras. In the Vanaprastham Ashrama, a man prepares to renounce the world by living in the jungles as a hermit. In the Sanyasam Ashrama, the man renounces worldly affairs completely, cutting himself away from the world and becoming a wandering saint.

The duties one has to do during each stage are known as Ashrama Dharma. All Ashrama Dharmas are laid down by the Dharma Sutra. In the Gautama Smriti, which is a part of the Dharma Sutras, there are forty ceremonial rites in the Garhastyam Ashrama, but according to the Griha Sutras the total number of ceremonial rites in the Garhastyam Ashrama is sixteen. The Ashrama Dharmas guide a man to the final goal of God-realization.

DO HINDUS PRACTICE NON-VIOLENCE?

There is an oft-quoted Hindu saying, "Ahimsa Paramo Dharma," which means "Non-violence is the highest duty." Long before Jesus Christ, Hinduism taught people to return good for evil. Scores of passages from the Mahabharata and the Mahabhagavatam can be quoted in support.

Ahimsa, or non-violence, is for those who are brave and strong. To flee from a bully and brute and to call it non-violence is the worst form of self-deception. Non-violence actually teaches the mastery of spiritual strength over brute strength. The spirit of non-violence is prevalent among all religions. It is evident throughout the teachings of Christ and also the lives of the Sufi saints. True Ahimsa implies gentleness, courtesy, kindness, hospitality, humanity and love. Mahatma Gandhi is the greatest apostle of Ahimsa in modern times. He used Ahimsa effectively in his freedom fight against the British. Non-violence has two sides, as I said above. On the negative side, it even means running away from righteousness and duty for fear of afflicting pain on creatures. On the positive side, it means perfect selfless love towards every creature. Non-violence should never be used to cover up cowardice.

IS THERE A HINDU DIET CODE?

According to Hinduism, food is divided into three categories: Sattvic, Rajastic and Tamasic.

Tamasic is the worst food of all. The food that is left over and contaminated is usually called Tamasic food. These foods are supposed to produce jealousy and greed among men.

Food that consists of the meat of animals is called Rajastic food. Rajastic food also consists of spices, onions, garlic, hot peppers, pickles, and other similar foods. Rajastic foods are supposed to produce activity and strong emotional qualities among men.

Sattvic foods are those foods which do not agitate your stomach at all. Much of the Sattvic food consists of fruits, nuts, and vegetables. These foods are supposed to produce calmness and nobility among men. Hindu diet codes, not moral codes, strictly prohibit the consumption of beef and pork. As per those codes, eating fruits and vegetables increases one's magnetism. From what we can understand today about diets, we are sure that the ancient Hindu saints had a very good idea about food in general and its effect on the body and thinking patterns of man. Expression of the soul is dependent on the body, and the body is dependent on food. So for proper spiritual development, a proper diet is a must for everyone.

63 ॐ
Untouchables

WHO ARE THE UNTOUCHABLES?

When the Aryans settled on the banks of the Indus, Ganges and Brahmaputra, they were forced to divide their society into four distinct groups based on labor for the smooth functioning of society. They were:

1. Brahmanas--priestly class to work in temples, study and propagate religion
2. Kshatriyas--royal and fighter class to rule and defend society.
3. Vaishyas--business class to see that all commodities are properly distributed
4. Shudras--to help all other classes in their respective duties

According to Manu, Brahma created the Brahmanas from his face, the Kshatriyas from his arms, the Vaishyas from his thighs and the Shudras from his feet. In Chapter 4, verse 13 of the Bhagavad Gita, Lord Krishna says, "According to the three Gunas (Sattvic, Rajastic and Tamasic) and the proper division of labor, the Chathur Varna ("four-colored") society was created by me." The division of labor was a very good idea, but over the course of time it degenerated. Some say that a fifth division of people emerged in Hindu society over time, and these people were known as outcasts or untouchables. Another group of historians says that it was the Shudras who became the untouchables. Mahatma Gandhi called the untouchables by the name Harijans (children of God) and fought for their emancipation. In fact Gandhi once said, "I do not want to be reborn, but if I have to be reborn, I would like to be reborn an untouchable so that I may have their sorrows, sufferings, and the affronts levelled against them in order that I may endeavor to free myself and them from their miserable condition."

There is nothing in Hinduism as complex as the caste system. It is indeed the greatest curse on Hinduism. Once upon a time, India had three thousand castes and twenty-five thousand sub-castes. There were even 1,800 Brahmin castes in India. What a shame! Even different Brahmin castes did not mingle among themselves socially or otherwise in ancient times. Last of all, ancient India has the untouchables. Mahatma Gandhi said, "Untouchability is a crime against God and men." Ambedkar once wrote, out of his own experience, "To the untouchables, Hinduism is a veritable chamber of horrors."

The government of India abolished the practice of untouchability in 1949 with the statement, "Untouchability is abolished and its practice in any form is abolished," and today Harijans are well taken care of in government circles. Untouchability stood against all Hindu ideals and principles. It only helped conversions from Hinduism to other religions, even though the color of human skin is still dividing nations and communities throughout this world. So the caste system is not unique to Hinduism, but is part and parcel of the human race.

ARE YOU SAYING THAT THE CASTE SYSTEM WAS DEVELOPED BY MANU WITH THE INTENT OF DIVISION OF LABOR ONLY AND THAT THE DIVISION WAS NOT DONE BY THE COLOR OF THE HUMAN SKIN?

To begin with, as I told you before, no Hindu is happy about the existence of the caste system in Hinduism, even though you can witness racial prejudices in every society in the world. Anyway, nobody knows what the actual reason was for Manu to place so much stress on the caste system. Did he do that for the proper division of labor among the nomad tribes settled down on the banks of the Indus and Ganges Rivers? Or did he do that to control and humiliate the dark-colored Dravidians of South India? All of us can only speculate one way or another.

If you look at the caste system as a color system, there are a few ingredients to prove that. One of the chief ingredients in the caste division is the notion of purity, with Brahmins as the purest and Shudras as the least pure. Surprisingly, the word caste came from the Portuguese word "casta," meaning "pure race." Also, Varna means "color." In the Hindu scriptures, the caste system is called Chathur Varna, meaning "four colors." It should be assumed that the Aryans, who settled on the banks of Indus, found their skin color was far lighter than the native Dravidians, who were black. So they divided the society on the basis of the color of the human skin. In fact, Manu wrote that Brahmanas are white, Kshatriyas are red, Vaishyas are brown and Shudras are black in color.

Manu might have started it, but most Hindu saints did not do anything to stop the deterioration of the society due to the caste system. Even one of the greatest philosophers of Hinduism, Adi Sankara of Kerala, seems to have supported the caste system. In fact, legends say that once Sankara angrily asked an untouchable to move out of his way and that untouchable talked back. "Dear Sir! What do you want to move? Body or soul?" To which Sankara said, "The untouchable who speaks like that can be nobody else but my Guru, Veda Vyasa," and prostrated in front of him. The legend might have been written as an episode in Sankara's life, but we have to treat it as a revelation that even Sankara indirectly supported the caste system. If he was against the caste system, then he would not have asked the untouchable to move away from his path.

Rishis came from all classes of people. Of course, there have been many great saints in India who came from lower castes. Veda Vyasa was the son of Sathyavathi, who was a fisherwoman. Of course, his father was Sage Parasara. Valmiki was a robber who was transformed by Sage Narada, and as such we have no idea to which caste Valmiki belonged. The South Indian saint Thiruvalluar, who wrote Thirukural, was only a weaver.

Anyway, after Manu formulated the caste system, it grew by leaps and bounds all over India. Numerous castes have their own theories of their own origin. The caste system in India even affected the converts to Christianity and Islam, for even they practiced some form of caste system among themselves after conversion.

64 ❧
Truth--A Virtue

IS BEING TRUTHFUL ANOTHER CARDINAL VIRTUE OF HINDUISM?

Hinduism states "Satyameva Jayate," meaning "Truth alone triumphs." Being truthful to oneself is one of the most important teachings of Hinduism. The greatest apostle of truth in modern times was none other than Mahatma Gandhi. His autobiography, *My Experiments With Truth*, is just that. The greatest follower of truth in ancient times was King Harishchandra. It is said that this great king gave up his kingdom, wife and only son for upholding the truth (his promise) to Sage Vishwamitra. According to the Narada Smriti, truth is the best means of purification of the soul. It says that if the telling of a truth and a thousand horse sacrifices are put in a balance and weighed, it will be found that the truth weighs more. Truth, according to Manu, is the best austerity a human being can perform, and a man of truth attains the state of Godhead when living in the body. It is the lack of truth or the uttering of falsehood that makes our lives miserable. Whenever we lie, we are actually punishing ourselves to momentarily gain some object for which we will pay dearly in the future with a multitude of problems. It is a habit on the part of many to tell lies, but in their own minds they suffer with guilty consciences.

DON'T YOU THINK IT IS VERY DIFFICULT INDEED TO TELL TRUTHS AND LIVE IN MODERN TIMES?

Well, there is no rule that you should always utter truth, even to the extent of making others' lives miserable. For example, if you see a mother with a very ugly child, you don't have to say to her, "What an ugly child you have!" Here that truth is unnecessary. Instead if you say,

"I pray to God to bless your child with health and happiness," you are telling another truth and you avoid unnecessarily hurting the feelings of the mother. You could also avoid any comment at all.

If you are a car salesman, tell the people the limitations of the car you are selling along with the good points of the car. By telling the truth, you, as a salesman, will be able to sell a lot of cars as long as your cars have some positive points to them. If you cheat people in your profession, always believe that others can cheat you a thousand times in their profession also. For example, an auto mechanic can give you back your car with the brakes half done and that could result in a fatal accident. The babysitter who takes care of your infant can be inattentive and that could even result in the death of your infant. I admit that once in a while the truth will hurt momentarily, but in the long run it will pay you well. For example, if you do not like the behavior pattern of one of your friends, you are better off telling that truth than trying to cover it up with lies and later suffering for that. So it is better on your part to tell the truth and live by it even if that will result in your getting hurt once in a while.

Story of Ganges

WHAT IS SO IMPORTANT ABOUT THE GANGES?

The Ganges is considered to be a goddess and is supposed to be one of the consorts of Lord Siva. The River Ganges, popularly known as Mother Ganges, was the mother of Bhishma, the great hero of the Mahabharata. Hinduism in its infancy used to worship the River Ganges, and the practice still holds. The Ganges is known as the river of heaven because she agreed to come down from there to earth. According to mythology, she was brought down from heaven by a king named Bhagirata in order to purify the ashes of his ancestors. It is said that Mother Ganges came down reluctantly and that she flowed through the matted locks of Lord Siva in order to break down her force; otherwise the earth would have been shattered by her direct impact. Some Hindus believe that the indwelling spirit causes the water in the Ganges to move. The Ganges comes roaring down the Indian plains, but the source of the river, popularly known as Gangotri, is a silent lake.

There are many myths about the Ganges and those myths are passed on from generation to generation. Mythology states that if a dying man takes a drop of Ganges water, he is assured of heaven when he dies. As per mythology, bathing in the Ganges is supposed to wash away all one's sins. Since the river contains a lot of minerals, it has many medicinal qualities. The total length of the Ganges is 1,557 miles.

Sri Yantra

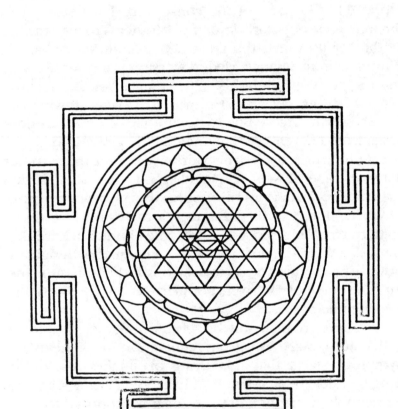

66 ॐ
Hindu Pilgrimages

WHAT IS THE MEANING OF TIRTHA YATRA?

Tirtha literally means "crossing place" or "ford," and Yatra means "travel" or "pilgrimage." The ford in a river is the safest point to cross the river. Anyway, a visit to sacred places is considered a Tirtha Yatra. Most of the important places of pilgrimage in India are located along the banks of great rivers like the Ganges, Narmada, Godavari, Kaveri and Brahmaputra. Tirtha Yatra is not only the physical act of visiting holy places but implies mental and moral discipline as well. Hindus go on pilgrimages for purification and redemption from sin as per mythological traditions. Some of the most important points of pilgrimage in India are Badrinath (Uttar Pradesh) in the north, Puri in the east, Rameshwaram in the south and Dwaraka in the west. Any trip to the Himalayas is considered a pilgrimage since it is known as Devalaya or "the abode of gods." In the Himalayas, the most important point of pilgrimage is Gangotri, the point at which the River Ganges starts.

The Puranas are the indispensable source of information about the sacred places of ancient India. The Guruvayur Temple and Sabarimala in Kerala, the Sri Venkateswara Temple in Tirupati, Kasi, Hardwar, Pandharpur in Maharashtra and other locations can be considered important places of Hindu pilgrimage. The most important Hindu pilgrimage takes place during the Kumbha Mela Festival, and also the Maha Kumbha Mela Festival which occurs once every twelve years.

67 ஜ
Kumbha Mela Festival

WHAT IS THE KUMBHA MELA FESTIVAL?

It is the greatest Hindu pilgrim festival that takes place once in three years. According to the Guinness Book of World Records, this festival is the largest religious gathering on earth. It is a riverside religious festival rotated between four places: Allahabad (on the banks of the Ganges, Yamuna and the mythical Saraswathi), Hardwar (Ganges), Ujjain (Sipra) and Nasik (Godavari). The festival that is held in Allahabad every twelve years is known as Maha Kumbha Mela. It is normally celebrated when a rare planetary configuration occurs: Jupiter in Taurus, the sun and moon in Capricorn, and a series of complicated calculations of Hindu astrology. Taking a bath in those rivers during the Kumbha Mela is considered to be a great spiritual act. Adi Sankaracharya himself gave a lot of importance to this festival and exhorted holy men to meet during the Kumbha Mela for free exchange of views. This Mela attracts millions of people right from Digambaras (naked Jain saints) to the Sanyasin who live high in the Himalayan caves throughout the year. In 1954 at the Maha Kumbha Mela at Allahabad, the crowd was estimated at many millions and such was the rush that more than five hundred people were killed in a stampede.

It is said that once upon a time, the Devas (gods of heaven) and Asuras (demons) fought for a Kumbha (pot) of Amrita (life-giving elixir) that came out during the churning of the milky ocean. Then Vishnu saved the Amrita from the demons and gave it to the Devas. During their stay on earth, the Devas rested the pot at four places, thus sanctifying the four sites of the Kumbha Mela. That mythological incident started the famous festival.

Vishnu Yantra

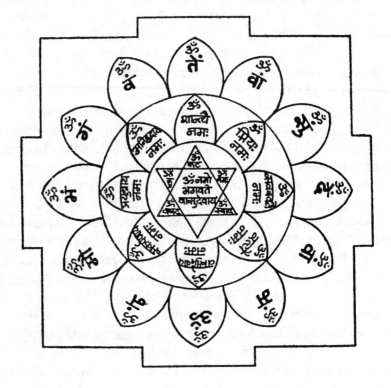

68 ಸ್ಥ
Benaras--Holy City of Hindus

WHICH IS THE HOLY CITY OF THE HINDUS?

A large number of cities in India are holy cities to Hindus, and among them Benaras is the most sacred and most popular. It stands on the banks of the Ganges between Delhi and Calcutta. The ancient name of the city is Kasi, the luminous city of lights. The Sanskrit and Hindi name of the city is Varanasi. A thirty-six-mile road circles the most sacred parts of this city. Benaras has thousands of temples, of which the Kasi Vishwanatha temple is the most famous. The most important part of a pilgrimage to Benaras consists of taking a bath in the holy waters of the Ganges. Along the river there are at least seventy bathing ghats (landings or banks). It is said that taking a bath in the Ganges at Benaras washes away all sins.

Benaras is the oldest living city in the world. It attracts people from all over the five continents. It is said that saints and prophets like the Buddha, Mahavira and Sankara went to Benaras to worship and teach. Benaras is said to be the city of Lord Siva, the God of Annihilation, so it is especially sacred to followers of Siva.

After visiting Benaras, Mark Twain said, "Benaras is older than history, older than tradition, older than legend, and looks twice as old as all of them put together."

69 ঽ
Hindu Holy Festivals

WHAT ARE THE HOLY HINDU FESTIVALS?

Hindu festivals are known as Utsava in Sanskrit. During the time of festivals, communities set aside mundane matters and rejoiced together, honoring both the Supreme God in one of His various forms and the change of seasons. Since Hindu festivals are associated with the worship of a particular deity, each festival falls on a date which is astrologically auspicious for that particular deity. There are many Hindu festivals and their importance differs from place to place. Holi is a religious festival of North India, and it is not celebrated in South India. To give you another example, Onam (flower festival) is a very important religious festival in the state of Kerala, but the rest of India does not celebrate it. Similarly, the holy festival Pongal is strictly restricted to Tamil Nadu.

Deepavali or Diwali, the festival of lights, is an important Hindu festival celebrated during the month of Kartika (October/November). It is one of the most widely celebrated festivals in the world, being a national holiday in India, Fiji and Trinidad. Deepa mean "light" and Avali means "row," so Deepavali means "row of lights." There are many mythological stories behind the Deepavali or Diwali celebration. For some, Deepavali is the celebration of the triumphant return of Lord Rama and his consort Sita to the kingdom of Ayodhya after the annihilation of Ravana, the demon-king of Ceylon (Sri Lanka). During this celebration, people light rows of small candles or oil lamps along balconies and windows to welcome Lord Rama and Sita home.

Some celebrate Deepavali as the joyous celebration of the death of the titan of hell, Narakasura, at the hands of Lord Krishna. The story about the annihilation of

Narakasura is written in the Sabha Parva of the Mahabharata. According to the legends, Narakasura, the son of earth, was the king of Pragjyotishapura. By the boons he received from Brahma and Siva, he conquered and plundered not only the earth but heaven as well. Narakasura robbed the earrings of Aditi, the mother of the gods, apart from all the other havoc he caused all over earth and heaven. Finally, all the saints and Devas supplicated Lord Krishna at Dwaraka to kill Narakasura. In a fierce battle, Krishna, aided by his queen Satyabhama as his charioteer, killed Narakasura. After the death of Narakasura, his mother prayed to Lord Krishna that her son's downfall might be brought to the memory of all the people in the world as a day of celebration of the good. Thus Deepavali is the celebration of the deliverance of earth and heaven from the clutches of Narakasura.

Deepavali is also considered a festival to worship Lakshmi, the consort of Lord Vishnu and the Goddess of Wealth. A special Goddess Lakshmi Pooja is performed in most Hindu homes during this festival. During Deepavali people visit friends and exchange sweets and gifts.

The Holi festival also has a mythological background. It is said that once the world was ruled by a demon-king, Hiranyakashipu. He proclaimed himself as God and made everyone pray to him, but his son, Prahlada, persisted in worshipping Lord Vishnu. As per the order of Hiranyakasipu, a female demon named Holika, who believed herself to be immune to the ravages of fire, carried Prahlada into fire. It is said that due to the blessings of Lord Vishnu, Prahlada came out untouched by the fire, whereas Holika was burnt to ashes. The Holi festival celebrates this mythological event. Some say that this festival is in honor of Kama Deva, the God of Sexual Desire. Whatever the legends say, the Holi festival, celebrated during February/March, is one of the most important festivals of North India. A bonfire is also lit on the eve of Holi. During the day following Holi, people throw colored water and bright herbal powders at one another. Just as in the Deepavali festival, during this festival people exchange gifts and sweets.

The Onam festival is celebrated in the state of Kerala only to mark the end of the summer monsoons. This festival also has a mythological origin. It is said that once upon a time, the world was ruled by a demon-king named Mahabali who made the world better than heaven. That was against the rule, since the world was not supposed to be better than heaven, and the God of Heaven, Indra, was much annoyed. So to set matters straight, Lord Vishnu came down as Vamana (dwarf) and begged King Mahabali for the amount of land which he could cover in three small steps. Without any thought, King Mahabali agreed. Then Vamana suddenly grew to unimaginable proportions and stepped over both heaven and earth in two giant steps. Vamana then pushed King Mahabali down to the world underneath known as Patala. Just before King Mahabali was pushed out of this earth, he was given permission by Vamana to visit his people once every year. The Onam festival is a celebration of welcoming Mahabali to his lost kingdom. During this festival, beautiful floral decorations in concentric circles are made in every house and boat races are held throughout Kerala. The Lord of the Onam, called Thrikakkarappan, is usually made of mud, in an almost shapeless shape, with a square bottom, four faces and a pointed top. The four faces depict the four Ashramas or stages of a man's life. The ascent from the square bottom to the pointed top indicates the ascent of man from his animal tendencies to a highly spiritualistic stage through the four stages of Kaumaram (bachelor student), Garhastyam (married householder), Vanaprastham (hermit) and Sanyasam (wandering renunciate). A twenty-one course feast is the most important part of the

Onam festival. The Malayalees (people of Kerala) make this festival an opportunity for reuniting their families.

The Pongal festival is an important festival held during January/February in the state of Tamil Nadu. It is a three-day festival celebrated at the time of the rice harvest. The Thaipusam festival is a religious festival honoring Lord Subramaniyan, son of Lord Siva, and is celebrated in the Batu Cave Temple of Malaysia. Hundreds of Hindus shave their heads and slide steel rods into their faces during this celebration. The Ram Navami festival is to celebrate the birth of Lord Rama, the seventh incarnation of Lord Vishnu, during March/April. Devotees engage in non-stop reading of the Ramayana. In the evening they attend a performance called Ramalila, recounting the deeds of Rama. This festival is especially popular in Uttar Pradesh.

The Raksha Bandhan celebration happens during July/August. During this celebration a sister ties a Rakhi--a kind of handspun cotton thread dyed yellow with turmeric--around the wrist of her brother, who in return gives her a present of clothing or cash or jewelry and becomes responsible for her safety. The Rakhi can be given to anyone, even someone outside the Hindu community. Raksha Bandhan is the Hindu community's way of protecting the welfare of the women.

The fourth day of Leo or Simha (August/September), Ganesh Chathurthi, is celebrated around the world as the birthday of Lord Ganesha, the elephant-headed God of Wisdom and remover of obstacles. One of the most important part of the festival is making clay images of Ganesha and worshipping them for seven or ten days. On the last day, these images are ceremoniously immersed in the ocean or in a lake. This celebration signifies the raising of consciousness from the material level (clay image) to cosmic consciousness (ocean).

Navaratri is known as the "Festival of Nights" honoring the goddesses, beginning on the ninth day of the month of Virgo or Kanya (September/October). Total worship lasts for nine days, out of which the first three are devoted to Durga (the Goddess of Valor), the next three days to Lakshmi (the Goddess of Wealth) and the next three days to Saraswathi (the Goddess of Knowledge). The images of the goddesses are created, worshipped and then immersed in the sea or a lake. In North India during the nights of this celebration the Garbha dance is performed. In South India, houses are decorated and toys by the name of Bomma Kolam are displayed. The tenth day is known as Vijaya Dasami, Dasara or Dussera.

Dasara is another name for the nine-day Navaratri festival which is celebrated in many parts of India, especially in Mysore in the state of Karnataka. Dasara is the celebration of the victory of Goddess Durga (Kali) over the demon in the form of a buffalo named Mahishasura. It is said that Goddess Durga took nine days and nights to annihilate the demon. In the northern parts of India, Dasara is a celebration of the victory of Lord Rama over the demon-king Ravana of Sri Lanka. During Dasara special Poojas are conducted in Hindu temples as well as in Hindu homes. The Dasara festival lasts for a week.

There are still more religious festivals in India. Sivaratri (February/March) is a festival honoring Lord Siva. It is celebrated throughout India. Krishna Janmashtami (August/September) is the celebration of the birthday of Lord Krishna. Vasant Panchami (January/February) is a spring festival honoring Goddess Saraswathi. Guru Purnima (June/July) is the celebration of showing gratitude to Gurus and masters.

70 ❧
Hindu Rituals

WHAT ARE THE RITUALS IN HINDUISM?

Ritual is the colorful art of worshipping a deity. The two most popular rituals are Pooja and Yajna. Pooja is the commonest form of ritual. The Vedas do not speak about Pooja, which contains elaborate forms of worship for homes and temples. One of the main parts of this ritual is the offering of many articles called Upacaras (offerings with honor) to the deity. The Upacaras consist of food, perfumed water, Tulsi leaves, sandalwood paste, incense, flowers, ash and clothes. The person who conducts the Pooja in a temple is called a Poojari. Arati is another important part of the Pooja ceremony. It is a very common ritualistic waving of lights before the image of the deity. After the Pooja, the householder or Poojari distributes offerings made to the deity, known as Prasad, to fellow devotees. Prasad consists of food as well as herbal powders.

Yajnas are performed at temporary altars constructed as per Tantric laws. These altars are made exclusively for Yajnas, and as soon as the Yajna is over the altar is destroyed. Yajna involves no image or idol of God. A special Yantra (complex geometrical figure) is drawn on the altar and this Yantra personifies the deity of worship. Most Yajna rituals involve simultaneous chanting by many Brahmin priests.

There are two kinds of Yajnas, one done exclusively for public welfare and the other done for the good of the householders. Public Yajnas used to be sponsored by kings, but they are now sponsored by several Hindu temple managements and socio-religious organizations. One of the most popular domestic Yajnas is Ganapathi Homam. This Yajna is done in most Hindu homes once a year by a very capable Brahmin priest.

Yajna is usually done for material human welfare. Of course, by performing Yajnas, a devotee is indirectly brought closer to God, for he fully understands the power of God in his day-to-day affairs.

One of the very ancient rituals is known as Rajasuya Yajna or horse sacrifice. It is a Vedic ritual usually done during the coronations of kings. The term Rajasuya means "king-engendering." It is said in the Mahabharata that the Pandavas conducted the Rajasuya ritual under the guidance of Lord Krishna. In its entire course, this ritual lasts two years. Even though this ritual is associated with the coronations of kings, it also stresses the continuance of the cosmic rhythm of birth and life. Agnihotra is another domestic ritual still practiced by orthodox Brahmins.

Apart from all the rituals described above, there are a number of Vedic rituals collectively known as Samskaras, meaning "refinements." Actually, the closest word in English to the word Samskara is "sacrament." The Samskaras consist of all rituals from the time of birth to the time of death. There are at least sixteen Samskara rituals. They are:

1. Garbhadhana--ritual to guarantee conception.
2. Pumsavana--ritual to protect the fetus and to have a boy.
3. Simantonnayana--ritual done during the last month of pregnancy for the proper mental formation of the child.
4. Jatakarma--birth ritual involving the preparation of the astrological chart of the child.
5. Namakarana--ritual of naming the child. This ceremony is performed in the home, usually when the child is eleven to forty days old.
6. Nishkramana--ritual of taking the child out of the house for the first time.

7. Annaprasana--the first feeding of rice, usually done in front of the god in a temple.
8. Chudakarana--ritual of first cutting of the hair.
9. Karnavedha--ritual of boring the earlobes of the child for putting in gold earrings.
10. Vidyarambha--the beginning of the child learning the alphabet.
11. Upanayana--the holy thread ritual by which the boy becomes a Dwija or "twice-born." This ceremony is performed when the boy is between the ages of nine and fifteen.
12. Vedarambha--commencement of Vedic studies.
13. Keshanta--ritual of first shaving of the head.
14. Samavartana--ritual of home-coming after completion of Vedic studies.
15. Viveha--the marriage ritual.
16. Anthyesthi--funeral rites.

Rituals performed at death are collectively known as Shraddha. These rituals last twelve days. Immediately after death the corpse is cremated and the funeral pyre is lit by the deceased's eldest son. The remaining ceremonies are conducted to ease the problems for the soul's journey to the world of the ancestors. The ceremonies consist of offering small rice balls to birds, like the crows. The crows are supposed to be departed souls. The Shraddha rituals are very ancient, going back to early Vedic times. Shraddha is done every year for the sake of the departed soul.

Tirtha Yatra, or visiting holy places, is another very important ritual in every Hindu's life. Hinduism prescribes many rituals appropriate to a variety of circumstances, castes and regions.

DADDY, WHAT IS KUMBHABHISHEKAM?

Kumbhabhishekam is a very important ritual of temple consecration associated with temple construction. The ritual literally means "anointing of the pot." During the construction of the temples at Pittsburgh and New York, this ritual was performed. Kumbhabhishekam is associated with very powerful symbolism. The rituals of Kumbhabhishekam are performed in a series of eight sequences starting with a ritual named Swastivachanam, which is a ritual welcoming all guests.

71 🍂
Hindu Marriages

ARE HINDU MARRIAGES ARRANGED?

Most Hindu marriages are arranged by the parents. There was a time when bride and groom would meet at the wedding for the first time. That system has changed now. Nowadays the parents of both bride and groom first meet and discuss the forthcoming marriage. Then the boy and girl meet. If they like each other and only if they like each other, the wedding plans proceed. If either does not like the other, the wedding plans are immediately dropped. The following is the most important part of any marriage, and that is the checking of the astrological charts of both the boy and the girl to see that both charts match each other perfectly. If the family astrologer sounds an alarm, the wedding is called off. After all this, the wedding takes place in an elaborate ceremony.

Hindus do not believe in any kind of courtship before marriage. The belief among them is that love develops gradually after marriage and not before. The sincere love one sees in a Hindu household proves that point beyond doubt. Of course, the tradition of "arranged" marriages is breaking down in India now and "falling in love and marrying" is common at least among educated people.

Hindu weddings differ from place to place. The ceremony is usually held at the bride's house and sometimes even held in a temple. The wedding date for a Hindu marriage is fixed only after careful astrological calculations. The ceremony is performed before a fire lit in a special metal vessel or a lamp. Usually a Hindu priest conducts the wedding ceremony by reciting hymns from the scriptures written in Sanskrit. As a part of the ceremony, the bride and groom exchange rings and the groom presents the bride with saris. The bride and groom garland each other and at the end of the ceremony the couple walks around the fire three times. Among some castes, the couple walks around the fire seven times (Saptapadi).

Since there are many castes and sub-castes in the Hindu community, the wedding ceremony differs from place to place. Some marriage ceremonies last an hour, while others may take days to finish. There was a time when child marriages were prevalent in India, but now such marriage is a crime, punishable by imprisonment.

DO ARRANGED MARRIAGES WORK?

Statistics show that there is not even one percent of divorces among Hindus now. Arranged marriages work because Hindus believe that the union of marriage is predetermined and is a form of Karma. They also work because Hindus, unlike many others, try very hard not to break a wedlock. In Hindu marriages the union is not between a boy and a girl, but between two families. The girl is given in marriage to a family and not to a boy. Of course, like any other place in the world, India too is changing due to Western ideas of instant love and divorce, and as such the divorce rate among Hindus may increase as years pass.

72 &
Mysterious Brahman

WHAT IS THIS MYSTERIOUS BRAHMAN?

There is nothing in Hinduism more mysterious than Brahman. Brahman means "the one without a second." Of all the names given to God in scriptures, Brahman is the most obscure. In the Upanishads, Brahman is the Absolute One which makes all things known. According to Advaita philosophy, Brahman alone is real, and all the rest is unreal and illusion or Maya. Trying to understand Brahman with a human mind is like trying to look at the eye with which one sees everything. To know Brahman, one must experience one's oneness with the Brahman through one of the methods of God-realization. In the Upanishads, Neti-Neti ("not this-not this") is the method by which Brahman is explained.

DADDY, ARE BRAHMAN AND ATMAN ONE AND THE SAME?

They are actually one and the same. The individual soul within the body is known as the Self or Atman. It is also known as Jeevatman. The soul that is bound by Karmas is known as Atman. When that soul breaks loose from the bondage of Karmas, then it attains salvation or becomes one with Brahman or Paramatman. To give you an approximate example, I should say that if the electricity in your computer can be called Atman, then the total electrical energy in the entire utility network is Brahman. As I told you before, by no means will you be able to understand these words with your mind since we are talking about things far above and beyond the mind.

AFTER HEARING YOUR EXPLANATION ABOUT BRAHMAN AND ATMAN, I FEEL GOD IS ENERGY. WHAT DO YOU THINK?

Well, it is erroneous to make a definition like that since God is beyond any definitions and the concept of understanding or realizing Him is above the mind. Even so, I should say that almost all the time God acts as if He is energy, complying with the unwritten laws of the universe. These unwritten laws act in a similar manner all the time. A newborn baby who touches a live conductor of electricity gets an electric shock; so too does the scientist who may have done twenty years of research on electricity alone.

The energy concept of God makes Him in tune with modern science. The laws of Newton, Maxwell and Einstein suddenly become as religious as the Code of Manu or the Upanishads. The latest research into Alpha, Beta and Gamma brain waves also gives us a correlation between happiness and brain waves. In one of the books written on Raja Yoga, it is said that all happiness and realization lie in the head, so try to tap the vast resources of happiness in the head by meditation.

Raja Yoga, Mantras, Tantras, the existence of the coiled Kundalini power, Chakras and auras point towards the direction of God as energy. The energy concept is seen in the Holy Bible too. Anyway, all those who knew God never defined God, so we cannot conclude that God is energy or something else, but the energy concept of God is a good topic for discussion.

"Aham Brahmasmin" and Other Mantras

I KNOW THAT THERE ARE SOME LINES THAT HINDU SAINTS USE IN THEIR SERMONS. CAN YOU EXPLAIN ALL OF THEM TO ME? FOR EXAMPLE, WHAT IS THE MEANING OF "AHAM BRAHMASMIN"?

The actual meaning of "Aham Brahmasmin" is "I am Brahman, the Spirit." Of course, anyone can say that line very easily, but only God-realized masters experience it. All of us, even though we are pure spirit or energy, still find it difficult to fight the illusion (Maya) which says "I am the body."

Anyway, the idea expressed in the words "Aham Brahmasmin" can be explained in another way. Look at a dead body and a living body. Both are identical, but the living body has something that the dead body does not have. That which is missing in the dead body is the spirit, Brahman, but at the same time, when Brahman is present in the body, it creates the greatest illusion that "I am the body."

I will give you another example. Look at your computer. It does all kinds of wonders for you, but if you accidentally switch off the main circuit-breaker, your expensive computer is a dead machine. So, here the electric current is the Brahman. We know that it acts differently in different people or creatures according to their Karmas. Similarly, the same electric current is a thinker in a computer, a heater in your electric iron and a cooler in your air conditioner.

WHAT IS THE MEANING OF "TAT TVAM ASI"?

"That thou art" is the meaning of the above line. This statement is an indirect repetition of "Aham Brahmasmin," meaning "I am Brahman." As you can see, both statements are one and the same. Brahman alone exists; everything else is Maya. "Tat Tvam Asi" is actually quoted from the Chandogya Upanishad, "That subtle essence is the self of this entire world. That is real, that is self. That thou art."

WHAT DO YOU MEAN BY "SAT-CHIT-ANANDA"?

"Absolute existence--absolute knowledge--absolute bliss." Saints usually use this statement to arouse in devotees spiritual feelings and to break away from material bondage.

WHAT IS THE MEANING OF "SATYAM-SHIVAM-SUNDARAM"?

"Truth--bliss--beauty." This statement again expresses the true nature of one who is one with Brahman. A God-realized person will experience "truth--bliss--beauty" all the time.

IS "HAM AHAM SAH" A MANTRA?

Yes, it is a Mantra. It means "I am he, he is I." This Mantra came from the word Hamsa. Hamsa means swan. It is a symbol of Brahman. Those who attain cosmic consciousness are often called Paramahamsa, or "Great Swan." This mantra is similar to the Hebrew word Jehovah (Old Testament) which means "I am."

"I Am God"

DADDY, MANY NEW AGERS ALWAYS SAY "I AM GOD."
WHAT DO THEY MEAN? CAN YOU EXPLAIN?

They are actually repeating two Hindu sayings by
stating "I am God." One is "Aham Brahmasmin," meaning
"I am Brahman," the Infinite. The other one is "Tat Tvam
Asi," "That thou art," meaning that the individual soul is
indeed the Supreme Soul.

If one does not understand the whole story, "I am
God" will sound stupid and egoistic. Hindus believe that
within every body there is an imperishable soul named
Atman. This soul is deluded by its past and present
Karmas or actions. As such, it forgets that it is a part and
parcel of the universal soul, which is called Paramatman or
Brahman or God. According to Hinduism, by various ways
one should realize that the soul within oneself is part and
parcel of the Universal Soul. So all Hindus try to realize
that fact. That realization is called salvation in Hinduism.

The closest comparison of Atman and Paramatman
is "the electricity within a computer and the electricity in
the entire network of the power company." Electricity
within the computer is the same electricity within the
power company network throughout the world. So if you
know all about the electricity within the computer, then
you know all about the electricity all over the world.
Nobody says that the electricity within a light can do
miracles, except to give the filament the capacity to give
light and heat. So the individual soul, captured within the
body, is conditioned by Karmic laws. That is the reason
why neither Christ nor Buddha nor Krishna could
transform the world by one single act. All great masters
have shown us the way but they were never able to
explain the ultimate goal. This ultimate goal is beyond the
mind of man, beyond the vocabulary of any language on

earth. Man can explain only what he can compare with. As such, the ultimate goal will always remain a mystery.

Anyway, by just saying "I am God," nobody realizes God. All of
us have to work at realizing that by good actions, good thoughts and meditation. Hinduism does not offer any easy alternatives. So if you hear someone say that there is an easy way, he/she is telling a lie.

Jehovah said to an inquiring Moses who asked Him His name, "I am who I am" (Exodus 3:14). Jesus Christ said the same thing by saying that "Before Abraham was, I am." Those who heard Christ exploded with anger, condemning him for making himself equivalent to God, and the wrath of his enemies only grew when Jesus said, "I and the Father are one" (John 10:30). Jesus Christ made more than seven statements beginning with "I am" in the New Testament. Lord Krishna used the same lines several times in the Bhagavad Gita. Totally lost by these words (like Moses), Krishna's disciple Arjuna asked, "Who are you?" Then Lord Krishna showed him his Viswaroopa which was indeed the sum total of the whole universe, with its past, present and future. Even the Islamic mystics Sufis uttered the words "I am God," and that resulted in their execution. So the statement "I am God" has been repeated throughout history by many saints who have indeed experienced oneness with God.

Jesus Christ was indeed God on earth. In Saint Thomas' Gospel, Christ said, "He who drinks from my mouth will become as I am and I shall be he." By those lines, Christ is stating to mankind that he who follows him will achieve Christ Consciousness or Cosmic Consciousness. Because Jesus Christ had limitations due to Karmic laws, those who surrounded him never fully understood his greatness or magnanimity. Since Christ and Buddha had problems explaining their true identity, those who achieved Christ Consciousness may not necessarily be recognized by the material world.

In the Zohar ("The Book of Splendor"), the mystical teachings of Judaism, one reads that if one contemplates on the things in mystical meditation, everything is revealed as one. Several times Jesus said, "God is Spirit." He also said, "The Father abiding in me doeth His works." So, all that show that God is within you and that everything is God.

"I am God" is repeated in several Upanishads in different formats. "Tat Tvam Asi," or "That thou art," is one of the important sayings among them. Hindus believe in the fundamental unity of all experience and all existence. Salvation is the knowledge or realization of one's own identify with God.

A Hindu, by stating "I am God," is only repeating his own oneness with God or his true nature. It is stupidity to think that by just uttering this without proper meditation one can achieve the state of Christ Consciousness. Again, by stating "I am God" if someone is developing false ego, that person is working totally against his or her objective of becoming one with God. Using "I am God" to gratify one's own emotional urges will only create problems.

Western mystic Meister Eckhart, who was fascinated by Hinduism, explained the law of identifying oneself as God, saying that "the eye with which one sees God is the same eye with which God sees him."

IF WHAT YOU SAY IS THE TRUTH, WHY DO SOME CHRISTIAN THEOLOGIANS VEHEMENTLY ATTACK THE STATEMENT "I AM GOD"?

That is because most Christian theologians do not know the difference between the Hindu and Christian concepts of God. In Hinduism, Brahman or God has no qualities or attributes. It is timeless and it has no consciousness or "I" feelings. Buddhists do not even recognize the word Brahman, stating that such definitions are above the mind of man. Buddhism does not even have any concept of God. But in Hebrew-Christian circles, even though God is explained as spirit, the majority worship God as a very personal God in the form a loving holy father.

In Genesis God said, "Let us make man in our own image." So the Jewish-Christian God has an image of a father figure with human attributes. Christianity is full of words like "God loves," "God is merciful," etc. Even though in Hindu books of devotion you will come across similar lines, a Yogi will say that such personal descriptions of the Infinite are qualities which people admire in other people. Hinduism states that there is nothing wrong in pursuing a personal God, but as the devotee progresses in his/her devotion, he/she will begin to see God as a formless, nameless being. Even in the writings of Ramakrishna Paramahamsa, who worshipped Kali, and Chaitanya Mahaprabhu, who worshipped Vital, one can come across a God without any name or form.

Once again, I wish to point out to you that claiming to be God in the Hebrew-Christian context is utter nonsense. A Hindu never states the line "Aham Brahmasmin" with the belief that his false ego is in charge of the whole universe. The only thing he is stating is that he is not the false ego with a body, but the eternal soul, which is part and parcel of God. Once again, the only example I can give is the comparison between the electric current in the light bulb and the electrical energy in the whole network of the power company. The light bulb's light and heat are due to the presence of the electrical current in it, and that current is the exact replica of the electricity in any part of the network. At the same time, electricity within the light has no independent standing.

Like the power within each one of us is part and parcel of God, the electricity within the light bulb is in fact part and parcel of the network electricity.

The lack of knowledge of the true Hindu concept of God makes some Christian theologians attack the statement "I am God," asking people like Shirley Maclaine to make a snowflake or perform other "miracles." What new agers like Shirley Maclaine are saying is utter nonsense if you look at it from the Hebrew-Christian definition of God, but their statements have a lot of meaning if you look at them from the Hindu, Buddhist and Taoist teachings.

Some people who toy with the idea of a perfect world with clear-cut boundaries have very serious problems in understanding the Hindu-Buddhist concept of God. Hinduism and Buddhism very clearly state that the world is duality: good and bad, light and darkness, etc. As such, the only peace man will see is within himself, which has nothing to do with the happenings around him.

It is a shame to witness arguments and counter-arguments on the question of the "I am God" statement without searching for the fundamental aspects of that age-old statement.

75 ॐ
What Do You Mean By "Born Again"?

IS THERE A TERM IN HINDUISM LIKE "BORN AGAIN"?

Long, long ago, the Christian term "born again" was exclusively used within the church as an important part of the church's phraseology. Now it is widely used even in commercials, just like the word "Guru." The actual word in the Greek version of the New Testament is Anothen, meaning "born from above" or "born of God." Jesus said, "Except a man be born again, he cannot see the kingdom of God" (John 3:3), and added, "Marvel not that I said unto thee, Ye must be born again" (John 3:7). The closest word in Hinduism to what Jesus said is Dwija. The actual meaning of Dwija is "twice born."

"Who is a Dwija? A Brahmin. Who is a Brahmin? He or she who knows Brahman. What is Brahman? That which is infinite...God." So in a nutshell, he who knows God is twice born, or he who is twice born will automatically realize God. According to Hinduism, unless there is an absolute change in consciousness and absolute self-purification, nobody can achieve God-realization. So, it is to be assumed that omnipresent Jesus Christ was referring to a complete change of consciousness rather than any ritualistic or symbolic gestures. He who is born again is a Christian as well as a Brahmin.

World Religions

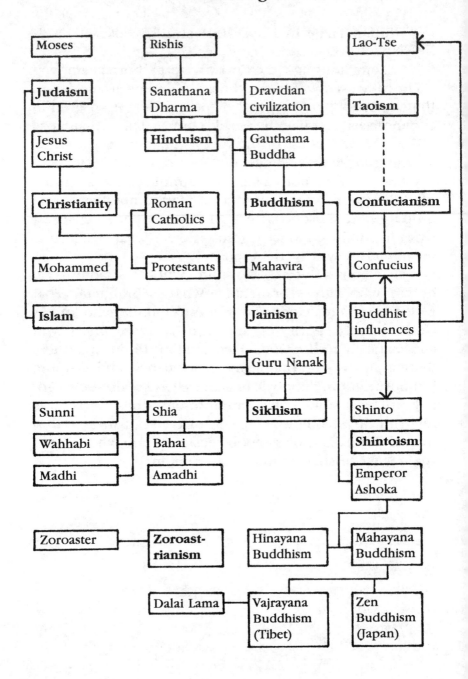

Sin in Hinduism

DO HINDUS BELIEVE IN THE WORDS "SIN" AND "SINNER"?

Except in mythology, in no other scriptures are there any references to sin. Hinduism very scientifically deals with sin, explaining the law of Karma, of cause and effect. All the parables in mythology explain how to deal with sins in a very positive manner. When the child puts his hand in fire, he gets burned. His action here is due to ignorance of the power of fire. The child did not commit a sin, but due to ignorance of the truth that fire burns, he did a bad Karma and he had the result of getting burned. Hinduism looks at all actions in the manner of the example quoted above. We all sin or do bad Karmas due to ignorance. Ignorance is the root of all evil. Knowledge eradicates ignorance. That is the way the idea of sin is explained in Hinduism. Christianity has stressed sin and fear of God and hell. Hinduism, as I said before, stands against the doctrine of sin. Swami Ramakrishna Paramahamsa always looked down upon the Western idea that human beings are sinners. The Bhagavad Gita says, "Even if thou art the worst of sinners, thou shalt cross the ocean of sin by the bark of wisdom" (Chapter 4:36). Adi Sankaracharya, in his doctrine of Advaita, looked at ignorance as Maya or illusion, and time and again wrote that knowledge is the only answer to all human problems. Hinduism forbids guilty consciousness in any form.

The scriptures state that even God cannot save a man who goes under self-pity and guilty consciousness. An advanced Yogi will look at a devotee, prostitute and murderer alike, because he knows that we are all part of an evolutionary process. Some are far ahead and going very fast towards God, and some are at the starting gate and going at a snail's pace to God. Some are divine in form and some are in the mental state of beasts even though they have human forms.

The Bhagavad Gita states, "Yoga--union with the Divine--is for all." So we all will achieve salvation one day. Only the time factor differs from one individual to another. God has given us free will, so that we can decide when to reach God. Some experiment with their lives and take millions of years to reach God, and some mentally comprehend the truth and reach God very fast by following the methods discovered by Rishis and Christ-like masters. So to the Hindu who believes in the truth "Salvation is for all," the words "sin" and "sinner" do not mean much at all.

DADDY, WHAT IS MAYA?

Son, the word meaning of Maya is illusion. The world is Maya, meaning that it is always changing from what it is into something else without ceasing. Hindus do not say that the world is unimportant, but they emphasize the fact that the world we see is not the real world. The true world is beyond description and beyond the concept of time. Hinduism does not advocate running away from the world either. It asks its followers to work in the world until they achieve true knowledge.

According to Hinduism, we witness duality in the world, such as right and wrong, good and bad, and yin and yang due to Maya. In fact, the whole story of Adam and Eve in Genesis deals with Maya. God said to Adam that he could eat the fruit of every tree in the garden except the tree of knowledge of good and evil (Genesis 2:15). Adam disobeyed, and by eating that forbidden fruit Adam and Eve came to know right and wrong, good and bad, etc. That caused the downfall of man. That capability to discern right and wrong in Hinduism is duality perception, which is indeed Maya. What Adam and Eve attained in the garden by eating the forbidden fruit was false knowledge, and it is that false knowledge which is causing the downfall of every man. So Maya is indeed the "original sin." That is the reason why man became aware of his nakedness in the Garden of Eden and lost his knowledge of his true nature. The serpent only depicts the inner weakness in man to indulge in material things. There is no subject more liable to cause the Christian theologians to tear their hair out, and Christians to profess their outspoken unbelief, than original sin. But if the Christian theologians try to explain original sin as false knowledge or Maya, many Christians will understand the magnanimity of symbolism behind the story of Adam and Eve.

We all suffer due to Maya or duality perception. Maya makes us forget our true nature. It was Adi Sankara who used the word Maya to a very large extent to explain his Advaita philosophy. According to Sankara, God or Brahman alone is real, and everything else is Maya. According to Sankara, Maya is false knowledge. Once again, that is the knowledge Adam and Eve received in the Garden of Eden by eating the forbidden fruit. Sankara said that Maya disappears when a person comes across true knowledge. In one of the Upanishads, it is written that nature or Prakriti is Maya and the Almighty is the wielder of Maya. Maya is a word used often used by Hindus. Unluckily, some use this word for selfish motives. Some do not work at all and explain their ideology with the statement, "The material world is Maya and hence no work is necessary." This is dead against the teachings of the Bhagavad Gita. The Gita specifically states that no man will reach the state of inaction (Nishkarmata) by shunning duties (Svadharma) because man by nature does actions all the time (Chapter 3:4). Maya indeed is the original sin described in Genesis, and true knowledge is the only way to get rid of it.

78 ❧
Creation and Annihilation of the Universe

ACCORDING TO HINDUISM, WHAT IS TIME?

According to Hinduism, Brahman alone is timeless. All the rest, which emerged from Brahman, will change shape and form in time. Birth and death are part and parcel of creation. They are also a part of time.

According to the Code of Manu, the universe undergoes endless cycles of birth and destruction. As per Manu: "When the eyelids move eighteen times, the time elapsed is called a Kashta; thirty Kashtas make one Kala; thirty Kalas make one Muhurta; thirty Muhurtas make a day and night."

Hinduism was influenced by Greek astronomy in its calculations of time. The seven-day week was introduced in India by the Greeks, and India started following it during the Gupta dynasty period (320-480 A.D.). The zodiac signs were also brought to India by the Greeks.

WHAT IS BRAHMA MUHURTA?

The time between 3 a.m. and 6 a.m. is considered to be Brahma Muhurta. It is supposed to be the most auspicious time of the day. It is said that during this period of time all celestial beings take rest and there is very little thought activity in the ethereal world. As such, this period is considered the best time for meditation and for spiritual activities. It is said that any problem can be solved if you try to solve it during this period of time.

PLEASE DESCRIBE "KALPA" AND "YUGA" IN DETAIL.

Time immemorial is measured in cycles called Kalpas. A Kalpa is a day and night for Brahma, the Lord of Creation. After each Kalpa, there is another Kalpa.

Each Kalpa is divided into two thousand Mahayugas. Each Mahayuga is divided into four Yugas or ages. They are Krita or Sathya, Treta, Dvapara, and Kali. Lord Krishna lived in the Dvapara Yuga. We are now in the Kali Yuga. At the end of the Kali Yuga, the universe will be destroyed by Pralaya (deluge) to start the cosmic creation once again. Things in the universe deteriorate from Yuga to Yuga.

Krita or Sathya Yuga is characterized by truth and righteousness. It is the best age to live. Everyone belongs to one caste. There is no sexual intercourse in this age. Children, like all other things, come by mere wishing. The color of this age is white. Men live for four thousand years. Men have only one Veda.

Treta Yuga has a decreased form of righteousness in comparison with Krita Yuga. Knowledge is the chief virtue of this age. Procreation happens by touch. The color of this age is red. Men live for three thousand years. Men have four Vedas now.

Dvapara Yuga has a further decrease of truthfulness. Men are subjected to disease and misery. The caste system started in this age. Children are born out of sexual intercourse. The color of this age is yellow. The scriptures of this age are Puranas. Men live about two thousand years.

Kali Yuga is the worst of all Yugas and is supposed to have started in 3102 B.C. at the time of the accession of King Pareeshit to the throne of Hastinapura. Truth and righteousness will cease to exist in this age. The color of this age is black. The scriptures of this age are Tantras. Everything is sexual in this age. Homosexuality will take over heterosexuality as a way of life in this age. Women will rule in this age. Men live up to one hundred years.

Krita Yuga is four times the length of Kali Yuga. Its length is 1,728,000 human years. Treta Yuga is three times the length of Kali Yuga. Its length is 1,296,000 human years. Dvapara Yuga is two times the length of Kali Yuga. Its length is 864,000 human years. Kali Yuga's length is 432,000 human years. So the length of one Mahayuga is 4,320,000 human years.

A Brahma, or Lord of Creation, lives for one hundred Brahma years (each of made up of 360 Brahma days). After that he dies. So a Brahma lives for 36,000 Kalpas, or 36,000 x 2,000 x 4,320,000 human years--i.e., a Brahma lives for 311.04 trillion human years. After the death of each Brahma, there is a Mahapralaya or great deluge, when all the universe is destroyed. Then a new Brahma appears and creation starts all over again.

As per legends, when one Brahma changes, a saint named Romesha (hairy saint) loses one hair. When he loses all the hairs on his body, he dies. When one Romesha saint dies, Sage Ashtavakra (eight curves in the body) loses one curve. When he loses all the eight curves, he dies. So time devours everything!

DADDY, I AM VERY MUCH CONFUSED. ON ONE SIDE YOU ARE SAYING REPEATEDLY THAT THE UNIVERSE AND CREATION ARE CREATED AND DESTROYED TIME AND TIME AGAIN. BUT YOU ALSO GIVE THE IMPRESSION THAT WE HAVE TO WORRY ABOUT SALVATION. IF EVERYTHING IS PURELY INSTRUMENTAL IN NATURE, THEN WHY SHOULD ANYONE WORRY ABOUT SALVATION?

To begin with, please do not say that we are "worried" about salvation. Do not even say that we are concerned about salvation. Will you ever say that the Mississippi River is worried or concerned about reaching the Gulf of Mexico? No, because you know that, as per the laws of physics, the Mississippi River has no other alternative but to seek and merge with the Gulf of Mexico. It is the river's nature. The same ideology stands when explaining the nature of seeking salvation. The individual soul (Jeevatman) by nature seeks to reach the absolute soul (Paramatman). If you ask me if it is purely instrumental, the answer is yes, it is instrumental. By our human will, we can delay or accelerate our soul's merging with the Absolute but we have no choice. According to the Bhagavad Gita, Yoga, or union with the Divine or the Absolute, is for all. As I said before, the only difference is the time factor between the best and worst among us. Some will attain salvation with this life and some will take millions of lives to attain salvation. Now coming back to the first part of your question, I think the naked truth of the instrumentality of the universe such as the repeated birth and death of the universe reaffirms the fact that the urge to seek salvation among us is purely instrumental or involuntary or natural.

As long as we feel pleasure or pain and as long as we feel that this physical body is the ultimate "I," we are not going to be content with life as it is. So the urge to seek perennial happiness and peace is inborn in all of us. Of course, this seeking of everlasting happiness and peace will definitely start on a trial and error basis. Remember, each time I brought you a toy when you were a small boy, you felt you achieved all the happiness in the world. Look at you now. You feel a brand new sports car will give you all the happiness in the world. In a few years' time, when you have that car, you will want to have something else. What I said above is true regarding you, me, and everyone else. This seeking of happiness in material objects will continue until we find happiness and peace within ourselves. We make many mistakes in our search for everlasting happiness and peace. The wise ones among us will learn with a few mistakes and others will repeat the same mistakes over and over again. So it is in the nature of all of us to seek salvation and we have no choice. All of us are purely instrumental.

79 ஐ
Pralaya--The Hindu Armageddon

DO HINDUS BELIEVE IN ARMAGEDDON?

Hinduism also talks about the biblical Armageddon (Revelation 16:16) as Pralaya (great deluge). Very descriptive details of Pralaya are written in the Srimad Mahabhagavatam. As far as Hinduism is concerned, Pralaya is not something that shows despair but hope. Hindus firmly believe in the law of Karma and Pralaya as a necessity to take care of the collective Karmas of multitudes of people. Even the Yadavas (blood-relations of Lord Krishna) and Krishna himself were wiped out of this earth when their actions warranted their extinction from the earth.

Hindus also believe in the cyclical nature of creation and annihilation of the universe. In the Code of Manu, it is written that the universe and creation come and go in a cyclical order. There is no end to this drama of the creation and annihilation of the universe. As I have mentioned, there are four periods of time called Yugas: Krita or Sathya Yuga, Treta Yuga, Dvapara Yuga and Kali Yuga. The total time period of the four Yugas is called a Kalpa. At the end of each Kalpa or Kali Yuga, the universe is destroyed by Pralaya, or great floods. Then another Kalpa begins. It is said that at the time of Pralaya, Lord Vishnu will take his tenth Avatar known as Kalki (the man on the white horse). It is said that the state of affairs will be the worst now, in Kali Yuga.

End of the World as per Hinduism

Hinduism believes in the perpetual creation and annihilation of the universe. According to Hinduism, we are presently in Kali Yuga. Our world will come to an end in approximately 427,000 years, when Lord Vishnu will appear as Kalki (the Man on the White Horse) and destroy the world by fire and flood.

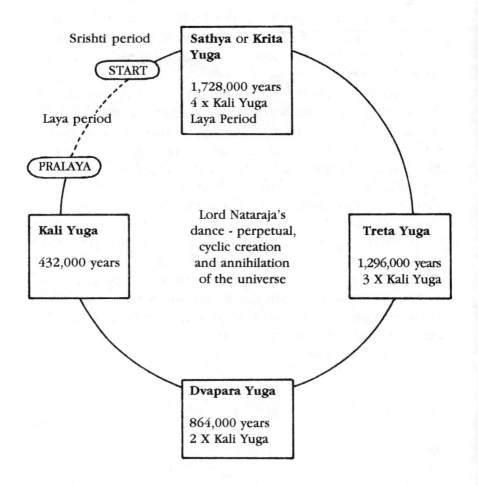

Devils and Ghosts

DOES HINDUISM BELIEVE IN THE EXISTENCE OF SATAN
OR THE DEVIL?

According to Hinduism, a devil is Maya. In
Christianity, it is said that Satan "fell from heaven." In the
Bible, it is described as follows: "He was a murderer from
the beginning, and abode not in the truth, because there
is no truth in him. When he speaketh a lie, he speaketh
of his own: for he is a liar, and the father of it" (John
8:44). The Hebrew word Satan means "to oppose or
harass" someone, especially by accusing him. So as per
early Christianity, Satan means "accuser" or "prosecutor."
The early church was persecuted by the Romans and their
pagan religion, and so the early church called Romans by
the name Satan. In fact, even the true meaning of "devil"
is "a slanderous accuser." The devil was depicted in
Christian art in the sixth century, appearing as an angelic
figure in miniatures and frescoes. But during the Middle
Ages, the devil was portrayed as an ugly and horrifying
monster. As per the New Catholic Encyclopedia, even the
proverbial Antichrist is the one who opposes the work of
God, especially that accomplished by Jesus Christ. The
Antichrist could even very well be a spirit or force rather
than a person, according to the New Catholic
Encyclopedia. Bertrand Russell once said that God and
Satan are essentially human figures, the one a projection
of ourselves, the other of our enemies.

Hinduism recognizes the Satanic force as the effect
of Maya, which is caused by ignorance. Meditation is one
of the ways to get out of this delusion. Anyway, Hinduism
does not regard the devil as the personification of a
dangerous being, but only as a negative force standing
against the spiritual upliftment of man.

Who creates the demonic forces in the world? We ourselves, individually and collectively by our selfish and destructive thoughts, words and actions, give birth to a multitude of demons. Hinduism calls these demons Kritiyas. These demonic forces attack the weak and young among us. This is the reason why Hindu saints say that by hating someone we may be unknowingly destroying the sanctity of the home, and even contributing to the destruction of the well-being of younger and weaker members of the family. If a whole nation personifies itself with hatred towards someone, that nation will ultimately meet with disaster.

DO YOU MEAN TO SAY THAT THERE ARE ABSOLUTELY NO GHOSTS IN HINDUISM?

Well, when I was telling you about demons, I was trying to give you a proper explanation based on very advanced Hindu scriptures. But if you pick up mythology, it is full of ghosts and demonic beings. There are mainly Pretas and Bhutas, which are actually the departed souls of people.

Pretas are souls which left their bodies and by their own fault cannot enter any new body. Pretas are supposed to be under constant pain and they enjoy visiting dirty places. It is said that they easily influence people with weak minds. Bhutas are souls of people who left after an accidental death. Bhutas, like Pretas, are trouble-makers, and it is said that both Pretas and Bhutas do not go to places where God-fearing people live. I know it will be difficult for you to believe in Pretas or Bhutas and I can understand your frame of mind. Mythology, as I told you before, is full of stories and it is up to you to believe in anything you want.

81 ह

The Swastika and Hinduism

IS THE SWASTIKA ACTUALLY A HINDU SYMBOL?

The symbol Swastika ("luck" or "well-being" in Sanskrit) is a symbol of Aryan culture or Hinduism. It is an auspicious symbol for Hindus, Buddhists and Jains. Hindus and Jains draw Swastika marks on books, doors, offerings, etc. It has also been found on Byzantine buildings, Celtic monuments and Greek coins. It has even been found in some American Indian burial grounds in the U.S.A. It served as a powerful emblem in Britain from 3000 B.C. to 300 A.D. It is said that early Christians even used it as an emblem on the walls of the catacombs, in which they secretly practiced their faith away from the Roman persecutors.

The Swastika figure is in the form of a Greek cross with the ends of the arms bent at right angles. The right-handed Swastika moves in a clockwise direction and the left-handed Swastika moves in a counter-clockwise direction. This symbol creates an impression of perpetual motion. The right-handed Swastika is considered a solar symbol or a fire symbol. The left-handed Swastika is sometimes considered an evil omen. According to Max Muller, this dualism in the Swastika is intended to represent both the vernal and autumnal sun. Each type, in its turn, was employed to ensure the sun's safe passage and return. In Scandinavian countries the Swastika represented the hammer of Thor, the northern god of thunder and lightning.

Usually all Swastikas are white on a black background, but during the Nazi regime, a black left-handed, titled Swastika or "Hakenkreuz" became the characteristic emblem of the Nazi party. Hitler took over this sign in 1920 from the German Baltic Corps and adopted it as a badge on the helmets of the armies serving in Finland. Anyway, now the Swastika is the most hated symbol in the world. Nobody can say for sure whether it was the misuse of the Hindu Swastika's power that caused the rise and fall of Adolf Hitler.

Hare Krishnas

WHO ARE THE HARE KRISHNAS?

From the age of the Brahmanas, Hindus believed that creation came from the word AUM and that the Godhead is triune, with the Mother Goddess apart from this Trinity. The Trinity is Lord Brahma (Lord of Creation), Lord Vishnu (Lord of Preservation), and Lord Siva (Lord of Annihilation). The Mother Goddess is known as Sakti. Three main groups arose in Hinduism, namely Vaishnavites (those who worship Vishnu), Saivites (those who worship Siva), and Saktiates (those who worship the Mother Goddess). Three scriptures associated with those groups were developed, namely the Vaishnava Agamas, Saiva Agamas and Sakta Agamas. The Sakta Agamas are also known as the Tantras.

Some historians state that the Vaishnava movement degenerated in time due to constant battles with Saivites, as well as to the Deva Dasi system, where women from good families were used as temple prostitutes under the guise of serving Lord Vishnu and practicing the Tantras. The emergence of Buddhism as the prime religion among the people due to Emperor Ashoka also contributed to the downfall of Vaishnavism. In recent years, a great saint from India, Swami A.C. Bhakti Vedanta Swami Prabhupada, revived the ancient Vaishnava movement as "The International Society for Krishna Consciousness" or ISKON. The popular name of the society is the Hare Krishnas, meaning "victory to Lord Krishna."

CAN YOU PLEASE DESCRIBE HARE KRISHNAS FURTHER?

First let me repeat to you the real name of that society--The International Society for Krishna Consciousness or ISKON. The Hare Krishna society is one of the most ascetic and ritualistic sects in the world. Sometimes one wonders how the Hare Krishna society attracts devotees with its very strict moral and ethical codes. There is absolutely no drinking, smoking or casual sex allowed to members of the society. The public chanting of the Mantra "Hare Krishna, Hare Krishna, Krishna Krishna Hare Hare; Hare Rama, Hare Rama, Rama Rama Hare Hare" is one of the important activities of the devotees. According to the Srimad Bhagavatam, anyone who utters this Mantra and also anyone who happens to listen to this Mantra will be blessed by God.

In addition to public chanting, each devotee repeats the same Mantra 1,728 times every single day. The chanting is counted by a string of one hundred and eight Tulsi beads. So the string is counted through sixteen times each day. Hare Krishna devotees do even menial jobs as offerings to Lord Krishna. They cleanse their bodies at least twice a day, and even among married people sex is allowed only for progeny. Like any other society, controversies still plague this society. Some people claim that their children were brainwashed by this pious society, but nobody can say exactly how much truth there is in those allegations. Hare Krishna devotees are pure vegetarians, and practice non-violence.

Anyone who is concerned about the nature and motives of the Hare Krishna movement must read *The Dark Lord: Cult Images and the Hare Krishnas in America* by Larry D. Shinn (Westminster Press, Philadelphia). This book warns people against unjustified fears concerning all Eastern religious sects in the West.

83 ॐ
Drugs and Hinduism

WHAT DOES HINDUISM SAY ABOUT USING DRUGS TO
GET HIGH?

Hinduism very clearly understands the power of
drugs and Hindu saints knew which herbs in fact give the
so-called "high" feeling among users. The only drink
mentioned in the Rig Veda which some consider to be a
narcotic beverage is Soma juice. Nobody knows exactly
from which plant it was produced nor what kind of
intoxicating properties it had. Anyway, right now Hindus
look down upon the consumption of drugs like LSD,
heroin and "crack" as means to attaining different levels of
consciousness. The reason is that even though certain
drugs can bring a man to a higher level of consciousness,
that chemically-induced higher consciousness is
momentary and dangerous. People using drugs usually go
into depressive states of mind after a few moments of
"chemical paradise." So hours and days of mental agony
for a few moments of higher experience are not the
answer. Drugs, according to Tantric literature, result in
the sudden shooting up of Kundalini power in the
Sushumna nerve, but since the ordinary body is not
conditioned to accept sudden outbursts of power within
itself, it reacts with physical and mental disorder. That is
the reason why a drug addict undergoes violent
hallucinations and suffers permanent damage to the brain.
So if any drug at all is used, it should only be under the
advice of a competent medical doctor or under the
guidance of a Guru who has thorough knowledge of
herbal medicine and Ayurveda.

Let me repeat that Hinduism strictly forbids the use
of drugs in meditation. In some forms of Hindu
meditation, even stimulants like coffee and tea are
forbidden.

Elements and Sacred Plants of Hinduism

WHAT IS MATTER MADE OF?

According to Hinduism, matter is made of five elements. They are:

1. Prithvi--Earth (solid)
2. Jala--Water (liquid)
3. Tejas--Fire (light)
4. Vayu--Air (gas)
5. Akasha--Ether (space)

These elements are popularly known as Panchabhutas or Pancha Tattvas. There is something very strange about these elements. Look at the electron configuration of all the elements, beginning with the first element--solid--and ending with Akasha or space. You will see a gradual increase of free electrons in the atomic structure of the elements. No one can say whether it is a strange coincidence or whether the Hindu saints did know something about the variation of free electrons in the atomic structure of these elements. According to Hinduism, at the time of Pralaya the manifested universe will break down into its elements and it will stay in that state until another universe is born and life begins again.

DO HINDUS HAVE SACRED PLANTS?

Hindus look with respect at the Banyan tree, which lives for more than four hundred years. They consider the Pipal tree sacred, believing that Brahma resides in its trunk. The Bel tree is associated with the worship of Lord Siva.

The small Tulsi plant is the most important of all plants. It is associated with Lord Vishnu, and the leaves are offered to Lord Vishnu in daily worship. The presence of a Tulsi or basil plant is a must in every devoted Hindu's house.

Birth of Creation as per Hinduism

HOW DID CREATION START, AS PER HINDUISM? IS IT
DIFFERENT FROM MODERN THEORIES?

Scriptures say that Brahman is the ultimate reality
which is none other than the cosmic word AUM. The
blowing of the conch shells and the ringing of the temple
bells represent the cosmic sound.

In Christianity, Genesis explains the beginning of
creation. As per Hindu scriptures, the first universe that
came out of AUM was the Causal Universe. From the
Causal Universe came the Astral Universe. From the Astral
Universe came the Material Universe. As per mythology,
the whole creation was created by Lord Brahma, and he
himself took birth from the umbilical cord of Lord Vishnu
(the God of Preservation). There are quite a lot of stories
in mythology about creation.

The Chandogya Upanishad says, "In the beginning
this world was merely non-being" (3:19:1). "To what does
this world go back? To space...verily, all things here arise
out of space. They disappear back into space, for space
alone is greater than these. Space is the final destination"
(1:9:1). Some astronomers believe that the universe came
into existence about fifteen billion years ago as a result of
a violent explosion of a few infinitesimal hydrogen
molecules. This theory is known as the "Big Bang theory,"
and it reminds us of the Hindu idea that everything came
from Brahman which is "subtler than the atom, greater
than the greatest" (Katha Upanishad 2:20). Of course, the
Big Bang theory does not explain how hydrogen atoms
came into existence in the first place. Astronomers also
think that our solar system came into existence about five
billion years ago and that Planet Earth came into existence
about four and a half billion years ago. As per the
scientists, at present all the planets and stars are moving

farther and farther apart. This phenomenon is known as the "Expanding Theory of the Universe."

Will this phenomenon change and the universe start to contract one day? It may happen, but nobody can give a definite answer. Now astronomers are discovering galaxies trillions of light years away. A light year is the distance traveled by a ray of light in one year. A ray of light travels 186,000 miles in one second. Each galaxy consists of billions of solar systems and there are several billions of galaxies in the universe. We may never find a signboard saying, "Stop, the universe ends here." Again, we do not know whether all those galaxies put together with our galaxy only make up an atom of a superior galaxy, and whether that superior galaxy is only an atom of a mightier galaxy and so on.

Modern astronomy, with its day-to-day amazing and mind-boggling discoveries, makes all of us look like micro-microorganisms and our life period on earth like micro-microfractions of a second, which is exactly what you see in Hinduism with its details of Yugas, Kalpas and perpetual creation and annihilation of the universe.

The more we know about the world around us nowadays, the more we realize how little we know about the creation and annihilation of the universe.

86

The Hindu Search for God

DOES ONE HAVE TO GO TO THE FORESTS TO REALIZE GOD?

In none of the Hindu scriptures is it said that one has to run away from one's earthly belongings and duty (Svadharma) to achieve God-realization. In fact, the Bhagavad Gita advocates doing one's own duty. After the great Bhagavad Gita discourse, Arjuna did not become a hermit; instead he fought a fierce war. Almost at the end of the Bhagavad Gita discourse, Lord Krishna says to Arjuna, "Mam Anusmara Yudhyacha" ("Remembering me, fight the war"), which means, "thinking of God, do one's own duty." So nowhere is it said that one has to run to the jungles in search of God. Of course, Hinduism says that the change of mentality from material to spiritual is slow, like a glutton worm which eats three to four times its weight and finally becomes a butterfly. So changes should be made gradually without frustration. Hinduism advocates the statement, "You can possess things, but do not be possessed by them." King Janaka is a perfect example. On one side, he was a materialistic king of his century, and on the other, he was one of the greatest Yogis India has ever seen. Understand, the Yogi who fights for his loincloth in the bitter winter of the Himalayas is no better than the cunning businessman. Both are possessed by greed and anger. So, change of consciousness is more important than change of outward appearances or change of lifestyle.

DADDY, DO YOU MEAN TO SAY THAT GOD CANNOT COME TO US UNLESS WE CHANGE OUR CONSCIOUSNESS?

That is exactly what I want to tell you again. Even Swami Vivekananda had problems when his master Sri Ramakrishna Paramahamsa made him see God for the first time, since his consciousness then was not at the highest level. Vivekananda, then known as Narendra, tormented everyone with his inquisitive question, "Have you seen God?" Sri Ramakrishna Paramahamsa alone answered Vivekananda, "Son, I see him like I see you" and touched the forehead of Vivekananda. Narendra, who had troubled so many Yogis with his penetrating questions about God, then uttered the cry of a lamb. It is said that the power was too much for the great offspring of India to bear and he implored, "Leave me, Sir, I have my mother, father and others at home" (see *The Life of Swami Vivekananda* by his Western and Eastern disciples). There is no easy way out. God is close to us and yet He cannot come to us. We keep Him away from us. Christ said, "Behold, I stand at the door and knock: If any man hear my voice and open the door, I will come in to him" (Revelation 3:20). Those words reaffirm the fact that without individual effort, without changing the consciousness, God cannot come to anyone, even though God is so close to everyone of us.

DADDY, IS SCRIPTURAL KNOWLEDGE A PREREQUISITE FOR GOD-REALIZATION?

No, not at all. Anyone who sincerely seeks the absolute truth will finally realize the absolute truth, even if he/she is totally ignorant of the Vedas and Upanishads. All religious scriptures are only aids in the pursuit of truth and they are not a "must" in search of the ultimate truth.

Jesus Christ very emphatically said, "Seek, and ye shall find; knock and it shall be opened unto you" (Matthew 7:7).

So, whether a person is well-versed in the scriptures or not, if he/she is sincere in desiring to know the truth, he/she will finally realize the truth. God appears in front of anyone who surrenders his personal will to divine will. In so many verses in the Bhagavad Gita, Lord Krishna teaches very easy ways by which one can attain the Absolute. In verse 9:22, Lord Krishna says that he himself undertakes the burden of the day-to-day problems of a devotee who dedicates himself to Him (God) by surrendering his free will. In verses 12:6-7, Krishna says, "Those who surrender all actions to Me and regard Me as the supreme goal and worship Me with whole-hearted devotion will be saved by Me from repeated births and deaths." In another verse he says, "Give up all righteous and non-righteous actions and come unto Me; take refuge in Me. Then I shall free you from all sins; grieve not" (Gita, 18:66).

Through all those lines God is asking for unquestionable, whole-hearted devotion from the aspirant and there is no mention of studying the scripture at all. There is nothing wrong with studying the scriptures, but it is wrong to feel that people who are ignorant of the scriptures have no chance for salvation. That is the reason why, in Hinduism, all methods of God-realization are equally important. The devotional lamentation of a Bhakti Yogi, the selfless actions of a Karma Yogi, the Pranayama exercises of a Raja Yogi and the scriptural contemplation of a Jnana Yogi are all treated with the same respect throughout Hinduism. Meera Bhajans, Advaita philosophy and Patanjali's Yoga Sutra have equal status in Hinduism.

DADDY, WHAT DO YOU OR ANYONE TRY TO ACHIEVE THROUGH THE PRACTICE OF HINDUISM?

It is easy to say "salvation," but that is the ultimate goal. Right now, we are trying to achieve peace and harmony in life. In a way we are trying to have a stress-free life. The Hindu way of life aids that effort. Those who follow Hinduism are generally calm at heart and they express their calmness in their day-to-day life. They do not scream and shout when their dinner is not served on time or if they are caught in a traffic jam or if they have just lost their job. Once in a while they also get agitated, but that state of mind is only temporary. As I told you before, it is quite easy to follow Hinduism, because Hinduism believes that ignorance is the root of all evils and true knowledge is the answer to all problems. First, try to understand the truth, and then try to practice and realize that truth.

So, most of us who adhere to Hinduism are not trying to become Gurus or hermits or philosophers. We are just trying to have a stress-free, peaceful life. If that is achieved, then one has really profited by the study of Hinduism. The methods described are very simple, and anyone can practice them. I hope I have made my point very clear to you.

87

Day-to-Day Problems and Hinduism

DADDY, DO YOU THINK MY PROBLEMS ARE SIMPLE?

From where did you get that idea? Your problems, my problems and even the problems of a newborn are equally important. I know that you are under a lot of pressure in school as well as at home. At school you have to listen to every mundane thing your classmates tell you and at home you have a totally different situation. So the clash of ideas itself can generate hundreds of problem for you. You want to be one among your friends at school, in a way "to do in Rome as the Romans do," and at home you want to toe the line your father and mother dictate to you. I am also under pressure in my place of work. So, we all have problems and all problems are important. You will never see a true Yogi ridiculing anyone's problem. He will try to help by suggestions in tune with the scriptures. Whatever we do in every walk of life is very important. That is the reason why Manu put down the Ashrama Dharmas comprised of Kaumaram, Garhastyam, Vanaprastham and Sanyasam. Even great saints are not allowed to bypass any stage in their lives. Legends say that Veda Vyasa tried his best to stop his son Suka from jumping from Balyam (boyhood) to Sanyasam. Legends also say that Sankaracharya was delayed in climbing Sarvajna Peedam at Benaras since he couldn't answer questions from Goddess Saraswathi regarding Garhastyam Dharma (householder's duty). Sankaracharya was forced to leave his body and occupy the dead body of a Brahmin householder in Kashmir for about a year, so that he could answer all questions regarding Garhastya Dharma. So every minute of our life is important from childhood to old age. The stages of life you and I are in are as important as the stage of life of a renunciate sitting on the banks of the Ganges.

We are all seeking perfection in action, and religion provides us with so many suggestions on how to tackle our day-to-day problems. As I have told you so many times, it is you who have to decide what is good for you and which part of the religion is well suited to you. Some can just think of Lord Krishna and go into a trance, but for many, such a way of meditation is unthinkable. So let me repeat that your problems, my problems and even the problems of a newborn are equally important. Hinduism only gives us suggestions on how to tackle them and it never orders us what to do. You and I have absolute freedom to do whatever we want in our lives, but if we are not careful, if we do not listen to the ideas written in the scriptures, we may make errors with grave consequences. That is all.

88

Misrepresentation of Hinduism

DADDY, WHAT IS WRONG WITH HINDUISM TODAY?

There is nothing wrong with Hinduism at all. Some people misunderstand the essence of Hinduism, and that creates problems and misery among people. For example, some run away from their duties and call themselves Sanyasins or Sadhus and lead a beggar's life. The Gita specifically states that no one will reach the state of inaction (Nishkarmata) by shunning duties, because man by nature does actions all the time. It is also wrong to believe that Hinduism can be understood only if clothed in a kavi robe and never in a three-piece suit.

Karma and fate are two most misused words among Hindus. Some refuse to use their free will at all, and lead the lives of earthworms under the guise of total surrender to God. By not using their free will, they become victims of their own emotions and the whole country pays for their laziness. Doing wrong actions and then bringing in scriptures to support them is another mistake some do.

Some among the younger generation look at Hinduism as a taboo, only to be touched when they hit sixty. They perceive Hinduism as being full of dogmas without even reading one line from the Vedas or Upanishads.

Some Hindus mix up mythology, Vedic and Upanishadic teachings. That creates unnecessary arguments about scriptures. Arguing about mythological stories is the most stupid act of all.

DADDY, WHENEVER PEOPLE TALK ABOUT HINDUISM, THEY BRING UP THINGS LIKE THE "HOLY COW,"

UNTOUCHABLES AND THE MANY GODS, AND CONCLUDE THAT HINDUISM IS A STUPID RELIGION. ARE THEY RIGHT?

They are right in much the same way as concluding that New York means Harlem and Times Square. Those ugly, downtrodden places are parts of New York City, but we all know that they do not represent the real New York. Broadway, museums, art galleries and thousands of God-fearing multi-colored citizens make New York. The same argument goes for Hinduism. Of course, since Hinduism is a slowly-developed thinking process which gave absolute freedom of thought and action to its followers, it has so many contradictory aspects. The holy cow and the caste system are parts of Hinduism, but they do not constitute Hinduism. Even mythology is actually intended for common people who cannot understand the truths in the Vedas and Upanishads.

Advaita philosophy, the Bhagavad Gita, Raja Yoga, Pranayama, Mantras, etc. are the pillars of Hinduism. Anyone who does not want to discuss them is only searching for dirt and getting dirt, barrels and barrels of it.

Most critics look at Hinduism with a preconceived notion and a colored vision. By doing so, they are actually degrading themselves to the level of the Romans who accused Jesus Christ of blasphemy. What a shame!

89 æ
Does Science Have Answers?

DADDY, DO YOU THINK THAT SCIENCE WILL HAVE
ANSWERS TO ALL RIDDLES OF LIFE ONE DAY?

I don't know the answer and I do not think even
renowned scientists will venture to answer that question.
Of course we have come a long way with our research in
molecular biology and genetics. Today, we know that the
nucleus of every normal human cell contains twenty-three
pairs of chromosomes, each of which is a thread-like
structure made up of about eighty thousand genes. Since
1953, we know that these genes are made up of DNA
(double-helix molecule of deoxyribonucleic acid) and at
regular intervals along a strand of DNA, one of just four
nitrogen based chemicals are attached. Those chemicals,
abbreviated A, G, C, and T, are the "letters" of the genetic
code. But science still does not know exactly how this
genetic code works, and scientists are still working on
methods to properly sequence them. Definitely, we hope
understanding the genetic codes will lay the groundwork
for conquering most of the diseases and also solving many
of the riddles of life. "Is there light the end of the tunnel?"
is a baffling question. Each time science discovers
something, it opens up another thousand questions. We
have to wait and see what answers science will bring to
the riddle of life.

Concluding Advice

DADDY, FOR THE PAST SIX OR SEVEN HOURS YOU HAVE
ANSWERED ALL MY QUESTIONS. PLEASE ANSWER THIS
LAST QUESTION FOR ME. DO YOU REALLY THINK I
SHOULD STUDY AND PRACTICE HINDUISM?

Son, until you are nineteen years old, I may compel
you to read and understand Hinduism because I feel it is
my duty to show you all the right things in life, but I am
not going to answer "yes" or "no" to your question.
Whether you should follow Hinduism for the rest of your
life is up to you.

You have an analytical mind, so you decide about
your life. It is your turn to sit and analyze the world
around you. What do you see? At the dawn of the twenty-
first century, modern science is still groping in the dark.
It still has only theories about the beginning of the
universe; it still can't define death; its inventions are
creating more and more greed, anger, deceit and stress
among men.

Look at the question of aging, for example. Despite
all the research, scientists still do not know why people
age and die, although they believe that it is due to the
accumulation of breaks in the basic heredity substance
known as DNA.

Remember, modern science provides us with
aerosol cans and coolants like freon (CFC), which are
destroying the thin ozone layer around the world. The
ozone layer has protected the world for centuries from the
sun's deadly radiation. Right now, scientists have found
two holes in the ozone layer, one over Antarctica and the
other over the Arctic.

Remember, modern science, which has given us
nuclear energy, is still battling with the problems of
disposing the most deadly nuclear waste--which will be

with us for thousands of years to come, even after the day scientists discover a safe form of energy.

By no means do I wish to look down upon the great scientific achievements in genetic engineering or molecular biology or any other branch of science. I respect those great achievements and study them wholeheartedly like you and everyone else. The thing I abhor is the unnecessary glorification of science. At the end of the twentieth century, science may have only touched the tip of the great iceberg of knowledge. Remember, there are at least one hundred billion galaxies in the universe and each of them consists of billions of stars. We may never see a signboard saying, "Stop, the universe ends here."

We are still in search of the ultimate atomic unit, even though at present it is the quark. Remember that each drop of water consists of hundreds of life-forms. Each time the astronomers look through powerful telescopes they are discovering new galaxies. Each time biologists look through more powerful microscopes, they see new life- forms. That is what is happening in the scientific world today. So, modern science is still in a blind man's state. We cannot deliver our lives to science to govern one hundred percent, since it itself does not know where it is going. Genetic engineering could lead us to a trouble-free life or it could make our lives a genetic nightmare. Believe me, I am just stating the facts and there is not even one iota of prejudice in my statements.

Seeing the true nature of the world, my question to you is: Aren't you better off getting into life armed with the knowledge taught by Hinduism? Please understand that when I talk about Hinduism, I am not talking about ritualistic worship or ceremonial gestures. I am not even talking about trips to temples or holy places. I am strictly talking about the knowledge that the Vedas and Bhagavad

Gita offer. After studying them, try to study other true religions like Christianity. I am also not asking you to dump the comforts materialism provides you. I am only requesting that you study the truths taught in Hinduism, since Hinduism is not a religion but a way of life. Later, if you find a better way to answer all the problems, if you see science can solve all riddles in life, you may dump Hinduism and all other religions. Good luck! Please remember, the most important aspect of Hinduism is being truthful to yourself. If you lack that quality, you will be able to grasp neither religion nor science.

ORDER FORM

To: Halo Books
     73691 Sawmill Canyon Way
     Palm Desert, CA 92260

I enclose check/money order payable to Halo Books in the amount of $_____ for books noted on list below. (Add $2.50 for shipping one book and $1.75 for each additional books. California residents please include 8% sales tax.

Mail to:
Name_____
Street address_____
Town _____ State_____ ZIP _____
Please send:

____copies of AM I A HINDU?
          The Hinduism primer
          Viswanathan $16.95 ea

____copies of TIME HAPPENS,
          You could not have picked
          a better time to be fiftysomething
          Coombs $13.95 ea

_____copies of A GARDEN OF WOMAN'S
WISDOM, *A Secret Haven for Renewal*
Veltri $12.95 ea

_____copies of SUDDENLY SINGLE,
A Lifeline for Anyone
Who Has Lost a Love
Larson $15.95 ea

_____copies of THIS ISN'T EXACTLY WHAT I
HAD IN MIND, GOD,
How to get your life back on track
Larson $14.95 ea

_____copies of IF HE LOVES ME, WHY DOESN'T
HE TELL ME?
Larson $12.95 ea

_____copies of TEENAGE SURVIVAL MANUAL,
Being in charge of your
own mind and body
Coombs $15.95 ea

_____copies of YOUR SEXUAL HEALTH
What teenagers need to know about sexually-
transmitted diseases and pregnancy
McClosky $15.95 ea

For a free catalog of all Halo Books in print,
write address above. Thank you.